TEMPLARS

TEMPLARS

THE KNIGHTS WHO MADE BRITAIN

STEVE TIBBLE

YALE UNIVERSITY PRESS
NEW HAVEN AND LONDON

For information about this and other Yale University Press publications, please contact:
U.S. Office: sales.press@yale.edu   yalebooks.com
Europe Office: sales@yaleup.co.uk   yalebooks.co.uk

Set in Adobe Garamond Pro by IDSUK (DataConnection) Ltd
Printed in Great Britain by TJ Books, Padstow, Cornwall

Library of Congress Control Number: 2023937772

ISBN 978-0-300-26445-6

A catalogue record for this book is available from the British Library.

10 9 8 7 6 5 4 3 2 1

◆

CONTENTS

CONTENTS

❖

MAPS AND PLATES

MAPS

PLATES

6. Empress Mathilda, from the Benefactors' Book of St Albans Abbey, *c.* 1380, British Library, Cotton Nero D. VII, f.7. © British Library Board. All Rights Reserved / Bridgeman Images.

7. Bisham commandery, Berkshire, photo by Anthony McCallum. WyrdLight.com / CC BY-SA 3.0.

8. Cressing commandery, interior of barley barn, 2019. Michael Coppins / CC BY-SA 4.0.

9. Cressing commandery, exterior of wheat barn, 2019. Michael Coppins / CC BY-SA 4.0.

10. Interior of New Temple, London, 2014. David Iliff / CC BY-SA 3.0.

11. Exterior of New Temple, London, 2014. Matthias Süßen / CC BY-SA 3.0.

12. Garway commandery, 2018. Richard Waller / CC BY-SA 4.0.

13. The Becket casket, *c.* 1180–90. © Victoria and Albert Museum, London.

14. Stained glass panel showing the murder of Becket, Canterbury Cathedral, thirteenth century.

15. Miniature in four compartments with portraits of English kings, from Matthew Paris, *Historia Anglorum*, 1250–1259. British Library, MS Royal 14 C. VII, f.9.

16. The battle of Mont Gisard, from William of Tyre, *History of the Crusades*, VI, f.259. Limédia Galeries.

17. The battle of Gisors, from Mahiet and the Master of the Cambrai Missal, *Les Grandes chroniques de France*, 1332–50. British Library, Royal 16 G. VI, f.360.

18. King John of England hunting a stag with hounds, fourteenth century. British Library, Cotton Claudius D. II, f.116. © British Library Board. All Rights Reserved / Bridgeman Images.

19. The fall of Château Gaillard and the loss of Normandy, *c.* 1330. France, Castres, Municipal Library, Ms. 3 f.259. BVMM / CC-BY-NC 3.0.

20. King John's tomb, Worcester Cathedral, 2014. Hugh Llewelyn / CC BY-SA 2.0.

21. Head of the effigy of William Marshal, 1st earl of Pembroke, in Temple church, London, 2006. Kjetilbjørnsrud / CC BY-SA 3.0.

22. Henry III 'long cross' penny. The Portable Antiquities Scheme / The Trustees of the British Museum / CC BY-SA 3.0.

23. Balsall commandery, 2012. Oosoom / CC BY-SA 3.0.

24. Philip d'Aubigny's tomb at the Holy Sepulchre, 1925. American Colony (Jerusalem), Library of Congress Prints and Photographs Division Washington, D.C. 20540 USA, LC-DIG-matpc-08516.

25. Sedilia of Westminster Abbey thought to depict Edward I. © Dean and Chapter of Westminster.

26. Edward I of England and Eleanor of Castile, from Matthew Paris, *Chronica Roffense* (*Flores Historiarum* made at Rochester), early fourteenth century, British Library, Cotton Nero D. II, f.179v. © British Library Board. All Rights Reserved / Bridgeman Images.

27. Denney commandery, 2004. Rob enwiki / CC BY-SA 3.0.

28. The arrests in France by Virgil Master and his atelier, from *Chroniques de France ou de St Denis*, late fourteenth century. British Library, MS Royal 20 C. VII, f.42v.

29. The death of James of Molay by Virgil Master and his atelier, from *Chroniques de France ou de St Denis*, late fourteenth century. British Library, MS Royal 20 C. VII, f.48.

30. Rosslyn chapel, Scotland, 2022. Anthonyrandell / CC BY-SA 4.0.

31. Interior of Rosslyn chapel, photo by J. Thomson, 1860–9. © Victoria and Albert Museum, London.

◇

FOREWORD

There is no shortage of books on the Templars. On the contrary, there are far too many.

The problem lies in the fact that most are closer to fiction than to the true story. This is a great shame, and completely unnecessary – the reality of the Templar achievement, in Britain and beyond, is so rich and so extraordinary that it needs no embellishment. There is undoubtedly a lot of fun to be had with the obsessions of popular culture – with Holy Grails, Assassins and Illuminati. But it is important not to confuse it with history.

This book tries to redress that balance and to create a more rounded view of the British Templars. Luckily, there is a mass of excellent work to call upon in the quest to regain a sense of sanity. Two authors in particular are both authoritative researchers and beacons of rationality in this field.

Professor Helen Nicholson is the leading academic working in the field of British (and other) Templar studies. She is astonishingly productive. Her vast output of highly readable and academically robust books and papers on the subject is both deeply impressive and suitably daunting.

Particularly helpfully for the current study, she has edited and trans-lated the transcripts of the interrogations undertaken in Britain as part of the final trial and dissolution of the order. This fascinating two-volume work allows an insight into the minds of the often frightened or embit-tered men associated with the British Templars. These documents, combined with the large number of analytical papers that followed its publication, give a unique insight into the final days of the order in Britain.[1]

Professor Malcolm Barber is the other doyen of the field. He has written two of the major works that form the starting point for any serious discussion of the Templars – *The New Knighthood: A History of the Order of the Temple* (1994) and *The Trial of the Templars* (2nd edition, 2006). Malcolm's unpretentious but quietly professional approach to the study of medieval history has been an inspiration to several generations of scholars. His kind support in the writing of this book and his seemingly effortless nudges (both at the initial idea stage and as the work progressed) have been invaluable.

Professor Jonathan Harris has given some very clear and extraordinarily helpful guidance in his usual understated and charming manner. His good company and quiet insights during some of the darker days of the recent Covid lockdown (suitably socially distanced, of course) made the task of writing far easier. Professor Peter Edbury has also kindly brought his dry wit and encyclopaedic knowledge of the crusades to the project. The end product is certainly far better for their help.

Other academic friends and colleagues have been far more supportive than I could have ever reasonably expected. Professor Jonathan Phillips has been his usual charming and supportive self – he has made extremely helpful comments throughout. Dr Nick Hopkinson has given far too freely of his expert knowledge of British history in this period and steered me away from some of my more obvious mistakes, particularly about the financial institutions of medieval England. Dr James Doherty has very kindly shared his research into King Stephen's links to the crusading movement. Ronan O'Reilly has helped with the Irish aspects of the Templars in Britain, and our mutual Italian friend Alessandro Scalone has given invaluable guidance about papal policy. Charles Masefield and Robert Mitchelmore have both been kind but assiduous as non-specialist readers – their comments have been much appreciated.

Dr Faith Tibble has been as kind and supportive as ever – she has kept me on track throughout and helped me find my way when I was in danger of becoming lost. Finally, I am also extremely fortunate that this book has been something of a pet project for the wonderful Heather McCallum of Yale University Press. She knew that the real achievements of the British Templars deserve to be far better known – none of this would have happened without her.

London and Hereford, 2023

1. The Templars in Britain (After Proceedings II [Nicholson 2011] and Walker 1990)

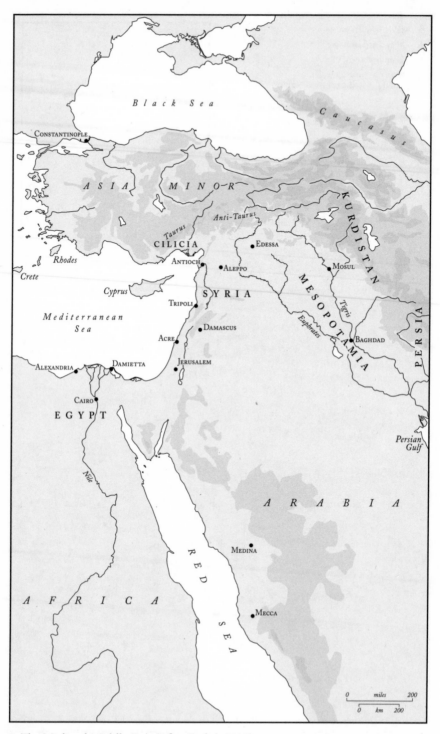

2. The Medieval Middle East (After Barber 2012)

3 Crusader States: The Latin Kingdom of Jerusalem (After Barber 2012)

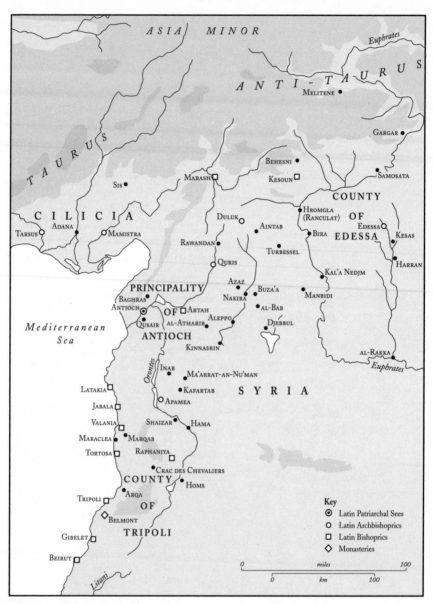

4 Crusader States: Antioch, Tripoli and Edessa (After Barber 2012)

1

✧

THE BRITISH TEMPLARS

Galilee, 4 July 1187.

The dry heat caught the stench of blood and death and held it close to the earth – the fear was palpable and, for many, overwhelming. The men, already severely dehydrated, were almost finished. Even the dying had little energy left for screams, just animal sounds of pain and muttered, delirious talk of mothers – but whether this was their own or the Virgin Mary, even they probably did not know.[1]

Many had dropped out of the ranks. The militia had begun to bunch together, edging up the nearby hillside. They were refusing to come down. Everyone could see that the battle was lost. They just wanted to find a way to get through it alive: 'We are not coming,' they said, when they were ordered to return to the ranks, 'because we are dying of thirst and unable to fight.'[2]

Most of the horses were already dead – some, very visibly, from numerous arrow wounds, and others, less obviously, from the heat and lack of water. The remaining Templar cavalry formed up in a thin, all too fragile line. Next to them were the men of the other main military order, the Hospitallers, and the last survivors of the crusader knights from the Latin Kingdom of Jerusalem.

Some of the brothers quietly mouthed a prayer to give them the strength and courage they needed. Most were just desperate to do their duty and avoid showing weakness in front of their comrades. A few made eye contact with their friends on either side. But looks had to express what emotions of fear or affection needed to be communicated. Few words were spoken. The famous Templar discipline, even in these last moments, was fierce – what little energy was left needed to be channelled into the coming fight.

There were fewer than 200 men in these dusty, ragged ranks. Preparing to charge a Muslim army of perhaps some 30,000 men, they must have known that they were going to lose. But the Templars were arguably the best heavy cavalry in the world. And, more to the point, they were out of options. This was the bravery of despair.

Complete silence fell in the ranks for the last few seconds. Time stood still. Then the standards signalled the order to charge. The tiny crusader squadrons lurched forwards, heads down as they careered into a storm of arrows.

Against all the odds, even this forlorn charge, and another which followed it, were enough to cause concern amongst their enemies. Al-Afdal, Saladin's son, was at his father's side at the time. He later spoke movingly to the historian Ibn al-Athir of their impact:

> They made a formidable charge against the Muslims facing them, so that they drove them back to my father. I looked towards him and he was overcome by grief and his complexion pale . . . The Muslims rallied, returned to the fight and climbed the hill. When I saw that the [crusaders] withdrew, pursued by the Muslims, I shouted for joy, 'We have beaten them!' But the Franks rallied and charged again like the first time and drove the Muslims back to my father. He acted as he had on the first occasion and the Muslims turned upon the Franks and drove them back to the hill. I again shouted, 'We have beaten them!' but my father rounded on me and said, 'Be quiet! We have not beaten them until that tent [the crusader command post] falls.'

Bravery was not enough against such odds. As the Templars and their comrades charged, they took more and more casualties. Eventually too few horses remained for the men to be able to fight mounted. The Templar brothers and the other knights set up tent ropes and overturned wagons as obstacles – they carried on fighting on foot for as long as they could.[3]

But there was only one realistic outcome.

The Frankish army was forced to surrender. The dazed survivors were bound and taken into captivity. The courage of the Templars had made a huge impact on their enemies. There was one final and unwelcome back-handed compliment. Saladin decided that the British Templars and their comrades from the other European provinces must die 'because they were the fiercest fighters of all the Franks'.[4]

The prisoners were executed on the battlefield.

York, 1310.

A different place. A very different story.

The rector of the church of Crofton, near Wakefield, was testifying under oath. He said that he had heard (second-hand, of course) that a Templar had confessed to having had sex with others from the order. Even more sensationally, the same brother knight revealed that he and his comrades had insulted and spat upon the crucifix. Bizarrely, and this was the big surprise, the Templar was also reported to have said that 'a certain image was shown to him like a certain calf placed on a sort of altar, and he was told that he should kiss the image and venerate it, which he did'.

Strangely, there was even corroboration of this seemingly outlandish claim. John of Nassington, a knight from York, had a very similar story. He testified that he had been told that the Templars had invited the knights and officials of York to a 'great banquet' at their manor house at Hirst. There 'they were told that many brothers of the said Order had assembled there for a certain solemn feast that they used to hold, at which they adored a certain calf'. And, as if to make an extraordinary anecdote even more lurid, the context from other witnesses made clear that 'adoring' a satanic creature such as this involved kissing its anus.[5]

These two stories ostensibly have little in common. British Templars and their patrons had fought and died on the battlefields of the Holy Land. The struggle to save the Christian Middle East had been partly financed by British money – money that had been gathered, transported and stored with the help of the Templars. And yet they had also, or so it was said, engaged in devil-worshipping rituals and bestiality – they were traitors to everything that Christianity stood for.

How did a small band of brave and intensely orthodox warriors become the centre of satanic cults? And how, in the space of a little over a hundred years, did the British Templars make the journey from crusaders to conspiracists?

This book is the story of these remarkable men, and that even more remarkable journey.

We need to be clear from the outset that there were two very distinct groups of 'British Templars'.

One group, the order's British soldiers in the front-line military arm, had the 'glamorous' but dangerous job of fighting in its armies and manning its castle garrisons in the East – these Templar volunteers performed heroic acts of outstanding bravery in the defence of the Holy Land.

But they were supported in their increasingly forlorn endeavours by the less dramatic but vital work undertaken on their behalf by their fellow brothers back in Britain. This other group, the British Templars on the 'home front', had the task of running farms, organising financial support and, often more importantly, lobbying the governments of England and Scotland. These were the Templar brothers who sent money and volunteers to aid the war effort and used their influence to ensure that British kings and queens did as much as possible to help the crusading movement.

The Templars were warriors in the East, but farmers, administrators and lobbyists in the West – and, like the British Templars themselves, this book similarly strives to be polarised but harmoniously balanced.

These two groups of men have very different stories to tell, but neither story makes sense without the other. *Templars: The Knights of Britain* tries to bring these two very distinctive aspects of the order together, hopefully in a way that allows each of their experiences to be told within the context of the other – the military achievements alongside the agricultural advances, the individual acts of heroism alongside the more shadowy activities of the Templar lawyers, diplomats and bankers who advised kings and helped finance their expeditions.

The objectives behind their different activities, however disparate they may appear at first glance, were often far closer than one might imagine. It is pointless, say, to examine Templar estate management or banking transactions without fully understanding the context of what those farms and financial dealings were for.

Inevitably, the Templars had their own provincial organisations and tactical objectives within each of the different states of western Europe and the Christian Middle East. Wherever they operated, the Templars were necessarily, unavoidably, active participants in local politics – in this case the governments and power struggles of the British Isles. But these relationships and assets were primarily just a means to a far more ambitious end.

Most importantly, and regardless of their local relationships and allegiances, they were called to a higher master – the papacy. And they were dedicated to a higher cause – the broader struggle to defend the frontiers of Christendom.

This dichotomy meant that they were often tactically 'national' within their host states, but the heart of their strategic objectives was fundamentally 'international' in nature.

In the British Isles, for instance, as in the other provinces of the West, the Templars were primarily diplomats and fundraisers. They were locally based administrators and professionals, focused on generating goodwill and resources for the brutal wars that raged unceasingly in the Holy Land. But in the East the role of the British Templars was very different: they were dedicated soldiers, fighting as volunteers in an international army alongside comrades gathered from across western Europe. They were warriors single-mindedly focused on the military requirements of the defence of the Christian East.

It is important to remember that the Templars were, above all else, a *military order*.

And the embarrassingly large clue to the nature of their role, the very reason for their existence, lies in that descriptor.

Despite the impression given on the internet and by an entire industry of conspiracy theorists, they were not established to guard the Holy Grail, nor to create a thriving global cult revelling in the arcane delights of satanic worship. Neither, more prosaically and even more disappointingly, were they the medieval equivalent of a Club Med for the bored younger sons of the European landed gentry.

They were indeed military. The Templars were the nearest thing that Europe could come up with to create a (semi) professional standing army to help defend the Holy Land – and they were the best means to gather resources from across the different states of western Europe and funnel them to where they were needed most.

But they were also a monastic order. The British Templars were Catholic (or 'Latin') Christians. They were not intellectuals or theologians – their interests were more firmly focused on the material world, particularly the violent struggle for the Levant. Most did not know Latin, and in church services the majority of the brothers would have been spectators. But they were expected to devote themselves to prayer and to the service of God. And, as members of a monastic order, they swore vows of obedience, chastity and poverty. They said prayers at fixed times each day (the 'Hours'), and they attended a daily religious service at which they prayed for the souls of their patrons and the members of the order who had gone before them.[6]

It is in the strange and often tense consequences of this extraordinary blending – the potentially toxic mixture of pacifistic monasticism and hyper-violent elite warfare – that the Templars lived, prayed and fought.

This book is similarly split – and for very similar reasons. If one were to write purely about the Templars *in* Britain (rather than the activities of the British Templars as a whole), one would have a study that was largely focused on the management of agricultural estates, interlaced with some administrative and legal manoeuvring at court. It would neglect their core objectives and downplay the truly important issues that the Templars faced.

Above all, it would skate over the most profound aspect of the order's purpose: the need to defend those parts of the Middle East, the old heartlands of Christianity, which had been recaptured during the extraordinary (and exceptionally lucky) armed pilgrimage of 1095–9 which later became known as the First Crusade. As so often with issues of medieval strategy, their broader goals were often unspoken (or at least unwritten) but nonetheless real.

This book, like the Templars themselves, must juggle 'local' perspectives while continually remaining aware of the bigger picture.

NATIONALISM AND THE BRITISH TEMPLARS

Part of reconciling local perspectives with an international agenda involves rethinking what we mean by nationalism and national identities in a medieval context.

It is important to understand just how different medieval views of ethnicity, nationalism and culture were from ours. The British Isles are our case in point, of course, and they provide a particularly useful perspective on how to view (and how not to view) such things.

It is easy to be confused by ostensibly similar boundaries and ideas. There was a kingdom called England, the dominant military and political force in Britain. There was a kingdom of Scotland, with a Scottish king and Scottish inhabitants. And there were lands called Wales and Ireland, both with fluctuating relationships with their neighbours, and particularly with the English. This all sounds very familiar to our ears.

When we read of English Templar knights taking over lands in Wales or (to an even greater extent) Ireland, we are perhaps tempted to see this through a prism of English 'proto-colonialism'. We might be aware of the close relationships between the Templars and the English crown during the Anglo-Scottish wars and again assume that there is some quasi-nationalistic agenda at play.

In fact, such ideas, tempting as they are as a shorthand explanation for events, are almost entirely wrong. True, there was always power play at work – when is there not? As we shall see, the Templars' default position was to align themselves with the most powerful players within their province of Britain – and this predominant power was usually the English crown.

But there was little that was truly nationalistic about all this. Most of the ruling classes across the whole of Britain at this time were Anglo-Norman rather than 'English', 'Scottish' or 'Welsh'. The Anglo-Normans in charge of England were the richest and most powerful in the British Isles and they acted accordingly. But the nobility and kings of Scotland were also largely Anglo-Norman in language, culture and ethnicity. They were fighting for the interests of their (largely Anglo-Norman) friends and families every bit as much as for some anachronistic sense of 'nationalism'.

The same was also true in Wales or Ireland – large parts of their ruling classes were Anglo-Norman by blood and language. The fault lines were always far more complex than, say, 'English' versus 'Scottish' or 'Irish'.

The clearest example of this is perhaps to be found in the structure of the Templars themselves. The Templars in Ireland and Scotland were seen as subordinate parts of the broader Templar province of England. There were Templar commanders (or masters) in both locations, but they were almost exclusively 'Englishmen' (or, rather, Anglo-Normans), chosen or approved by the (Anglo-Norman) brothers operating out of the order's provincial headquarters in London. When Walter the Bachelor, the Templar master in Ireland, was accused of theft, for instance, he was ordered back to England and imprisoned in London. The papacy took a similarly robust view – it explicitly treated Britain as a single province, subject to the commander of England, 'so that the whole is one commandery' [*ita quod totum est una preceptoria*].[7]

Wherever they operated, the British Templars were neither 'English' nor 'oppressors', or at least not in the way that we might use such words. They were not even 'foreigners', except in a general sense that applied to most of the (Anglo-Norman) British ruling classes. Instead, they were members of an international monastic order, doing the best they could to marshal the resources of fractious islands in the cause of defending the Latin East.

This was also usually true of those in Britain who supported them – families, networks and religious structures were all more important than the romantic notions of local nationalism propagated by nineteenth-century novelists and their political successors. On the contrary, despite all the modern conspiracy theories that place them within nationalist agendas, the Templars were pan-national rather than provincial – the order looked up at the bigger picture and out towards the East, rather than down into parochialism.

Paradoxically, as we shall see, helping to make the British Isles more peaceful and productive was a consequence of their actions. But it was a by-product rather than a primary goal.

Ultimately, the Templars wanted to operate within effective, stable societies. Such societies could generate more resources to be sent to the East (to help bolster up the crusader states). Ideally, they would also be ruled by kings and noblemen who were sufficiently undistracted to be persuaded to lead their armies on that same journey, out to the Holy Land.

A far-reaching consequence of this surprisingly internationalist agenda, however, was to help create more modern instruments of government on a provincial level. The interests of the order were fundamentally their own – but those interests often coincided with those of a stabilising and central-ising monarchy.

This was not an ideal world. Ultimately, anyone who wanted to generate help for the Latin East had to work with the material with which they were presented. In most of western Europe, the Templars were embedded in societies that had poor levels of communication and low productivity, presided over by more or less fractious elite groups: kings and queens, counts, earls and knights. Each man or woman, family or group jockeyed for position in their own tiny, splintered worlds.

However frustrating it might be, the local monarchies (which for the British Templars were the kings and queens of England and Scotland) almost invariably put their own interests first. In this situation, the Templars, and their papal masters, generally strove for improvement rather than perfection. They made the best of what they found. And they tried to make it better.

This usually meant supporting existing kings and the status quo of established political structures – the Templars instinctively grasped that it was in these structures that the best prospects for stability lay, and it was only in a situation of stability that help could be channelled to the East.

The Templar brothers were internationalists who inadvertently helped create nations. They were ferocious warriors who were also monks in a religion theoretically devoted to non-violence. And they were soldiers, capable of the most ferocious and hopeless charges, who helped create bureaucracy. Balancing these strangely antithetical characteristics was a permanent challenge.

This central core of irony, and the tension it represented, lay at the heart of the British Templars. We might try to drag the Templars into our modern world of national allegiances and politics, but they were internationalists at heart.

SOURCES

Like the British Templars, the nature of the sources is polarised – and they are divided along similar lines. In Britain itself, the 'home front', most of the sources are dry, agricultural records or financial statements. The characters of the British Templars going about their daily domestic duties are seen only in occasional glimpses.

The main exceptions to this are in the trial records dating to the suppression of the order from 1307 onwards. As we shall see, these occasionally give us insights, both mundane and extraordinary, into the lives of the brother knights.

However, given the exceptional nature of the process and the leading nature of the questions that the Templars were responding to, the information they provided to their interrogators needs to be treated with great caution. Then, as now, anything the brothers were 'encouraged' to say under interrogation is always suspect – this is particularly true in the French sources, for instance, reflecting an investigative process where the use of torture was rife, unlike that in Britain.

As we shall see, the different legal systems came up with very different results as a consequence. Torture is, of course, morally repugnant. But if anyone ever had residual doubts about its efficacy as a means of arriving at the truth, the trial of the Templars is a definitive case study. Even the bravest men really will say any number of lies to stop the pain.

The usual royal sources of first resort for English history in this period, the Pipe Rolls, the Liberate Rolls, the Close Rolls and so on, are less useful than one might expect. They shed some light on the Templars but tend to focus on the king's internal administrative processes.

The 'Inquest of 1185', on the other hand, a catalogue of the order's possessions, which was set in train by Geoffrey Fitz Stephen, the master of the order in England, is very helpful. It gathers together a series of documents that shed light on the privileges and possessions of the order in England towards the end of the twelfth century. This is very usefully supplemented by the *Cartulaire général de l'Ordre du Temple*, which lists many of the grants received by the Templars in England, and by the records of the Hospitallers, who inherited much of the Templars' assets after their dissolution.[8]

For the British Templars in the East, however – those at the sharp end of the order's purpose – we have almost the opposite problem.

The Templars were the larger-than-life icons of the crusading movement. To a large extent they remain so to this day. The contemporary chronicles are full of the order's exploits – leading heroic charges, building castles as huge and awe-inspiring as modern aircraft carriers or dying as martyrs for Christendom. The Templars continually demanded attention through their actions. Inevitably, they had the high profile that accompanied it.

But the real strength of the Templars at war was that they were an *international* order, acting across and above the internal, provincial borders of Christendom – they were pursuing pan-European aims at a time when most political activity in the West was irredeemably localised and fragmented.

This unique (and uniquely useful) characteristic is reflected in the way they are treated within the chronicles of the time. We know that British Templars fought in the East, and we catch occasional glimpses of their activities. But the Templars were a pan-national order – mentions of their exploits in the Holy Land are numerous, but rarely focus on the 'nationality' of the individuals concerned.

Appropriately enough for an international order (but unhelpfully for someone writing a 'national' history), references to their activities in the crusader states are generally made about 'Templars', rather than, say, 'Italian Templars', 'French Templars' or 'British Templars'. National identities on the front line were not seen as being particularly important – they were subsumed and lost in much the same way as, for instance, the exploits of Spanish or Polish soldiers might be absorbed anonymously into a history of the French Foreign Legion.

Both sets of sources (administrative records in Britain and chronicles in the Latin East) can be found in the Select Bibliography at the end of this book. But the most obvious archive – the elephant no longer in the room – is the one that is missing.

The Templars' own records have, except for a few pieces of accidental flotsam, disappeared without trace. This is incredibly frustrating. We know that the Templars had substantial archives. They were formidable lawyers as well as outstanding warriors. Their records would have been scrupulously filed and protected – they had depositories of documents proving all the many privileges and properties that the order had acquired. These were precious and jealously guarded.

But almost nothing remains. Two hundred years of mundane records were supplanted by the febrile confessions that were forced from the brother knights as the order was suppressed.

The Templars might be dead but the vacuum created by the loss of their archives, combined with the bizarre accusations that were made against them, created the perfect breeding ground in which conspiracy theories could flourish.[9]

2

❖

CRUSADE AND CONQUEST: 1099–1119

It began as it ended.

Invasions. Blood. Conflict. And a desperate attempt to save the Christian Middle East.

It was also the central irony of the age. The violent convulsion of Middle Eastern wars which we now call 'the crusades' was sustained by one of the world's most pacifistic religions – Christianity. And the shocking eruption of inter-cultural hatred that emerged was driven by love – albeit in a very specific and technical use of the word.

The idea of 'crusading as an act of love' sounds deeply Orwellian – just a shade away from a cardinal describing the papacy as doubleplus-good. But this was a world where peace required war. And a time when 'love' meant love of your God and love of your co-religionists and their communities. Love such as this might require you to give up your life in defence of your fellow man and often required a violent expression.[1]

In this context, it was no huge intellectual leap to suggest that monks could also be warriors. In fact, far from a leap, it was an entirely logical conclusion – merely an internally consistent consequence of the situation in which all parties found themselves in the early years of the twelfth century, across the war-torn towns and villages of Palestine and Syria later known as the crusader states.

The Templars epitomised this irony. They were the finest soldiers of the West, brave and highly skilled warriors. Their famous and rightly feared charge was the pivotal point of many battles. And yet they were also monks, clerics of a religion devoted to the concepts of love, peace and the possibility of redemption for all men.[2]

Even at the time, the incongruity did not go unnoticed.

THE FIRST CRUSADE

Appeals for help had been made for many years. Alexius, the emperor of Byzantium, was desperate for military assistance to face off an onslaught from Muslim (or at least nominally Muslim) Turkic tribesmen who were devastating Christian Anatolia. An expedition to help their fellow Christians had long been discussed in the West, with varying degrees of detail, realism and enthusiasm.

But on 27 November 1095, the time for action finally arrived. At the end of a Church Council in Clermont, Pope Urban II gathered a crowd of local people in an adjacent field and began the call to arms. Knights from across Christendom, he said, should be prepared to travel east to liberate the Holy Sepulchre, the tomb of Christ, from Muslim control, and to come to the aid of their fellow Christians.

The crusading movement was born.

The central ingredients of the Templar order were present from its inception: the necessity of having devoted Christian knights; the objective of an essentially defensive war to recover the ancient Christian heartlands; and the idea that even a pacifistic religion based on love could still call on violence to defend itself and its people. The Templar order was over two decades in the future, but its defining purpose can be seen from the very start.

The crusaders arrived in the Levant in 1097. The majority of the local populations in what became the crusader states were still Christian. But they had been demilitarised and ruled by Muslim overlords for long periods of time, sometimes centuries.

The world the crusaders blundered into was complex and chaotic. But it was this very chaos, and the Muslim disunity that it represented, that made the crusader states even temporarily viable.

The first waves of Muslim invaders had swept up from the south into the Middle East in the seventh century. They overran most of what is now Egypt, Palestine and Syria, and subjugated their mainly Christian populations. The Orthodox Christian Byzantine empire contested the possession of Syria, but a broad equilibrium was established.[3]

All this changed with the advent of the Turkic tribes.

Early in the eleventh century, the Seljuk Turks began to appear. They entered from the steppes in the north and north-east. From the 1020s onwards, these nomadic tribesmen drifted down into the region, first conquering the Iranian world and then attacking Christian Anatolia. By the 1070s they were heading south, attracted by the riches of the Arab-held city-states of Syria and contesting control of Palestine with the Egyptian Fatimid caliphate. Within a few years the Seljuk–Turkic state encompassed much of the known world, bordering Byzantium in the west and China in the east.

The Shi'ite Fatimid Egyptian empire, the incumbent rulers of Palestine, had long been at war with the Sunni Turkic invaders. Relationships between the two groups were poor – there was mutual and deep-seated cultural, racial and religious antagonism. Even amongst themselves, there were layers of fragmentation and mistrust.

Each Turkic warlord guarded his independence jealously and almost invariably placed his own interests first. The crusaders might be a nuisance, but they were often not the highest priority. They were no more foreign than the Turks themselves and could be enemies or allies as changing alliances or circumstances demanded. Far from being unique as 'intruders' upon local politics, the Europeans were just another group of players in the bloody world of medieval Middle Eastern politics.[4]

This endemic squabbling amongst the Muslim powers enabled the crusaders (or 'Franks' as they were often known) to carve out a place in the

Levant. But although this was helpful in the short term, it was also a longer-term problem. Such disunity was transient. It disguised the basic weaknesses of the crusaders. When the Muslim states began to coalesce, the true balance of power in the East would quickly become apparent.[5]

THE CRUSADER STATES

The First Crusade was always an unlikely expedition. The squabbling crusader armies, with only the most primitive logistical support, had marched across Europe and on through the Byzantine empire. From there they fought their way down through Anatolia, Syria, Lebanon and Palestine. But somehow it all worked. It was an astounding, some would say miraculous, success.

On 15 July 1099, Jerusalem, the Holy City and spiritual birthplace of Christianity, was liberated.

But it was immediately obvious that it could not be held indefinitely. It was sited inland. It was desperately underpopulated. And it had precarious supplies of food and water. The city was a military disaster just waiting to happen. Jerusalem could only be brought back into Christian hands in any sustainable way if it were part of a bigger, more demographically robust and militarily strong group of states which might be able to defend it and its people. The concept of the 'crusader states' was born.

The First Crusade had achieved far more than anyone might reasonably have expected. The Holy Land had been liberated in 1099. Some of the Christian territory lost to the Muslim invasions of the seventh to eleventh centuries had been recovered. But the victories of the crusade were never a satisfactory solution; rather, they just created an entirely new, and bigger, set of problems.

Most of the crusaders returned home to the West, happy to convince themselves that the vows of their supremely violent pilgrimage had been fulfilled. Few appreciated that saving the Middle East for Christendom was a *process* rather than an *event*. But holding territory on the very fringes of Europe was a far more difficult task than recapturing it.[6]

Some men stayed behind to defend the Holy Land, however. They established four political entities, which we now collectively call 'the crusader states'. To the north, and perilously inland, was the county of Edessa. Next to it, with the vital benefit of a coastline and ports which could help link it back to Europe, was the principality of Antioch (covering parts of what we now describe as Syria and southern Turkey). Further south, occupying most of what is now Lebanon, came the county of Tripoli.

But the most prestigious of the crusader states was even further south, sharing long and fragile borders with the Fatimid empire in Egypt and the Turkic-run states of Syria – the Latin Kingdom of Jerusalem (similar in extent to what we might now call Israel or Palestine).

It was clear to everyone that the crusader states faced huge military problems. What was perhaps less obvious, however, was the fact that these problems would only get worse over time.

The success of the First Crusade had been a huge stroke of luck – but the crusaders would need a lot more than luck if the new Christian states that they left behind were to survive.

THE MILITARY PREDICAMENT

The crusader states were all woefully undermanned and under-resourced.

If they were to survive, they would need massive military aid – but aid of a kind that had not been seen in the West since the fall of the Roman Empire.

The First Crusade had been able to recover much of the Christian Middle East, albeit as much by luck as by judgement. But, as a means of funnelling troops out to defend these gains, further crusades (in effect, a series of one-off military expeditions) were a far less effective mechanism.

Occasional reinforcements continued to come over from the West, but these crusaders were usually well-meaning military tourists. The normal pattern was to land at a congenial port, stay for a few months or a year while they acclimatised themselves and visited the religious sites. Then they returned home – perhaps leaving those they came to help vulnerable to retaliation.

Random interventions such as this could never be a substitute for a standing army. And it was a standing army that the crusader states needed above all else. There were castles to man and a pressing need for field armies with which to counter Muslim invasions. The primary requirement in the East, therefore, was a military one – the need to get high-quality soldiers and materiel on the ground, and on a long-term basis.

The scale of the problem was unprecedented. Standing armies were a barely distant memory in medieval Europe. But the military issues facing the European settlements in the Middle East were extraordinary in their size and scope.

Any solution would need to be similarly extraordinary.

3

BIRTH OF THE ORDER: 1099–1128

A bizarre, almost surreal, meeting took place in central Palestine in July 1099.

The First Crusade had finally reached Jerusalem. The city was under siege but had not yet been captured. The senior clergy and the secular leaders of the crusade gathered to take stock – and, most importantly, to decide who should be put in charge if Jerusalem was recovered.

Raymond d'Aguilers, chaplain to Count Raymond of Toulouse, was present at the meeting. He wrote in some detail about the way the discussions ebbed and flowed. The men were surrounded by Muslim states and armies, woefully outnumbered. And they were soon to have the dubious privilege of being in possession of an almost indefensible city.

In the face of this unenviable situation, an astonishing proposition was made.

The soldiers in the assembly quite naturally 'posed the question of the election of one of the princes [that is, a military leader] as a guardian of Jerusalem in case God gave it to us. It was argued that it was common effort which would win it, but it would be common neglect that would lose it if no one protected it.' So far, so sensible.

But the representatives of the church were having none of it. Instead, they proposed that Jerusalem, and presumably the lands around it, would become an ecclesiastical state, with ultimate power being wielded by the church leaders. In this optimistic scenario, the rulers would be papal appointees. Their instructions would be conveyed to a compliant military leader (an 'advocate'), who would be well resourced and eager to act upon their wishes.[1]

Nowadays, such an idea would be ridiculed as being obviously impractical – an absurd reflection of the overweening self-importance of the medieval clergy. Even at the time, amongst far more pious men, the idea was deemed to be extraordinarily unrealistic.

Eventually, common sense prevailed.

One of the army's military commanders, Godfrey of Bouillon, was elected as leader on 22 July 1099, after the city was back in Christian hands. Perhaps in deference to ecclesiastical sensitivities, and in recognition of his role as protector of Jerusalem, he took the title of *advocatus*, or *princeps*, rather than king – but there was no question of the Latin Kingdom of Jerusalem, a country in a permanent state of war, being run by a priest.

The original idea of making Jerusalem a religiously controlled state from its very inception is usually assumed to have been completely naive, even to the point of being slightly crazy. Or it is alternatively portrayed as the arrogant scheming of the local representatives of the church. Certainly, at that time, and in that place, it was absolutely inappropriate.[2]

CRAZY IDEAS FOR CRAZY TIMES?

But strangely, with hindsight, it was also surprisingly prescient.

With Jerusalem back in Christian hands, most of the army felt that their job had been done. They returned to Europe and were welcomed as heroes. The men were grateful to have survived. They were eager to see their homelands and families. It immediately became apparent that the defence of the Holy Land could not be adequately undertaken by the tiny number of crusaders left behind – ultimately it would require the full assistance and support of those the First Crusade had left behind in Europe.

But, given the fragmented and inefficient nature of the states that comprised western Europe, it was only the religious authorities (primarily the papacy) who could gather and funnel the resources required through to the Holy Land. Ironically, the idea of centralised military support being offered by the church for the defence of Christendom was inspired. Far from being naive, it was an astute and imaginative way of addressing the strategic problems facing the crusader states.

Setting up an ecclesiastical state was not feasible, particularly at that time of unending military emergency, but the religious leaders of the First Crusade had stumbled across the heart of the issue. There needed to be a mechanism by which the seemingly contradictory drivers of spiritual devotion and military muscle could be brought together to help defend the newly won lands.

NEW PROBLEMS, NEW SOLUTIONS – AND A NEW KNIGHTHOOD

As so often happens, the answer to this extraordinary conundrum emerged by happenstance – and it evolved so slowly and organically that most contemporaries did not even recognise what was happening.

It was a small start. A good, practical idea, rather than a grand, strategic plan. So small, in fact, that European chroniclers in Jerusalem at the time, men who knew the individuals concerned, did not even comment on it.

But the idea of the Templars was born.

The chronicler Archbishop William of Tyre was no fan of the order. Writing in the 1180s, many years after the event, he is, nonetheless, our main source for their origin story. He disliked the powerful and semi-independent organisation they grew to be. But even he was struck by the virtue of the initial idea.

The story was a simple one, and simply told. 'In this same year,' William wrote, ostensibly of 1118, but he possibly meant 1119, 'certain pious and God-fearing nobles of knightly rank, devoted to the Lord, professed the wish to live perpetually in poverty, chastity, and obedience . . . Foremost and most distinguished among these men were the venerable Hugh of Payns and Godfrey of Saint-Omer.'

These men were knights but they were nonetheless poor – their vow of personal poverty was taken seriously. 'Since they had neither a church nor a fixed place to live,' wrote William, 'the king [of Jerusalem] granted them a temporary home in his own palace, on the north side by the Temple of the Lord . . . The king and his nobles, as well as the patriarch and the prelates of the church, also provided from their own holdings certain stipends, the income of which was to provide these knights with food and clothing.'

For the first decade of their existence, the Templars looked more like a small group of eccentrics than a menacing army: 'nine years after the founding of this order, the knights were still in secular clothing. They wore such clothes as the people, for the salvation of their souls, gave to them.' Their appearance (mail shirts and armour worn over charitable donations of second-hand civilian clothing) reflected a strange, rather distant relationship with what was expected from a traditional Christian monastic order.

The crusaders (wrongly) thought that the al-Aqsa mosque was the biblical Temple of Solomon, so the members of this new order were initially known, with medieval directness, as 'the knights of the Temple of Solomon'. But by the 1140s a catchier and more iconic epithet begins to appear in the records – 'Templars'.

Although the notion that the order could become a semi-permanent army was still some way in the future, their objectives always involved the use of violence in a good cause. Their goal was that, 'as far as their strength permitted, they should keep the roads and highways safe from the menace of robbers and highwaymen, with particular regard for the protection of pilgrims'.

The growth of the young but enthusiastic group was painfully slow. Even when 'the Templars had been established for nine years, they were as yet only nine in number . . . After this period, however, they began to increase,' wrote William, 'and their possessions multiplied.'[3]

William's comments were inevitably speculative, given that he was writing some sixty years after the events he described. Interestingly, Fulcher of Chartres, a chronicler who was also a canon of the Holy Sepulchre, and who wrote a history covering most of the first three decades of the Latin Kingdom of Jerusalem, was silent about the Templars. In 1118 or 1119, when the order was born, Fulcher was living nearby. The Frankish population was small and he almost certainly knew Hugh and Godfrey on a personal basis. But he does not even mention them.

We do not need to search for hidden meanings in his silence, though many modern conspiracists inevitably do. The truth is far more mundane. The Templar order at this time was so small, so insignificant, that Fulcher probably just viewed them as being a few pious bodyguards – soldiers who were also, not uncommonly at a time of crusading fervour, religious enthusiasts. And perhaps he saw them as just one small part of the human flotsam of the early crusades, men adrift in the Middle East who were looking out for the safety of pilgrims and the protection of the precious relics to be found in Jerusalem.

Fulcher may not have been too far wrong if he did indeed believe that. Simon of Saint-Bertin, a Benedictine abbey in the home town of Godfrey of Saint-Omer, wrote in the 1130s that the founders of the order were knights who had fought their way across eastern Europe and the Middle East as part of the First Crusade – and that, on its completion, perhaps having seen and done too many things that they could not forget, Hugh and Godfrey had decided to renounce material possessions. Instead, they devoted themselves to the continuing protection of pilgrims and the Holy Land.[4]

Certainly, by the time Fulcher died (probably in 1128 or early 1129), the Templars were still just a tiny group of volunteers – an embryonic possibility of what they would later become. They had potential, but there was no reason at the time to believe that they would necessarily develop into anything more significant.[5]

Entirely predictably, a lack of references to the founders of the order has contributed to the myths and 'mystery' of the Templars' origins. Their absence from the chronicles was not due to any great secrecy, however –

their small numbers and relatively humble origins as individuals merely means that they did not appear frequently in the surviving records of the time. The brother knights, including the founders of the order, were not men who were overly wealthy or powerful.

And, strangely enough for an order that became known for its elite knights and occasionally arrogant demeanour, that continued to be the case. The Templars were usually eager recruits drawn from the lesser nobility and middle levels of society rather than from the very top. The brothers were far more likely to be the sons of wealthy peasants, poorer knights or the middle classes, rather than anyone grander. When the order was closed down, several of the British brothers claimed, under interrogation, that they could not understand French, let alone speak it or read it. Far from being evasive, this was probably just a consequence of their relatively humble origins.[6]

THE 'EVANGELICAL' TOUR OF HUGH OF PAYNS

Although the Templar order technically existed from 1118 or 1119 onwards, for the first decade after its foundation it was little more than an idea. The order had only a tiny number of volunteers with which to carry out its vastly overambitious objectives. It existed in borrowed clothes and borrowed accommodation. And it carried out its dangerous duties in relative anonymity. Its main support came from the near-bankrupt king of Jerusalem and his local clergy. The Templar order was born on the furthest fringes of Christendom – far from the glamorous courts and royal patronage of western Europe.

A step change was needed – and it was obvious that this change was not going to happen in the struggling Latin East. Something needed to be done to make the European powers take notice.

The turning point came in 1127.

In that year, Hugh of Payns, together with his royal sponsors in the Latin East, made the decision to launch a fundraising and recruitment drive in western Europe. It was a huge gamble. It involved many of the

Templars leaving the Holy Land, at a time when every fighting man was needed on the front line. If it worked, however, the rewards would be huge – the Templars could make the transition from being a tiny group of provincial enthusiasts to being one of the Christian world's greatest international corporations.

Damascus was the trigger for that transition. It was the biggest prize in front of the crusader leadership and its capture would be the best way to ensure that the nascent Christian states in the region had the critical mass to survive.

The city had been a prosperous Christian regional centre at the time of the Arab invasions. If it could be recovered, the crusader states would have enough land to attract desperately needed settlers into the region. And they would gain the geographic space to conduct a defence in depth in the face of inevitable Muslim attacks. At a single stroke, the prospect of a revitalised and sustainable Christian Middle East would become far more realistic.

Damascus was a tantalising objective. King Baldwin II, the tough and resourceful leader of the Latin Kingdom of Jerusalem, was understandably beguiled by it. By the mid-1120s, he began to put the planning in place for a coordinated assault on the city. To do this with any chance of success, however, he needed to get help from western Europe. Baldwin sent two diplomatic missions to the West in 1127 to call for help. Operationally, nothing was being left to chance.[7]

One delegation, led by the chancellor, William of Bures, and Guy Brisebarre, was primarily focused on Fulk, count of Anjou. Fulk was a powerful leader who was already known for his commitment to the crusading cause – he was to be offered the hand in marriage of Melisende, Baldwin's eldest daughter and the heiress to the throne of Jerusalem. Implicitly, Fulk was being positioned to succeed Baldwin as king.[8]

The other mission was led by Hugh of Payns and his obscure group of enthusiasts, with their strange blend of knighthood and monasticism. One of their objectives was explicit and well understood by contemporaries.

Hugh and the other ambassadors were, wrote William of Tyre, 'sent by the king and the chief men of the kingdom to the princes of the West for the purpose of rousing the people there to come to our assistance. Above all, they were to try to induce powerful men [*potentes*] to come to help us besiege Damascus.'

What William did not say, however, perhaps because of his antipathy towards the Templars and the power they later wielded, was that it was also a major awareness raising and recruitment drive for the order.[9]

Like Billy Graham's evangelical tours (which, with a strangely cyclical irony, became known as 'crusades'), the Templars took the opportunity to work their way around the European centres of power. The results were transformative.

The order was hugely committed to the mission. Hugh took five of his brother knights with him – tough, fighting men who would be powerful advocates when looking for recruits. These were empathetic figures with whom the western nobility and their kings could easily relate. This may not seem like a substantial embassy, but the order was so small at this stage that, by William of Tyre's own admission, the tiny contingent of six battle-weary men constituted the majority of the Templar brothers. Hugh was staking everything on this opportunity – now he could take his idea for a new kind of militant Christianity into the courts and palaces of Europe.

In practice, there was a big overlap between the two missions. Fulk was both a crusader and an ardent admirer of the Templars. He was possibly even an associate Templar brother himself by this time. Fulk had previously paid for the maintenance of 100 knights in the Latin East. He encouraged others to be generous with their money too. But, more importantly for the missions, in approaching him they knew they were pushing at an open door. Fulk and his men instantly signed up for the new expedition.

Both sets of emissaries from the kingdom of Jerusalem went to Le Mans. There, on Ascension Day, 31 May 1128, Fulk and his men publicly 'took the Cross' and vowed to go on crusade. Hugh stayed to help with the last-minute preparations for their expedition. With the assistance of the Templar brothers, soldiers with a deep understanding of military conditions in the Latin East, Fulk's small army started the long journey towards the crusader states.[10]

Although recruiting Fulk to the cause was the highlight of the diplomatic missions of 1127–8, this was just one part of the Templar recruitment drive. Energetic as ever, Hugh of Payns and his men continued to travel around western Europe, gathering practical help for the order – sourcing men, money, horses and other supplies. Most importantly of all, however, they built up profile and publicity. They established a highly desirable 'corporate brand', both within the church and, uniquely for a hybrid military–monastic order, amongst the warrior elite of Europe.

Their efforts were rewarded. In January 1129, the Council of Troyes was convened by Bernard of Clairvaux to allow Hugh of Payns to make his case. It was a huge success. The Templars were given papal approval and officially recognised as a religious order. This not only gave the Templars a sound organisational structure but also allowed them to start being given (and gratefully accepting) landed estates and other assets across Europe, together with all the rents and services associated with them.

They also received a range of different privileges and financial exemptions. Significantly in terms of their later poor relationships with many parts of the church, this often gave them tithes that would otherwise have gone to local ecclesiastical institutions. The motivation for these exemptions was good – it helped to divert as much money as possible to the defence of the East. But it also meant that the order's inception contained within it the seeds of much later unpopularity.

Hugh was clearly a charismatic speaker. Surrounded by his five brother knights, he 'conveyed from memory . . . the manner and observance of the small beginnings of his military order which owed its existence to Him who says, "I speak to you who am the beginning".' His audience was entranced. The idea of what the Templars stood for, and what they could become, had been planted. At last they had the calling card they needed for large-scale recruitment.[11]

Bernard, abbot of Clairvaux, normally gets the credit for helping to establish the Templars in the West. The Council of Troyes had been convened at his initiative and, soon after the Council had ended, Hugh of Payns very astutely asked Bernard to write a fulsome endorsement of the new order – though, far more diplomatically, Hugh preferred to describe it as a 'sermon of encouragement'.

This endorsement eventually took the shape of a famous treatise entitled 'In Praise of the New Knighthood'. The virtues of the Templars were set out in thirteen alluring chapters, each designed to persuade secular knights to play their part in the new cause. Bernard also devised a Rule for the extraordinary new order – a medieval 'code of conduct' for the brothers. The Rule included outline objectives and operating procedures to guide and regularise their lives as monks and as soldiers. It was all massively helpful.[12]

It is certainly true that Bernard played a very significant role in creating an aura of legitimacy for the Templars. He also succeeded in generating a mass of positive publicity for the order. The much lower-profile role played by King Baldwin II of Jerusalem was arguably just as important, however. His influence is largely overlooked because of an accident of fate: unlike the Vatican or the other religious archives in the West, very little of his correspondence has survived.

But it was Baldwin who had moved the Templars into the iconic al-Aqsa mosque, giving them a substantial base and, coincidentally, their name. He was the man with the imagination and vision to see that they could be a unique (and desperately needed) way of bringing the resources of the West to the aid of the East. Through the Templars, he helped devise a way of giving the martial enthusiasm of Europe's knights a spiritual tinge – the vital ingredient needed to keep them making the huge sacrifices required to defend the Holy Land. It was only because of Baldwin's foresight that the Templars were able to become such a powerful military force.

The mission was a triumph. The Templars were able to motivate 'many bands of noblemen' to follow them back to the East. These small armies gathered for the assault on Damascus, which Baldwin was trying to coordinate, and which eventually took place in 1129. Sadly for the participants, the attack was unsuccessful. Logistical problems, appalling weather and huge numbers of Turkic mercenary horse archers meant that the crusader army ground to a halt before it even reached the city.[13]

Importantly for our story, however, many of these brave and enthusiastic 'bands' of soldiers came from Britain, and Hugh's recruitment drive of 1128 can be seen as the start of the British Templars.[14]

A small unit of dedicated monastic warriors based in the Middle East had at last gone international.

It is easy to forget the enormity of that shift.

Extraordinarily for an age when few people ever left their villages, the Templars were to become a supranational army (a military order), fighting for a supranational organisation (the papacy), on behalf of a supranational idea (Christendom).

It was hardly a rapid-response force. Nothing about medieval communications or logistics was rapid. But, for the first time since the last Roman legionary in the western empire put down his sword, Europe had a mechanism by which pan-national forces could be deployed and sustained.

If anyone was going to be able to stabilise the dangerous frontiers of the Middle East, it was going to be the Templars. For the crusader states, help was on the way – just in time.

4

⟐

THE FOUNDATION YEARS: 1128–1135

There may have been British Templars before Hugh's arrival in 1128.

The English in particular had played a significant, although certainly not dominating, role in the First Crusade and the subsequent early expeditions to the East.

Inevitably, it is mainly the nobility who appear in the records – but they were accompanied by their anonymous retinues containing far larger numbers of Englishmen who served as soldiers, squires and mercenaries. Even some of the growing middle-classes were involved, helped by their money and access to shipping. Merchants and traders went on crusade, including Roger of Cornhill (still a famous City financial street), Andrew of London and Viels of Southampton. So it is certainly not impossible, given the enthusiasm for crusading at this time, that some of Hugh of Payn's original band of brothers were British.[1]

But it is unlikely.

The First Crusade was primarily a French affair and both Hugh of Payns and Godfrey of Saint-Omer were Frenchmen – instead it is far more likely that the vast majority, if not all, of the first generation of brothers were French. The British Templars were probably in the second wave of recruits.

The earliest reference to the Templars in Britain was a testament to the effectiveness of Hugh's bluff style of recruitment-preaching amongst the warrior classes – but the tone of the chronicles, written with the grim harshness of hindsight, was not encouraging.

While he was on his recruiting road trip around Europe, Hugh of Payns and his men had a very productive audience with King Henry I of England (r. 1100–1135). Not unusually (and this was a perennial problem for the crusading movement, of course), Henry was at war with France. In 1128 he spent much of the year campaigning in Normandy, but still found time to meet up with the charismatic emissaries from the Christian East.[2]

The Anglo-Saxon Chronicle noted that:

> Hugh of the Knights Templar came from Jerusalem to the king in Normandy; and the king received him with great ceremony and gave him great treasures of gold and silver, and sent him thereafter to England, where he was welcomed by all good men. He was given treasures by all, and in Scotland too; and by him much wealth, entirely in gold and silver, was sent to Jerusalem. He called for people to go out to Jerusalem. As a result, more people went, either with him or after him, than ever before since the time of the First Crusade, which was in the day of Pope Urban: yet little was achieved by it. He declared that a decisive battle was imminent between the Christians and the heathen, but, when all those multitudes got there, they were pitiably duped to find it was nothing but lies.[3]

There are two different levels of bitterness in this rather sad and disappointed chronicle entry. Firstly, perhaps, there was bitterness at the thought of Englishmen being taken abroad, to their deaths, by foreigners – and French foreigners at that. The chronicle was, after all, written at a time when cultural friction between Normans and Anglo-Saxons had not entirely disappeared.

The author was also saddened by the fact that young men had died in large numbers on a failed campaign – men who had died, moreover, in a faraway land that had little tangible meaning, either to themselves or the writer. He could not know that there were no lies. King Baldwin II had done everything he could, both militarily and diplomatically, to ensure that the campaign had a realistic prospect of success. But they had still not been able to capture Damascus. While the writer of the Anglo-Saxon Chronicle was hazy about the details, he was all too aware of its ignominious outcome.

This was a dangerous pointer for the future. The cause was just, so God would be on our side. The fault for any failure, so the harsh logic ran, must therefore lie with those who had failed to carry out His will. Frustration about an inability to achieve victory in what was, for all practical purposes, an unwinnable war, would return to dog the Templars throughout their existence.[4]

POLICING THE HOLY LAND

The resentful tone of the Anglo-Saxon Chronicle was a back-handed endorsement of King Baldwin's vision of what the Templars might be able to achieve. The order he envisaged would go some way towards ensuring that the young Frankish states were provided with additional military resources – a crude but useful approximation of a 'standing army'.

The success of Hugh's initial recruitment drive in the West demonstrated that this might indeed be possible. Exceeding Baldwin's expectations, over time the military orders assumed the lion's share of the responsibilities for the defence of the crusader states.

But, before we get drawn too far into the beguiling realms of huge battles, desperate charges and long-drawn-out sieges, it is perhaps worth reminding ourselves what the Templars were originally designed for. Strangely to modern eyes, the order was first established, in a rather prosaic and anticlimactic way, to act as what we would probably regard as police officers, not the elite warriors who later seared their way into legend.

The patriarch of Jerusalem seems to have encouraged Hugh and his men on the understanding that they would have a dual but interconnected role. Part of the time they would be acting as the in-house security team for the Holy Sepulchre and its precious relics. The rest of the time they would operate as a police force to protect pilgrims going to the holy places and other sites of interest to religious tourists. Above all, the approach roads to Jerusalem desperately needed to be kept free of bandits and enemy raiders.

In this the patriarch was not overreacting. The internal security situation was spectacularly poor in the early days of the crusader states.[5]

The enormity of the security problems was demonstrated by the level of military resources that needed to be devoted to the roads and the numbers of pilgrims and merchants who used them. Religious tourism and commerce provided much of the funding that underpinned the fragile viability of the state. So, protecting these groups was more than just about enforcing law and order – it was about safeguarding the very basis of the crusader societies.

The road from Jaffa to Jerusalem provides a good example of how the Templars' militarised policing worked in practice. The severity of the dangers encountered on the route was reflected in the intensity of the security that had to be provided. On the relatively short journey from Jaffa to Jerusalem, for instance, the order built no fewer than three roadside castles.[6]

Internal security was always an issue and in these early days the Templars were the best men for the job.

BODYGUARDS AND CONSIGLIERI: ORIGINS IN SCOTLAND

When Henry I met with Hugh of Payns and his Templar companions in 1128, he gave them permission to recruit and preach in England. He handed them letters of safe conduct and recommendation. He also granted them, according to the chronicler Robert of Torigni, annual contributions in arms and other materiel and lands near Avranches.[7]

Armed with this high-level endorsement, Hugh and his party set off. Detailed records of any other donations that Henry made have not survived. But it was in his reign that the Templars began to build a presence in England.

By the time Henry died in 1135, the Templars had a portfolio of properties. This included their first headquarters, later known as the Old
Temple, in Holborn. Probably more significantly, they had also established
a network of relationships that would stand them in good stead for the
next 200 years. These were the foundation years in which the Templars
began to clarify their role within the British Isles. They started to explore
the ways in which they could best use their local assets and influence to
help the cause of the Latin East.[8]

The Templars in Britain were headquartered in London, and the other
parts of the British Isles were generally subordinate to the order's operations in England – but the formula for determining how best to operate in
conjunction with local royal administrations was first established in
Scotland.

The records of the Templars in Scotland are far sparser than those relating
to England. The two main sources for the order in Britain are less than
helpful. The 1185 'Inquest', or review of assets, does not cover Scotland.
Neither do the inventories of 1308. Despite this, however, it is clear that the
Templars were quickly able to make very significant inroads into Scottish
governmental circles – the example of King David I of Scotland (r. 1124–
53) shows how the order began to influence policy from an early stage.

David had spent many of his formative years in England, before
becoming king of Scotland in 1124, at the relatively mature age of forty.
Hugh of Payns did a good job of ingratiating himself with the pious David
when he came to Scotland in 1128 – the king was fully persuaded of the
merits of the new military order. The Cistercian theologian Ailred of
Rievaulx was glowing in his account of the visit and the impact it had
upon the king. David, he wrote, 'trusted himself altogether to the advice
of [Templar] monks; and keeping beside him some good brethren,
renowned in warfare for the temple of Jerusalem, he made them guardians
of his morals by day and night'.[9]

This was just the beginning. King David's confidence in them rested at
least in part on loyalty and an alignment of interests – he recognised that

their default mode was to support the forces of centralisation. We know, for instance, that Templars in Scotland were habitually appointed to be the king's almoners (a form of financial officer with special responsibilities for charitable donations) by the late thirteenth century – and this tradition may well have been established by the devout King David.

There were other, even more tangible, signs of support. The king gave the order some of their earliest possessions in Scotland, dating from the time of Hugh's visit or very soon afterwards – these included their estate at Balantrodoch (now the unimaginatively named 'Temple' in Midlothian) and he probably gave them the church of Inchinnan in Renfrewshire. By the middle of the twelfth century, they had also been given scattered, albeit relatively small, pieces of land across much of Scotland and they owned property in many towns.

King David's interests went far beyond the easy rhythm of donations and confirmations, however – he was an active supporter of the broader crusading movement. We know that he was in correspondence with Bernard of Clairvaux, the Templars' famous ideological champion and PR spokesman. Only one letter, dated from 1136, now survives, but there were undoubtedly more.

Bernard was one of the key instigators of the Second Crusade, a counter-offensive launched after the Muslim capture of Edessa in 1144. He and David's Templar advisers probably helped lobby the king to join the army – and in this they almost succeeded. Ailred of Rievaulx wrote that King David was keen to join the crusade and that 'he would have renounced the Kingdom, laid down the sceptre, and joined the sacred army . . . if he had not been dissuaded by the . . . clamour and outcry of his whole kingdom; he was detained in body, but not in mind or will'.[10]

The king had been exiled in England and was heavily influenced by the style of government that he had found there. With the help of his Templar partners he introduced new structures into Scotland, increasing his authority as a ruler. They also helped him bring new, more orthodox practices into the religious hierarchy, simultaneously increasing both his own authority over the church and that of the Templars' masters, the papacy.

This was a relationship that delivered benefits for both parties. The Templars were comfortable working with kings of Norman heritage in governing their 'Celtic' possessions. The order's military muscle, network of houses and high-level connections in both church and state could be used to mutual benefit – by a king with ambitions to help increase his power and control, and by warrior monks seeking to improve the flow of men and money to the Latin East.

The Templars continued to be influential in Scotland long after the death of their first patron. King David was succeeded by his grandson, King Malcolm IV, in 1153 and the new king maintained the close relationship with the order – he confirmed the Templars' privileges and possessions and probably extended them. Representatives of the military orders appeared, for instance, for the first time as witnesses to Malcolm's charters.

The British Templars, both in the province itself and in the Holy Land, continued to lobby and cajole. In 1250, for instance, the master of the Templars in Scotland (styled as *magistri Templi in Scotia*, though he was probably not a Scot himself), wrote to Matthew Paris, the English chronicler, from the headquarters of the crusading army on campaign in Egypt. In the letter he conveyed news of the disastrous defeat of the armies of the Seventh Crusade at Mansourah in April of that year. Significantly, when reinforcements were dispatched to the Christian army a few months later, they included a detachment of Scottish knights from East Lothian. The Templars' powers of persuasion had clearly worked.[11]

The Templars kept conveying fresh news of the Holy Land back to Scotland, encouraging as many people as possible to help the crusading cause – either by volunteering in person or by making donations. Amongst the latter were the estates of Maryculter and Temple Liston (in West Lothian), together with a number of churches.[12]

The kings of Scotland had close and co-dependent links with the Templars. But, as in all other parts of the British Isles, we must be careful not to impose our own prejudices onto the true nature of that relationship. The vast majority of donations to the order in Scotland were made to the (largely Anglo-Norman) Templar knights by lords who were similarly of Anglo-Norman culture and descent. This was hardly the kind of 'nationalistic' enterprise that Victorian writers romanticised about.[13]

Even the 'Scottish' King David was of largely Anglo-Norman background and spent many years in England. His main support and patronage came from England, from the English king, Henry I, particularly in the latter part of his reign. His wife was an Anglo-Saxon and Anglo-Norman too, with the distinctly un-Scottish name of Maud. She was also, incidentally, countess of Huntingdon through her Anglo-Saxon father, Waltheof, earl of Huntingdon.

Similarly, there are no records of any Scottish family names amongst the Templar brothers serving in Scotland. There are a couple of instances of English-based brothers called 'de Scot', or 'Scotho', in the early fourteenth century, but there is no clear evidence that they were Scottish or had ever served the order in the north. There was a brother named 'Robert Scot', for instance, who had joined the order in the East some twenty-six years before he was interrogated as part of the Templar trials. He was later transferred to the West, but he was living in Cambridgeshire when the order was suppressed.[14]

There was also a brother named William of Scotho (or Skothow/Skotho) who seems to have been in the order for over twenty-eight years before it was suppressed. He may, on the face of it, have had Scottish connections. But he too was serving in Cambridgeshire when he was arrested in January 1308. The name 'Scotho', potentially of Scottish origins, was crossed out and changed to 'Stoke', a very common English name, in one manuscript. Alternatively, it might have been derived from the English word 'stot', meaning a steer or, occasionally, a horse. Tellingly, he is described more than once as being one of the Templar brothers 'of London'.[15]

Above all, the Templars were an international order and it is anachronistic (and misleading) to try to place them neatly within our current definitions of nationalism, frontiers and allegiances.

5

◈

A NEW ARMY IN THE HOLY LAND: 1135–1154

6 January 1148. The Second Crusade ground to a halt.

The French army of King Louis VII, one of the mightiest forces in Europe, was defeated and almost destroyed while trying to fight its way through to the Holy Land. These were skilled fighting men but, walking from Europe to the Levant, and encountering Turkic tactics for the first time, their experience counted for very little. As he should have done at the outset, the king decided to give tactical command of the army to those who had the best understanding of how to deal with Turkic harassment – the Templars.

The order was a small but elite task force within the army. They had contributed a contingent of some 130 men when Louis set off from Paris in 1147, presumably alongside larger numbers of their other retainers and hired troops. More importantly, they also brought their understanding of how to handle Turkic horse archers. Putting their battlefield experience into practice, the Templars had performed extremely well on the march. Unlike many of their brave but ill-disciplined colleagues, they were still in good fighting condition.

The Templars immediately put simple but effective organisational structures in place. They established a clear chain of command. Sub-commanders were nominated and assigned clear roles in different parts of the marching column. Each was given standardised numbers of troops. Extraordinarily, and indicating just how desperate the situation had become, everyone in the army was forced on oath to become a temporary lay brother of the Templars. An oath was not something taken lightly in the medieval world – all were now subject to the Templars' rules and famously strict military discipline.[1]

The reorganisation was accompanied by a crash course on how to deal with light cavalry. The discipline of the French host was tightened up. Archers and crossbowmen were deployed where the Templars knew they were most needed. Flanks were more assiduously protected. But the very basic nature of the remedial action that was now put in place says much about how disorganised the French had been before the Templars took control.

This was a turning point in the military history of the crusades – and it was the moment when the Templars transformed themselves from a small group of ecclesiastical bodyguards into the fighting backbone of the Christian Middle East.[2]

THE BIG PUSH

The growing strength and professionalism of these new Templar troops were sorely needed.

The early part of this period (broadly 1135–48) found the Templars and the Franks of the Holy Land in a permanent state of war with their neighbours. But this was still a war full of opportunities. Crusader armies were confident and aggressive. They were fresh from their successes on the coast. Further expansion inland was difficult, but did not seem to be impossible.

The rulers of the crusader states, welcoming any help they could get, quickly learned how to work in tandem with the Templars – and the Templars increased their military expertise and influence in the region accordingly.

Increasingly frustrating attempts were made to open up the interior. Each of the major Muslim cities in the region was attacked on several occasions. Aleppo was the target for two major campaigns (1124–5 and 1138); Shaizar was besieged twice (1138 and 1157); and Damascus was the objective for a coordinated assault in 1129 and later, in 1148, as part of the Second Crusade.

The crusader forces, hugely outnumbered and fighting inland at the end of vastly overextended supply lines, were unable to take any of the major cities. Frankish armies, and particularly their disciplined Templar contingents, looked suitably impressive when they were camped outside a Muslim city. But they remained outside. They never had the numbers to break in.

This lack of military momentum inevitably impacted on the order in the West. The flow of Templar soldiers from Britain and the other European provinces was speeding up. But what did these enthusiastic volunteers do when they arrived in the Middle East? And what difference did they make when they were on the battlefields of Syria and Palestine?

The contribution they made increased gradually over time, but it was soon apparent in two key areas – quality and quantity.

Injecting better-quality military practice was at the heart of what the Templars offered. This was particularly true in terms of the tactics needed to defeat light cavalry horse archers – a supremely dangerous kind of warrior almost unknown in western Europe. The order was not just making European troops better at what they already did. They used their new professionalism to change the entire way in which war was waged in the Holy Land.

The role of the new Templar troops at this stage should not be exaggerated. They were never a fully 'professional army' in the way that we would use the term. But they had better resources and a more corporate focus, which allowed them to take a longer view. At their best, they could rise above the compromises and complications of local issues.

The Templars also had the opportunity to develop and implement military best practice across large bodies of men – and this was a highly unusual luxury in the medieval world. They could identify the tactics that were most successful against Europe's newest and most dangerous enemy, the Muslim horse archers. And they could, by their example and training, introduce these new tactical responses into the West's crusader armies.

It is hard to be definitive about key points in time when these innovations were put into practice. With the partial exception of the Rule of the Templars, there are no surviving strategy papers or planning documents. But whenever we see military innovation, we find the Templars at the forefront of change.

When radical new castles were being built in the Holy Land, it was the warrior monks who took the lead in design. As 'Turcopole' horse archers (Christian light cavalry) were recruited to deal with enemy horsemen, it was again the Templars who were in the forefront – they employed them in large numbers and created the senior position of 'Turcopolier' officers to command them. And as professional crossbowmen began to be recruited into Frankish armies during the twelfth century, so the order became a major employer of their services.

Famously, of course, whenever a determined and coordinated charge was called for, the Templars were those trusted to take the lead. They led by example – these were men who combined unit cohesion with bravery and discipline with an aggressive spirit. Ironically, given their supposed fanaticism, whenever restraint was most called for, the Templars were there too. The command of the tail end of a fighting column was always the most dangerous position and the one most susceptible to severe provocation – it came to be given almost invariably to the military orders. Only they had the discipline needed for the task.[3]

The military sophistication of the Templars, and the burdens being placed upon them, had clearly grown enormously over the previous two decades.

Those burdens were only to increase. As the chronicler William of Tyre put it so succinctly, from this time onwards the military situation in the Holy Land 'became manifestly worse'.[4]

The Muslim enemies of the crusader states, whose disunity had allowed the Franks of the First Crusade to gain a foothold in the Middle East, began to coalesce under the leadership of a series of Turkic warlords. Foremost amongst these in the 1130s and 1140s was Zengi, atabeg of Mosul (r. 1127–46). He was a brutal but effective leader, and it was he who first captured a major Frankish city.

Zengi and his armies arrived outside Edessa, capital of the northernmost of the crusader states, at the end of November 1144. As always, the appalling lack of manpower was an issue. On 23 December, after a siege of twenty-eight days, the citadel and its garrison surrendered on terms. The entire county of Edessa east of the Euphrates collapsed in a matter of weeks.[5]

The shock waves of this disaster reverberated across Europe. There was an immediate desire to do something to help. As we have seen, attempts to reverse the tide of Muslim advances culminated in the call to arms that became known as the Second Crusade, and there was a determined attempt to take the offensive once more by capturing one of the main enemy centres – Damascus.

The extent of British participation in the crusades of this period is hard to establish in detail but it was certainly significant. Ralph of Mandeville, for instance, went to Jerusalem with a retinue of men at some point in the 1140s or 1150s, having raised money for the expedition from his British lands.[6]

British crusaders could rise to positions of great importance in the crusader states too. An Englishman named Ralph was appointed as bishop of Bethlehem from 1156, but we know that he had been prominent in royal service since the 1140s. He was chancellor of the Latin Kingdom of Jerusalem for nearly thirty years, one of the most senior offices of state.

Until his death in 1174, Ralph also pursued a variety of other clerical (and some decidedly unclerical) roles for a succession of kings in Jerusalem. These included that of diplomat and military leader – he was wounded during fighting in Egypt and was given the honour of carrying the True Cross into battle on at least one occasion. Perhaps reflecting Ralph's military proclivities, the English bishop was once described as being 'too worldly' (*nimis secularem*). William of Tyre, who succeeded Ralph as chancellor, knew the old English bishop well. He referred to him fondly as 'Ralph of happy memory' and as 'a man of liberal and genial nature'.[7]

Similarly, although we do not know the exact numbers of British Templars who participated in the Second Crusade or the siege of Damascus, there is every reason to believe that it was substantial. The Templars were a major driving force behind both enterprises and many British patrons of the order, and their military retinues, were active participants.

Some of the English contingent on the Second Crusade chose, appropriately enough given the Anglo-Norman heritage of their leaders, to join the French crusading army travelling to the Holy Land with King Louis VII. In Paris, on 27 April 1147, as the troops mustered for the long journey east, we find a supporter of the British Templars, Bernard Balliol, taking time out to give the order more lands at Hitchin. Military and spiritual preparations went very naturally together for these devout warriors.[8]

Other contingents mustered in southern England. Men from across the country gathered at Dartmouth in 1147. The siege of Lisbon, one of the few successes of the expedition, was undertaken with the help of many English crusaders led by 'four constables: the ships of Norfolk and Suffolk under Hervey de Glanvill; those of Kent under Simon of Dover; those of London under Andrew [probably Andrew Buccuinte, the justiciar of London]; and all the rest under Saher of Archelle'. And it was an Englishman, Gilbert of Hastings, who became the bishop of Lisbon once the city had been recovered.

Many of these men were close supporters of the Templars. Saher of Archelle, for instance, had given them lands in Lincolnshire and Kent; he had also made the strangely specific and rather anticlimactic gift of six hens and one sheep. Another crusader, William III of Warenne, gave them lands (this time in Lewes) before he too set off.[9]

And, finally, we know that Roger I of Mowbray, a participant in the Second Crusade and a dedicated warrior who spent much of his adult life in the Latin East, was a major donor to the British Templars – he gave them lands in at least three counties of England. Roger's extraordinary career as a pious soldier saw him fighting in the East over several decades – he went crusading no less than three times over a forty-year period.

As well as campaigning on the Second Crusade, Roger was back in the Holy Land in the 1170s at the court of King Amalric of Jerusalem, not coincidentally witnessing a charter for the Templars – he and his men were presumably taking part in the increasingly desperate Frankish invasions of Egypt at that time. He may also have had the misfortune to be part of the count of Flanders' lacklustre crusade of 1177.

Undeterred, the grizzled patron of the British Templars was still fighting in the East well into the 1180s – he was part of the Frankish field army that fought in the shadow of the Horns of Hattin in 1187 and was taken prisoner. Roger was ransomed but died soon afterwards. He had devoted his life and his treasure to supporting the order and fighting alongside the Templar brothers in the defence of the Latin East.[10]

When all these disparate British contingents set off on the Second Crusade, accompanied no doubt by British Templar brothers and their own small forces, the transfer of resources from West to East finally became real – the implicit function of the order in Britain was, at last, made explicit and militarily tangible.

The Second Crusade did not end well. The French and German survivors of the painful march across Europe and Anatolia limped on to the Holy Land. There they joined forces with the army of the Latin Kingdom of Jerusalem in their long-planned assault on Damascus – the attack eventually took place in July 1148. It quickly collapsed in the face of overwhelming Muslim numbers, however, and a gradual realisation that the city was incapable of being held, even in the unlikely event that it could be captured. The campaign dissolved amidst a flurry of mutual recriminations, much of which was directed at the Templars.[11]

The Templars had to ignore such criticism – there was no one else to take up their burden. Throughout the late 1140s and 1150s, the order took on huge financial and personal responsibilities. They fortified and manned large stretches of the vulnerable frontiers in Palestine and Syria. In the Latin Kingdom of Jerusalem, the order gradually came to take over large parts of the southern fortifications, including much of the defence network of the Sinai desert, which faced the Fatimid Egyptian caliphate.[12]

But after decades of sustaining attacks from the Fatimid garrison at Ascalon, the Franks were keen to go back on the offensive. The dramatic battle for control of southern Palestine reached a crescendo in 1153. The army of the Latin Kingdom of Jerusalem besieged Ascalon, the last Muslim bastion on the coast. With them were the Templars and as many men as the order could muster, including, one must suppose, as many of the British brothers as had survived the debacle at the gates of Damascus.

At a critical point in the siege, a small section of Ascalon's walls was damaged by fire. The Templars were manning the section of the siegeworks opposite the partial breach that emerged from the smoke. Brave to a fault (or, as some said, foolhardy), the master of the Templars and about forty of the brothers hacked their way into the city. But the rest of the army failed to follow through quickly enough. The way in behind them was sealed off.

Reports that eventually got back to Europe suggest that the Templar storming party managed to force their way through the crowded streets and make some form of last stand in the town square before the brothers were finally cut down. There were no survivors – the bodies of the order's knights were strung up outside the battlements to taunt the Christian besiegers.[13]

Despite this bloody setback, Ascalon was captured soon afterwards. But the incident contained two important warnings. Firstly, and most obviously, there was the issue of casualties. Although Templar armies might contain many men, most were squires, sergeants, Turcopole light cavalry or mercenaries. The brother knights were always to be found where the fighting was most fierce. As a result, the casualties they sustained were punishing. Forty knights might sound like a small number to our ears, in an age of large standing armies, but those dead warriors constituted a very large proportion of the Templar knights available for service in the field army of Jerusalem at this time.

After the bloodbath at Ascalon, most of the British Templars who had arrived just five years earlier with the Second Crusade were surely dead or incapacitated. The flow of new volunteers from Britain and the other provinces was a continual necessity. They were, literally, the lifeblood of the order.

The second warning was more subtle – less gory, perhaps, but more insidious and ultimately more dangerous. Even in death, however heroic, the Templars were not always popular. A large part of their role necessarily involved taking money from others to help fund the war effort and that was reflected in their reputation. Although the brothers themselves were poor and the money was diverted to an essential cause, speculation arose about their 'greed' and supposed treasure. And, as crack warriors, they were sometimes accused (perhaps with more justification) of being headstrong and proud, even to the point of arrogance.

When the brave Templar foray into Ascalon failed, far from praising the brothers, the main local Frankish chronicler merely used it as a pretext to criticise what he saw as their avarice and selfishness. They had charged in and actively stopped others following, he suggested highly implausibly, because they wanted to keep all the plunder to themselves.

One can write this reaction off as a personal grudge – the author was, after all, a clergyman who had lost a lot of his revenues to the Templars. But it also represented a deeper problem and the beginnings of a wariness towards the order in some quarters. This was an unhelpful reputation, meaning the Templars might not have as many friends as they expected when they needed them.[14]

Popular or not, however, the fate of the Latin East was on a permanent knife-edge. Now, more than ever, the Templars in Britain were expected to do everything they could to support the cause in what was increasingly a total war.

6

STEPHEN AND MATHILDA – A GROWING INFLUENCE: 1135–1154

The creation of this new military and spiritual elite force did not go unrecognised on the home fronts of Europe.

Despite the inevitable disputes about privileges and money, the vast majority of the clergy were still enthusiastic supporters of the Templars in those early days. An English monk writing in Normandy was clearly a fan. He wrote with glowing praise that they 'face martyrdom every day' in their fighting on God's behalf, and that they were 'admirable knights who devote their lives to the bodily and spiritual service of God'.[1]

Most agreed that the flowering of Templar influence in Britain and in the other provinces of western Europe could not have come at a better time. The Templars in Britain might not 'face martyrdom every day' but their role was increasingly vital.

BUILDING A BRITISH BASE

Strangely enough, the unprepossessing reign of King Stephen in England, and the period of English history ominously known as 'the anarchy', created opportunities for extending the influence of the order.

The Templars took that opportunity. As the ruling families of England broke into factions and turned in on themselves, the brothers began to play an increasingly active role in government. They used their political capital to act as mediators and exerted their influence to nudge the country towards more stable governance.[2]

As was so often the case, the problems arose from succession issues. On 1 January 1127, King Henry I held a Great Council. All the prominent magnates of the kingdom were there, including his nephew Stephen, the count of Boulogne. Also present were the rulers of the nearby principalities – King David of Scotland, the duke of Brittany and the count of Perche. The assembled power brokers were required to swear an oath supporting the claim of Henry's daughter, Empress Mathilda, as the rightful heir to the throne in the event of the king's death.[3]

So far so good. An orderly succession had been planned and agreed.

But when put to the test, the entire structure collapsed. King Henry fell ill while hunting on 25 November 1135. A week later, on 1 December, he died. The speed of his decline and death, combined with the lack of a written testament, lent a dangerous fragility to the transition of power, which had seemed so stable just a few days earlier.

Vows were quickly forgotten. Count Stephen seized his main chance.

Stephen was in his county of Boulogne when Henry died. He moved quickly to London, arriving there perhaps by 3 or 4 December. The merchants of the city were all too conscious of the young count's charm and, even more tangibly, of the commercial connections offered by his extensive holdings in nearby Essex – the alluring prospects of increased cross-Channel trade only added to his attractiveness. Stephen was acclaimed as their king, and he entered London to the cheers of his new subjects.

Large parts of the church and nobility also backed Stephen's bid for the crown. They were happy to use the reason (or pretext) that stronger leadership was needed on the throne than could be provided by a woman. They also claimed, largely on hearsay evidence, that on his deathbed Henry had released his men from their oath and had instead nominated Stephen as his successor.

On 22 December 1135, Stephen was crowned king at Westminster Abbey. A new regime was in place. It was not quite a putsch, but its legitimacy was always in question – and it was certainly dubious enough to store up trouble for the future.[4]

The power-grab kicked off a period of violent instability. Stephen's reign was marred by rebellions, invasions and open warfare. The list of conflicts included civil war with Mathilda's supporters, invasions and raids by Scottish armies fighting under King David I (Mathilda's uncle) and uprisings in Wales. Fighting continued, with varying degrees of intensity, throughout King Stephen's reign. The upheavals only ended a few months before he died, when, in 1153, he came to an agreement with his opponents. By the Treaty of Winchester, Stephen belatedly bought peace by recognising Henry, Mathilda's son, as his heir.[5]

A period of such profound unrest does not sound like a promising foundation upon which to start building a property empire, particularly one based on the charitable largesse of those involved in the fighting. It proved, however, to be a remarkable period of growth for the British Templars. They pursued a studied policy of principled neutrality in England. As they did so, their glowing reputation for heroism in the Holy Land was rewarded by many donations.

Stephen and Mathilda could not agree on many things, but they agreed that the Templars were doing good work in the East and needed support. All parties wanted to woo them, and everyone wanted to be visibly associated with them.

The Templars, for their part, tried to rise above the local conflicts. They focused instead on the two things that were most central to their corporate goals. These were to become the cornerstones of their policy in Britain over the decades ahead.

Externally, they concentrated on sending troops and materiel from their British province out to help the crusader states. And, internally, they looked to build up the network of assets that would allow them to do so – establishing an efficient structure of estate centres, known as commanderies (or preceptories), which would manage their smaller properties and gradually turn scattered, under-exploited landholdings into an integrated whole.

Politically, and in a way that also presaged the patterns of their future involvement with the English crown, the Templars were seen as being above the fray during the civil war. They were treated accordingly. This was not entirely irrational or undeserved. The order was indeed a trustworthy third party.

The master of the British Templars often became a mediator between the warring factions, trying to guide them towards a resolution that might help stabilise the country. The Templars could bridge divisions when other lines of communication had broken down – and there were times when that could be useful to everyone.

The growing enthusiasm and respect shown to the Templars was reflected in the growth of their physical presence on the ground. The office of master of the province was established. He was supported in making his more important decisions by a 'chapter', or Council, of senior brothers. London, and the London Temple, was the centre of the order throughout Britain and the master's base. Beyond London, the order quickly created a significant regional presence to help manage its growing estate network. Places such as Bisham in Berkshire, Dinsley in Hertfordshire, Temple Cowley in Oxford and Cressing in Essex all became significant Templar centres. Connections, power and property went easily hand in hand.[6]

The master of England (or 'master of all the Templar knights and brothers who are in England', as he was sometimes more clumsily called) was usually selected by the central Templar authorities. These authorities were based, quite rightly in view of their overarching strategic intent, in the eastern Mediterranean.

This decision was generally made in conjunction with advice from the local chapter. Perhaps not surprisingly, it often involved promoting the provincial deputy – this made a relatively uncontroversial and seamless transfer of power possible in most instances. In the thirteenth century, this happened at least twice in Britain, in the cases of master Alan Martel (deputy master c. 1219–22 and master 1222–8) and Robert of Samford (master 1228/9–50). Retired masters often carried on working in support of new masters, too, where it was helpful to the order. Their experience and relationships could continue to be leveraged across time. There were many advantages in being a corporation rather than a family firm.

Even the most senior brother knights were still expected to serve in the field, however. When military affairs in the Latin East were particularly frenetic, British masters might be called to help in the East. In these circumstances the decision as to who would replace them might, exceptionally, be made locally. The needs of the Holy Land were always paramount.[7]

BALANCING ACT: TWO KINGS, A QUEEN AND AN EMPRESS

The Templars played the difficult game of pleasing everyone extremely well. They were adept at maintaining their neutrality, whilst at the same time instinctively, and quietly, supporting the status quo as their default position.

They were helped in this by the way in which the crusading vision began to take hold in England – the idea that to fight in defence of the Holy Land was a beautiful, just and uniquely devout task. Crusading enthusiasm was high, and the Templars were Christendom's poster boys. Brother knights were the perfect vanguard for a movement that was both militarily muscular and spiritually compelling – their glamour was a powerful recruiting sergeant in establishing the order in Britain, even in the midst of civil war.

The notion that, while on crusade, 'to live is glory and to die is gain' was both abstract but also strangely tangible on an emotional level. Compelling family traditions of military devotion to the crusades, and to the British Templars, began in Stephen's reign and reverberated down through the years.[8]

King Stephen's Angevin opponents, Empress Mathilda and her son Henry, had close ties to the crusading movement. The order made efforts to remain on good terms with them, whenever possible – Templar interests, after all, transcended those of local family issues in the West. The king of Jerusalem, for instance, Fulk of Anjou (r. 1131–42), was both a Templar associate and Henry's grandfather. Not coincidentally, mother and son made significant grants to the Templars during the civil war. The empress gave the order pastures in Shotover Forest in Oxfordshire in the spring of 1141. Keen to emphasise the legitimacy of her cause, she ostentatiously made the gift for the soul of her father, King Henry I.[9]

Their example was inevitably followed by those of their party. One of Mathilda's leading supporters, her steward, Reginald of St Valéry, gave the Templars lands in Gloucestershire, money rents in Tarenteford and a church in Oxfordshire. Another of her backers, Henry of Hose, gave the order lands in Berkshire, at Sparsholt.[10]

Other major grants were also made by Empress Mathilda's men, including Miles of Gloucester at Lockeridge and William II of Braose at Sumpting. These were important additions to the order's property portfolio. The donation of the large estate at Hirst, which became the second Templar preceptory in Yorkshire, was made by Ranulf of Hastings, another of Mathilda's supporters. Significantly, Ranulf was himself the brother of Richard of Hastings, master of the British Templars (c. 1155–76/9). Connections meant a lot.[11]

Empress Mathilda and her supporters were good friends to the order. But, all things being equal, the Templars gravitated to the political status quo of the centralised power – regardless of their moral standing (or otherwise). Despite being neutral on one level, they also had the entirely rational objective of wanting to create an undistracted England – their ultimate interest lay in having a state that could participate as fully as possible in the crusading movement.

Not surprisingly, given this objective, the order's early masters in England made explicit efforts to ingratiate themselves with the king's party. Hugh of Argenstein was the first recorded Templar master in England (c. mid-1140s). He probably came from a Yorkshire family and received lands on behalf of the order from King Stephen and his wife in 1141 and

1145. He was succeeded as master by Osto of Saint-Omer (c. 1150–5), who was similarly keen to develop a close relationship with King Stephen. He did so very successfully.[12]

Relationships often seem intangible. But the success of these efforts was reflected by a very tangible metric – the number of estates they were given. Although the nobility on both sides of the civil war tried to ingratiate themselves with the Templars, it was the king's party that made the most effort. Of the grants made to the order in this period, over two-thirds were from Stephen and his men. Even with resources strained by their efforts in the civil war, the Templars were an important, and very visible, recipient of royal largesse.[13]

The order was helped in this by the close links that Stephen's household had with the crusading movement in general – and the Templars in particular. The house of Blois was related to the founder of the Templars, Hugh of Payns, and King Stephen was the eponymous son of one of the most controversial leaders of the First Crusade. His father had been accused of cowardice during the original expedition and, shamed by his wife, went back to rebuild his reputation soon afterwards.

True to the code of honour of his class, he died fighting against overwhelming odds – frightened or not, he was in the front line of the doomed Frankish cavalry charge at the second battle of Ramla in 1102. Despite the appalling casualties suffered by the crusader knights, Stephen senior managed to ride through the enemy lines and took refuge temporarily with King Baldwin I of Jerusalem and the other survivors in a small tower nearby. Egyptian cavalry surrounded the fugitives and they were quickly besieged. The king managed to escape overnight – a handful of picked bodyguards chopped a way out for him before they were completely cut off. But the next day, those left behind were forced to surrender.

Count Stephen was dragged out and bound. He was forced to kneel. Then he was beheaded. The knowledge of his father's last moments doubtless affected his son's view of the fight in the East. For him the cause was deeply personal and the Templars were the men who could pursue it on his behalf.[14]

King Stephen's uncle, Count Hugh of Troyes (the half-brother of Stephen's father), was an equally strong family link to the crusades in general and to the Templars in particular. Hugh was an unstoppable crusader. He went on independent expeditions to the Holy Land in 1104–7 and again in 1114–16. Significantly, it is possible that Hugh of Payns himself was on the latter crusade and chose to stay on in Jerusalem when most of the soldiers went home to Europe. In 1125 the indefatigable Count Hugh returned to the Latin East once again, this time to become a Templar (or Templar associate) alongside his old comrade Hugh of Payns. We last hear of Count Hugh in 1130, at which point, appropriately enough, he was still in Jerusalem.[15]

But the connections went even deeper than that. King Stephen's wife and fellow patron, Queen Mathilda of Boulogne (not to be confused with Empress Mathilda), was deeply immersed in the crusading movement. Her father had been a crusader and she was the niece of the first two rulers of the Latin Kingdom of Jerusalem – Godfrey of Bouillon and King Baldwin I. She had attachments of her own to the Holy Land – and she too was a devoted supporter of the Templars.[16]

These family links even impinged on her decisions about major affairs of state. On 2 February 1141, Stephen was surrounded by enemy forces at the end of the battle of Lincoln. He fought on until the men of his household had been killed or overwhelmed – the king was said to have bravely held off his opponents with an axe and, when that broke, with a sword. He was only taken down when he was concussed by a stone thrown at his helmet.

Negotiations for Stephen's release took place later in the year. Inevitably, these were fraught with difficulties. Tellingly, the queen suggested an extraordinary way in which the impasse might be broken. She proposed that, if Stephen were released, he might promise to immediately leave the country and fight in the crusader states instead. In the event such radical promises were not needed to secure his freedom. The matter was resolved by a high-level prisoner exchange – but the defence of the Holy Land clearly loomed large in her mind.[17]

Like his predecessor, Templar master Osto of Saint-Omer was well connected within the royal household. He was often to be found in the king's retinue and was one of the witnesses of the Treaty of Winchester. Perhaps not coincidentally, Osto came from a family who, as castellans of Saint-Omer, were vassals of King Stephen's house of Blois-Champagne. Osto was also related to the co-founder of the Templar order, Godfrey of Saint-Omer. His personal and family connections were deep and far-reaching.[18]

Even Stephen's ally King Louis VII of France was a strong supporter of the Templars and a close friend of Evrard of Barres, the order's grand master. Everywhere you look you find high-level bonds of familiarity and respect.

This respect was reflected in the generosity shown to the order by the king and his party. King Stephen himself was, perhaps not surprisingly, the most generous patron of all. He gave the Templars assets in Hertfordshire and Oxfordshire, in Essex, including a market at Witham, and what became the important preceptory of Eagle in Lincolnshire.

Stephen also confirmed very extensive lands and other assets given to the order by his wife and other patrons. These included mills in Bedfordshire, wastelands in Oxfordshire, lands in Hitchin in Hertfordshire and other lands in Essex, as well as the manor of Bisham in Berkshire.[19]

Queen Mathilda was a driving force in this process and a major donor in her own right. She played a vital role in establishing the Templar order in England. She gave the Templars a large estate and church at Cressing in 1137, which soon became one of their most important commanderies. Perhaps significantly, the grant of Cressing was made for the benefit of the soul of her crusader father, as well as those of herself and Stephen. By 1185 Cressing and Witham were being treated as a single estate, with eighty-five tenants farming the order's lands there.[20]

Similarly, the queen also made major grants of lands and mills at Dinsley in Hertfordshire to the Templars and helped establish the commandery at Cowley in Oxfordshire in 1139. By the time of the

1185 Inquest, three-quarters of the Cowley estate was let out to tenants, with the remainder held back as demesne land, retained for the direct use of the order. And, to round off the picture of a devout family predisposed towards the Templars, their son, Eustace of Boulogne, was also an enthusiastic donor. Queen Mathilda and her husband played a crucial part in kick-starting the order's estate network in large parts of England.[21]

Where the royal family showed their favour, other members of their household followed suit. Of the six men who held the role of constable under King Stephen, for instance, no fewer than five became Templar patrons: Miles of Gloucester gave them lands in Lockeridge (in 1141–3); Robert de Vere gave them a chapel in Lincolnshire and lands in Kent; Henry of Essex gave them land and a mill at Ewell, also in Kent; Robert II d'Oilli gave them money rents and land in Oxford; and Turgis d'Avranches, described as *regis constabularius*, gave the order lands at Hensington, in Oxfordshire.[22]

The donations kept flowing in. Philip of Harcourt, Stephen's chancellor from 1139 to 1140, gave the Templars the church and town of Shipley in Sussex, and William Martel, his steward, gave them properties in Somerset, Bedfordshire and London. Men and women who were unwilling or unable to go on crusade could still bask in some of the reflected glory by building associations with the British Templars.[23]

Significantly, the support of women was of great importance to the Templars in establishing their presence in England. Quite apart from the two Mathildas, we know that Agnes of Sibford became a patron and gave the Templars the church of Sibford and lands nearby in 1153.[24] Similarly, Adelizia of Louvain gave the order part of her estate at Stanton in Oxfordshire in 1139–44. Showing the strains of a war between fellow countrymen, Adelizia was the step-mother of Empress Mathilda, but had married into a family loyal to King Stephen. It is hard to say which party she belonged to in this time of political turmoil. Perhaps in matters of private piety such as this, it was of less significance than one might imagine.[25]

INNOVATORS ON THE LAND

These generous donations did not go to waste. The Templars showed no inclination to become passive, absentee landlords.[26]

The agricultural objectives of the order were focused and consistent. As late as the early fourteenth century, the Templar 'visitor' (a form of overseas inspector) was described as one who 'sells grain and timber and having accumulated money he transports it to overseas parts; and he does nothing else'. This was outstanding managerial clarity.[27]

Their proactive approach was not entirely unexpected. In the Latin East, monastic orders such as the Templars had quickly gained a reputation for creating productive agricultural settlements in areas that had been devastated by centuries of war and nomadic raiding.

Ominously enough, there was an entire vocabulary in the Holy Land to describe villages that had been destroyed or deserted – they were known as 'gastinae' in Latin, or 'Khirbet' in Arabic. In these unprepossessing places they had created thriving agricultural communities and, a particular goal for the Templars, a colonial militia that was highly motivated to defend their new lands and homes.[28]

In Britain, the Templars likewise did everything they could to maximise the productivity of their new estates. These landholdings might not directly produce soldiers, but indirectly they could generate money, which could be converted into military assets – mercenaries, equipment, horses and so on, all of which were desperately needed.

Three linked examples show just how transformative the British Templars could be in terms of urban development, town planning and agricultural best practice – and, within the obvious limitations of the time, they demonstrate how quickly and how thoroughly this pattern of development was played out across their estates.

Town building was a great way of increasing revenues from relatively modest initial assets. The town of Baldock, for instance, was created by the Templars on 150 acres of land given to them, together with a church, by

Gilbert of Clare, the earl of Pembroke, in 1148. By 1185 we know that it was already operating as a fully fledged borough, and in 1199 it received its official charter as a market.[29]

This development had not taken place by accident. No less than 117 tenants had been found to lease the surrounding lands, which had been carefully subdivided into 1.5-acre plots. As in the Latin East, settlers had been encouraged to move into the new venture by the offer of a favourable tax regime and access to land. In an age when social mobility of any kind was difficult, these settlers had the possibility to create a better life for themselves and their families. People came from as far afield as London to build a new stake.

The Templars had been astute in exploiting the location of their property – they correctly identified it as a prime spot upon which to build a new town. The land was at the junction of the main road leading from London to the north (the old Ermine Street of Roman times) and one of the country's major east–west routes, a road known as the Icknield Way.

As well as its growing agricultural value and urban assets, the prosperous market attracted a wide range of upmarket goods and trades. By the end of the twelfth century, the town had luxury products such as wine and gold for sale, as well as an abundance of the more traditional tradespeople – artisans included textile workers, leather goods specialists and blacksmiths (there were, for instance, no fewer than five smiths in business in the town by 1185).

Baldock was a huge financial success for the order. It had been developed from scratch and turned, by entrepreneurial insight and hard work, into a thriving community within a few short decades.

This was also true of the town of Witham in Essex. Witham had been given to the order at almost the same time as they had received Baldock: King Stephen made the donation in 1147–8. Significantly, the fact that both donations were quickly set aside for urban development implies an element of broader economic policy and planning on the British Templars' part.

Circumstances in Witham were, of course, different from those facing the order in Baldock. On the one hand, there was more initial infrastructure to work with in Witham. It had long been a settlement in its own right – the small town had been an Anglo-Saxon burgh before the Norman invasion. But its location was significantly less favourable. It was not on one of the major London trade routes, though it was, as was Baldock, on an ancient road – this time the route between the old Roman towns of Chelmsford and their provincial capital of Colchester.

The Templars did everything they could to maximise their new asset, however. They made great efforts to turn it into a regional trade centre. The order's produce was shipped into the town from across a wide area, including from their great barns at Cressing, just 3 miles north of Witham. Once they had reached market, these goods could be resold to traders and eventually make their way down to the even more profitable London market.

The Templars set up a manor house and started to build a new town around it, shifting the demographic gravity away from the old burgh. Eventually the settlement was moved yet again, this time, it seems, for purely economic reasons, to the crossing of the London Road over the River Brain.

As with Baldock, this development was carefully calculated, with many small plots of land and building sites being made available to new settlers. The planned nature of the enterprise was reflected in its name – the expanded town was often referred to, in the duly literal medieval way, as 'the Newlands'. It had an annual fair and included a small textile sector, merchants and travelling salesmen, as well as the more usual trades such as carpenters and butchers. The town seems to have been a financial success, both for the settlers and for their Templar landlords.[30]

Nearby Cressing is yet another example of how the Templars worked hard to exploit their lands' potential – this time for agricultural production rather than trade. The estate was an enormous one, comprising some 1,400 acres. There was already a village on the site, but the new preceptory complex was deliberately built some distance away so that it could visibly operate as a new and vibrant unit on its own.

Two of the preceptory's hugely imposing barns have survived and give a sense of the scale of the enterprise. The main barn timbers date from the thirteenth century and remain large even by modern standards. Most of the surrounding buildings have disappeared over the years, but we know that in medieval times they included a large manor house with its own chapel and gardens, a windmill and a watermill, a blacksmith, a dovecote, a separate bakery and (importantly, of course) a cider mill.[31]

As well as more usual farm animals on the estate, a catalogue of chattels at the commandery later included some more homely, and strangely domestic, animals. These were clearly valuable (and tasty) but ended up sounding like a medieval parody of 'The Twelve Days of Christmas' – the list included 'six old geese, eight goslings, one rooster, six hens, two peacocks, seven peahens [and] one hive of bees'.[32]

In the great barns and other buildings of the Cressing preceptory, produce from the huge estate, and perhaps from others further afield, was packaged and stored. From there, as we have seen, it could be sent down to the Templar market at Witham for onward sale to the wider regional market or, for the right goods trading at the right price, shipped down to London. Production, distribution and urban development: all were planned and maximised to generate higher productivity.

The British Templars were not content with the donations they received. They were continually sweating every asset to create additional resources for the struggle in the East.

7

❖

HENRY II – AGENTS OF THE CROWN:
1154–1177

1170 was a year of drama.

In June, a cataclysmic earthquake devastated large areas of the Middle East. Castles were severely damaged. Town walls were thrown over. Lives were shattered beyond repair. An age of piety saw the hand of God in this. People in the crusader states felt the chill omen of destruction in the air.

Omen or not, they were correct. By the end of the year the new Kurdish ruler of Egypt, a young, relatively untried man named Saladin, led his armies north.

On 9 December, he attacked the castle at Darum, on the frontier of the kingdom of Jerusalem. Specialist sappers and miners from Aleppo started to undermine the walls. Batteries of siege artillery swept the battlements. He harassed the garrison and destroyed the local Arab Christian and Frankish settlements before he and his army (said, in an exaggerated estimate, to be some 40,000 strong) moved off.

They headed north on 11 December. The plan was to intercept and destroy the crusader army of Jerusalem. King Amalric had set off to relieve Darum but had seriously underestimated the size of the enemy forces he would be facing. He rode out from the Templar citadel at Gaza with only 250 knights and 2,000 infantry, many of whom were presumably taken from the order's garrison. When he found out how badly outnumbered he was, Amalric refused to give battle. Instead, he pulled his men into a tight 'fighting-march' formation and struggled on. They finally managed to force their way through the surrounding Muslim cavalry and took refuge in Darum.

Saladin eventually withdrew to Egypt. His power base there was still fragile and he may have been nervous about leaving Cairo for too long.[1] But the pattern had been set. Saladin would be back, year after year. He would grind the crusader states down – and the Templars would become his special target. They were the men he respected and feared the most.

Two other events took place around the same time. At first glance, neither was so grand. Each involved just one death.

In a playground in the royal palace of Jerusalem, a nine-year-old child was engaged in rough games with his companions. He was clearly hurt when they pinched and scratched each other's arms. But he gave no indication of pain and no one fussed over him. It seemed trivial at the time. Ominously, he 'endured it altogether too patiently'. Some passed it off as bravery, thinking that this was the kind of stoicism that would stand him in good stead when he became a knight. But William of Tyre, his tutor, knew better.

William wrote of the event with barely suppressed emotion. 'It is impossible,' he later recalled, 'to refrain from tears while speaking of this great misfortune.' The child was the young Prince Baldwin, heir to the throne of Jerusalem. And this was not stoicism – it was a slow death.

He had leprosy. And in that disease lay the seeds of the destruction of the entire Latin East.[2]

At the same time, 2,500 miles away, a very different drama was being played out – one with a far more imminent death in store. Canterbury in December was bitterly cold. The stone of the cathedral was as hard and grim as the events that were about to take place. Four English knights, fresh from King Henry's court, paced the cloisters. They were in a dangerous state – angry, drunk and heavily armed. These were entitled men who were looking to settle an argument which they were intellectually incapable of winning with words. The priest they had been arguing with was their social inferior, just a jumped-up cleric from Cheapside. This London parvenue, with his patronising ripostes and self-righteous, stubborn manner, needed a lesson.

The cleric walked off into the cathedral. He thought he had won the debate and put them in their place. The knights followed. They argued with him more forcefully this time. If their weak logic and slow wits could not win the argument, maybe a few shoves and pushes would do the job instead.

They tried to bundle the priest out. He resisted. A scuffle ensued. Someone knocked the priest on the head. Blood flowed. The drunken knights were overcome by a toxic mix of alcohol and panic, rage and frustration. They pulled their swords and finished the job, barely aware of what they were doing.

Thomas Becket, archbishop of Canterbury and the leading prelate of the English church, died on the dark afternoon of 29 December 1170.[3]

Nothing in Henry's reign would ever be the same.

King Henry II was well placed to become an active leader for the crusading cause.

Crusading was a family affair for the king. He had strong links with the Holy Land. He was the grandson of King Fulk of Jerusalem, and two other crusader kings, Baldwin III and Amalric, were his uncles. They were also, in theory at least, even closer than one might expect uncles to be – the three rulers were near contemporaries, with Baldwin having been born in 1130, Henry in 1133 and Amalric in 1136. Of all the dynastic heads of Europe, Henry had the closest ties of blood with the rulers of the Latin East.[4]

Despite this, Henry had an ambiguous relationship with the crusading movement – we still do not know what he really felt about it. He was conventionally pious but no fanatic. Ultimately, he was a king who sometimes acted as if he was emotionally highly engaged with the defence of the Holy Land, but who strangely always had something better to do when the chance to go on a hugely expensive and dangerous crusade arose.

Henry chose to take the cross several times, particularly after the shock of the Becket affair derailed his relationship with much of the Christian world, so he clearly knew how to use virtue signalling when it suited him. And he often talked about leading an army on crusade to the Holy Land. But on every occasion this talk, perhaps suspiciously, coincided with an agenda dominated by domestic concerns, not the needs of the crusader states.

Some contemporaries became increasingly cynical about his true motivation, and rightly so. Henry was never shy about using the tease of (possibly, but always just possibly) going on crusade for his own advantage. In the end, however, that should not be too surprising. As with most western rulers, personal affairs and local issues usually came first.[5]

But whatever Henry's real thoughts, the crusader states certainly needed help from Britain in this period – either in the form of a crusade or, if that was not possible, through a steady flow of money and volunteers.

Critically, for much of Henry's reign the Franks were still significant players in the eastern Mediterranean, and there was a very real possibility of stabilising the Christian Middle East. The crusader states were under immense pressure, but they had a future worth fighting for.

England, and the British Templars, played a crucial part in this war effort. Henry might not have been able (or willing) to go on crusade himself, but the assets he provided were essential, and the British Templars were an important part of this process, cajoling, gathering and transferring resources to the East. Under Henry, the order was useful and rewarded for being so. The British Templars came into their own.

NEW LANDS, NEW POWER

England was an agricultural nation, so those rewards were partly manifested in land. In Henry's reign, the number of grants made to the Templars more than doubled.[6]

As always in the Middle Ages, patronage of the order was largely a family affair. Henry's uncle Robert, earl of Gloucester, had given the

British Templars lands in Bristol and his mother was similarly generous. Henry built on this tradition of patronage and became even more lavish himself. He gave them regular money donations in the form of an annual sum of one mark from each sheriff's farm, a source of income that carried on until the fourteenth century. Other members of the royal family followed his example – Henry's wife, Eleanor of Aquitaine, and his brother William were also patrons of the order.[7]

Henry gave the Templars significant rights to turn woods into arable land in many counties across England, a process known as *assarting*. These included 40 acres at Botewd in Shropshire and a grant that allowed them to assart 100 acres of woodland at Sharnbrook in Bedfordshire. The Templars' success in assarting Botewd is reflected in its modern name – Leebotwood (that is, 'The Clearing at Botta's Wood'). The king knew that the Templars were active and progressive managers of the land. It was in everyone's interest for the countryside to be made more productive.

Henry also gave the Templars several properties in London, including the church of St Clement Danes, a mill alongside the River Fleet and rents in London, as well as lands and other assets in Kent, Lincolnshire and Essex.[8]

Significantly, it was early in Henry's reign that the Templars established a new British headquarters at the heart of his realm. Their original administrative centre, the Old Temple church in Holborn, was soon felt to be inadequate for the needs of the rapidly growing order. By 1161 it had been sold to the bishop of Lincoln, at which point we find general chapter meetings being held in the *Novum templum*, just a couple of hundred yards south, by the River Thames. For the move to have taken place in 1161, the building of the new centre must have begun in the late 1150s at the latest.

The move to the New Temple may partly have been induced by competitive pressures. The order's Hospitaller rivals had recently built an impressive precinct in nearby Clerkenwell. This probably made the Templars' old base seem shabby by comparison. But it also reflected their new power and status. Increasing commercial and diplomatic activity was helped by the new building's prime location.

The competitive spirit may have extended beyond the boundaries of London, however. The Templar church in Paris, capital of the arch-rival of the English crown, has long since disappeared. We know that it was of a far simpler design, however, and significantly less ornate than its equivalent in London. The New Temple seems to have been designed by an architect from northern France with a mandate to create a state-of-the-art building that would make a statement, and Henry II seems to have been intimately involved in the initiative to create a new Templar base in his capital city.[9]

The king also took a particular interest in the order's preceptory in Garway, perhaps because of its frontier location on the Welsh borders. Landlords on the marches tended to be tough, and with good reason. He gave them a particularly wide-reaching right to assart some 2,000 acres of woodland around the order's new commandery and donated an estate, a house and a chapel there in the period running up to the climactic battle of Hattin in 1187. Over time, the Templars became an ever-more important force on the Welsh marches. Given their proven loyalty to the crown, they were probably acting as a check to the often wayward ambitions of the frontier lords who were their neighbours.

Many of the senior officeholders at Henry's court became similarly enthusiastic patrons of the British Templars. The list of donors is almost a roll-call of the great and the good in his reign: Seneschal Gilbert Malet; Robert, earl of Leicester, who was also justiciar and seneschal of Normandy; Chamberlain Ranulf Fitz Stephen; and Marshal John Gilbert. Thomas Becket, Henry's chancellor and (famously) later archbishop of Canterbury, gave the brothers lands in Ewell, together with a mill. Similarly, Dispenser William of Hastings gave the Templars meadows and, less generously perhaps, a piece of marshland in the appropriately named Hackney Marshes. The Templars owed a great deal to the patronage and example of Henry and his court.[10]

The Templars also benefited greatly from the support of British women. Not surprisingly, female participation in the military aspects of crusading was limited. There are, for example, no recorded instances of specific female crusaders in this period from Scotland, Ireland or Wales. There was, however, a great deal of female commitment to the crusading movement. A few English women became active crusaders, some of whom had very specific reasons for making the journey. The reason might be loyalty to a partner – Emma of Hereford and Godevere of Tosni both went east with their husbands. Piety could also be powerful. In 1185, Margaret of Beverley went on a pilgrimage to the Latin Kingdom of Jerusalem and got swept up in the tumultuous events that followed its military collapse in 1187. She helped defend the Holy City, very sensibly wearing a metal cooking pan on her head while she carried supplies of water to the Frankish soldiers defending the battlements.[11]

Unlike some other military orders, the Templars did not have any female houses associated with them – the nature of their calling made them particularly masculine in scope. Some women tried to join the Templars, but not in great numbers and it is not clear what their role would have been if they had succeeded in doing so. An elderly woman named Joan Chalfield applied to join the order at Saddlescombe in Sussex in the twelfth century, for instance, but there is no record as to whether her request was successful.[12]

There were other ways in which women could demonstrate their support for the Templars, however. The Inquest of 1185 shows that several women gave gifts to the Templars as part of a confraternity associated with the order. These included a widow named Matilda who gave them six pence and another Matilda (whose husband was also in a Templar confraternity) who gave four pence.[13]

Even those who were not members of a confraternity could be important patrons. Alice of Cundi, for instance, gave the order lands in Emingham (in Rutland). Cecilia of Crevequer, a major landowner (died by 1212), gave the order land in Haketorn in Lincolnshire. Her admiration for the Templars was infectious – Geoffrey of Neville, one of her tenants, gave the order lands nearby in Lesenby. Eleanor of Aquitaine, Henry II's wife, was also a patron – she gave the order 12 shillings to be collected in London.[14]

Commitment continued to transcend gender.

CONFLICT IN FRANCE: 1154–1162

Henry and the women and men of his court were generous in the lands they gave the British Templars but, perhaps even more importantly, the king gave the order power and influence. Alongside their new donations came a slew of privileges and appointments, which increasingly brought the order into the heart of government. The British Templars became counsellors, advisers, emissaries and money men. The order was quick to use its new-found influence to the full.

The Templars had invested in Henry's regime, even before it formally existed. They had acted as mediators between the warring parties in the struggle between King Stephen, Empress Mathilda and Henry. In 1153, respected by all sides, Osto of Saint-Omer, head of the order in Britain, had helped broker the Treaty of Winchester, by which the civil wars had been brought to an end, and, in doing so, the Templars were instrumental in ensuring that Henry was formally recognised as Stephen's heir. If the treaty was the prelude to the new regime, the Templars could argue that they had very visibly assisted at the birth.

Not surprisingly, the master and his men were well integrated into the workings of the new government. It seems likely that Osto of Saint-Omer had been elected master of the British Templars because of his close relationship with King Stephen. Probably for the same reason, however, his time in office came to an end when Henry, Stephen's enemy, came to the throne.

Osto, having played a high-profile role in regime change, stepped back soon after Henry's succession. He retired from office around 1155 and took up a less visible role within the order, whilst continuing to work behind the scenes.

This was an orderly and well-planned succession. Richard of Hastings became master of the Templars in Britain in his stead, at some point after January 1155. The appointment was both politically inspired and diplomatically astute. Master Richard made increasing, and increasingly successful, efforts to establish a close relationship with King Henry and his new administration.

Templar masters in the twelfth century were generally chosen from amongst those who had deep connections with the monarch, usually including family ties of vassalage. They also tended to be selected from those in the order who, like Richard of Hastings, had good connections with other ministers and members of government.

Both Richard and his predecessor Osto had made a conscious policy of ensuring that Templar knights and supporters were placed close by the side of the king, in positions of trust and influence. One of Richard's relatives, for example, had been the steward (*dapifer*) of Henry's mother, Empress Mathilda, herself a leading sponsor of the Templars. Similarly, another of his relatives, William of Hastings, was a steward with the rank of *dispenser* under Henry. Every effort was made to ensure that connections were used and that relationships with the crown were as productive as possible.[15]

Quite apart from the master himself, there were many other members of the Templar inner circle who were closely involved with the royal administration. Brother Gilbert of Hogestan, one of Richard of Hastings' close associates, became heavily involved in the process of collecting the crusading tax that became known as the 'Saladin Tithe' of 1188. Similarly, the preceptor of Hirst, Robert of Pirou, became one of King Henry's political agents. He was later sent to the Holy Land on Henry's behalf, presumably acting as an emissary for the king.

These roles usually came about through the easy medieval blend of family links and expediency. The Hastings family, for instance, were the founders of the commandery at Hirst in Yorkshire, and there were close links of loyalty and obligation between them and the Lacy family. Similarly, John of Rainville, another senior Templar, had connections to the family and acted as a private messenger for the king – his father, son and grandsons were all linked by service to the Lacys. Both the Rainville and the Hastings families were tenants of the family for at least some of their lands and, along with other Lacy tenants, they set up two of the major Templar houses in Britain – Newsham and Hirst.[16]

The strategy of becoming consciously embedded within the administration worked. The Templars were increasingly to be found at the heart of government. Richard of Hastings was often absent on the king's business, helping Henry manage different aspects of his Angevin empire. Richard installed deputies in his stead to manage the British Templars while he was away, sometimes even from other provinces of the order such as France.

Retiring from office did not mean retiring from the world of diplomacy. Even though the previous master, Osto of Saint-Omer, had taken a step back because of his close connections with King Stephen's regime, he continued to work with his successor. Richard of Hastings' first major project for his royal patron, for instance, was helping to resolve a crisis around the competing claims to the county of Toulouse and in this he also had the help of his old comrade Osto.[17]

All three of the major participants in the 'Toulouse question' had close connections with the Latin East and their bickering was profoundly unhelpful at a time when the Frankish states were in such peril. The recovery of rights that Henry believed were his was a predominant theme of the king's early wars on the Continent. Foremost amongst these was his 'right' to the county of Toulouse. Henry, through his wife, Eleanor of Aquitaine, had what he believed to be a compelling claim. The counts of Toulouse, he argued, had once been subject to the dukes of Aquitaine, and he was determined to regain those rights.

The existing count of Toulouse, unsurprisingly enough, thought differently. King Louis VII of France tried to mediate between the two parties, but failed. He too had his own interests. As always with elite medieval families, power politics and affairs of state merged seamlessly into family feuds. The countess of Toulouse was also Louis VII's sister. Eleanor of Aquitaine had previously been married to King Louis. Things were personal on multiple levels. Talking stopped and the crisis escalated. Henry declared war in the summer of 1159.

The British Templars worked tirelessly to mediate throughout this violent and (from the perspective of the crusading movement) extremely distracting conflict between two of the main provinces of Christendom. When Henry gave the order lands and a mill near Baynard's Castle in London (in a document signed in the English army's camp at Villemur in the late summer of 1159), he was probably making a tangible expression of his gratitude for their diplomatic activities.[18]

The brothers eventually helped broker a truce in the autumn, at the end of the campaigning season. The truce was due to run through until the following spring, in order to give the Templars and other diplomats time to establish a more lasting settlement. Thomas Becket, supported by the Templars, was able to thrash out a compromise, and a peace treaty was eventually signed in May 1160. No fewer than five British Templars acted as witnesses and guarantors to the treaty, including the present master and his predecessor.

Interestingly, the British Templars had a central role to play, not just in the shape of the treaty itself, but also in its implementation. The castles of the Vexin (some of the most heavily disputed areas of the Norman border with France) were an important issue of contention in the negotiations. It was eventually decided that the Templars, in their capacity as guarantors of the treaty, would hold the key castles of the county in trust. As tough military men, and as intermediaries who were respected by all the belligerents, the knights of the order were ideally placed to intervene in such matters.

Despite their supposed role as unbiased third parties, however, the order seems to have favoured the English. Henry's eldest son hurriedly married Princess Margaret, Louis VII's daughter. In strict accordance with the articles (if not the spirit) of the treaty, three senior British Templars, named by chronicler Roger of Howden as Richard of Hastings, Robert of Pirou and Osto of Saint-Omer (still working hard in retirement), handed the castles over to the English. It was no coincidence that all three men were closely connected to the crown. The French king was furious and expelled the three Templars. But the job was done – the castles were back in Henry's hands.[19]

Perhaps not surprisingly under these fractious circumstances, the peace did not last long. By the spring of 1161, both sides were once more gathering their troops on the borders of Normandy. Again, negotiations were stepped up before hostilities could begin in earnest. And, once again, Richard of Hastings, the master of the British Templars, seems to have been involved in progressing these delicate negotiations.[20]

The French king had his Templars and the English king had his, but the order, although it continued to have provincial interests, was ultimately trusted as being above the fray. Impartiality and fairness, delivered with the frank toughness of a warrior, were the key to making the order indispensable to all parties.

THE BECKET AFFAIR: 1164–1172

King Henry and Thomas Becket began to fall out in 1164. On one level their row developed over the relationship between the church and the English crown and their respective rights. But it was also far more emotional than that: this was a clash of two extremely talented and strong-willed personalities.

The Templars were once more needed as mediators. They knew that such vicious infighting would distract all parties from the needs of the crusading movement and impair their ability to provide military aid to the crusader states. They were proved to be all too correct in their assessment.[21]

The Templars tried hard to heal the breach. After Becket broke his promise to abide by the Constitutions of Clarendon, issued at the beginning of 1164, both the current and previous masters of the order in Britain intervened – Richard of Hastings and Osto of Saint-Omer went down on bended knees to persuade the archbishop to step back a little. They begged Becket not to precipitate another confrontation. The incongruous sight of these proud military monks kneeling in supplication produced the desired effect – Becket relented, for a while at least.

But the underlying problem remained. Becket eventually fled to France rather than face trial at the Council of Northampton. He stayed there for six years, firstly at the Cistercian abbey near Pontigny and latterly at Sens; the rift between church and state festered.

The king used the prospect of a crusade as a tantalising political lever with which to get the papacy, and the Templars, on his side. The Becket problem, he suggested, was such a distraction that it needed to be resolved (in the crown's favour, of course) before any crusade could be launched. This cleverly cast Becket in the role of the villain – the man whose stubborn behaviour was single-handedly preventing aid from reaching the Holy Land.[22]

Throughout this gruelling conflict, and partly as a result of these manoeuvrings, the influence of the Templars at the English court grew. A high-ranking Templar official, Geoffrey Fulcher, played a significant role in making peace overtures during the affair. He was one of the order's most senior diplomats and was clearly respected by both parties.[23]

The important role played by the Templars was recognised by other players in the process. John aux Bellesmains, the bishop of Poitiers and a cleric trusted by both Becket and the king, acted as a go-between. The bishop was clear in his opinion that the British Templars were embedded at the heart of the royal policy and that they were trying to get the rift between Henry and Becket resolved quickly. In one of his reports from 1165, for instance, he made comments about the security issues that needed to be addressed if the archbishop and the king were to meet in person. Bishop John wrote that he wanted to have a number of Templar brethren present, 'because it is said that the king now listens to their counsel very much'. John even went so far as to suggest that the Templars were effectively in charge of the process of mediation and that the negotiations were 'led through the said brothers.'[24]

Given the nature of their role and their desire for another crusade, the British Templars were inevitably suspected by some of taking a partisan position in favour of Henry. We know that in June 1170 Becket was warned, anonymously, that 'he should not trust the Templars, who would not dwell in simplicity and would rather be eager to prove the king's will than Becket's and they would tell him nothing but the lies of the king'.[25]

But these suspicions were never proven and any overt treachery by the order towards Thomas Becket or the English church as a whole was never uncovered. On the contrary, and despite John aux Bellesmains's misgivings, the Templars retained the trust of both parties. Becket used them as confidential couriers and acted as a benefactor to the order. At one point Becket even wrote that he had appealed to the king, as directly as he could, through the good offices of Templar diplomats and messengers.[26]

If Becket had any suspicions about the British Templars, it was more a fear on his part that they had been used as dupes by Henry rather than because of their own failings or treachery.

A fragile truce was established but none of the diplomatic work by the Templars and others was sufficient to stop the matter ending in bloodshed. In a single tumultuous event which did indeed, as the Templars had rightly feared, impinge directly on the crusading movement, four of Henry's knights hunted the stubborn archbishop down in his palace in Canterbury. On 29 December 1170, they brutally hacked him to death in front of many witnesses.

The murderers tried to make their penitence more tangible by giving lands to the Templars. Two of them went on pilgrimage to the East. There were even suggestions that they joined the order so that their violent inclinations could be put to better use. But the Becket affair did not end with the archbishop's death or with the supposed contrition of his killers.[27]

The shock of the murder rippled out across Europe. Henry's problems got exponentially worse. Once again, the Templars were at hand to try to stabilise matters. At least one Templar brother was in a delegation sent by Henry to appease the pope in France. These emissaries followed a previous group of English diplomats who had been negotiating with the pope's chamberlain, who was himself also a Templar knight. Connections counted and particularly so in the delicate world of medieval international relations.

The British Templars, fierce soldiers in the East, were remorseless peacemongers in the West, if only because it suited them to be so.

The order's mission was, at its simplest, to transform the energy of Europe into the resources needed to engage in the war with Islam in the East. Inevitably, they wanted good relations to be re-established between Becket and the king and between church and state. When that became impossible, after Becket's murder, they pursued the next best thing. They wanted to make peace between Henry and the papacy. And they wanted to use the moral outrage generated by the incident as leverage with which to extract as much money as possible from the English crown for the use of the crusading movement.

They succeeded on both counts – but only up to a point.

HENRY AND CRUSADING

During his increasingly bitter confrontations with Thomas Becket, and after the archbishop's death in 1170, Henry promised to go on crusade many times. There was active talk of an expedition in 1169, in 1172, in 1177, another in 1187 and again in 1188. The king continued to extract political rewards by vowing to go to the Holy Land – but he never actually went.

Historians still debate the seriousness and sincerity of his intentions. Ultimately, of course, he should be judged by how he acted rather than how he talked. Henry certainly derived benefits from taking crusading vows. He used them, for instance, to gain papal support in his conflict against his sons in 1173–4 – crusading vows were clearly being used as one of several instruments of political policy. It is easy to see why many of his contemporaries were unconvinced about his true intentions.

None of this necessarily implies that Henry was being entirely cynical, however. Humans are complicated. The political circumstances Henry faced were rarely favourable. Some have suggested that the king genuinely intended to go on crusade in the period 1169–74 and that he communicated his desire to do so to his uncle King Amalric of Jerusalem. From this distance, the truth is hard to discern. Perhaps the fairest assessment is to say that, all things being equal, Henry would have been willing, and maybe even eager at some points, to help the Frankish settlers in the East.[28]

But things were never 'equal'.

As we shall see, even once the reverberations of the tumultuous Becket affair had died down, Henry decided to lead his army west towards Ireland rather than heading east to support the Holy Land. The king could argue, with some justification, that he always had more pressing local matters to attend to.[29]

Religious fervour was not necessarily enough to outweigh the prospect of political advantage but, as a man of his era, there was genuine piety, nonetheless. Although Henry might not be motivated enough to go east in person, he could send very welcome supplies of money and materiel instead. Regular payments from the English crown started in 1172, in the aftermath of the disastrous Becket affair. These shipments provided a growing war chest (literally) for the beleaguered Latin Kingdom of Jerusalem.

Once again, the Templars were central to this process. Although the order, as warriors of the papacy, was as outraged by the assassination of Becket as the rest of Christendom, they put its consequences to good use. In 1172, at the conference of Avranches, Henry agreed to pay huge sums of money to the Templars to assist in the defence of the Holy Land – enough to pay for the upkeep of 200 knights for a year.

Although this figure does not sound overly generous by current standards (and the size of modern armies), it is worth noting that the entire knightly contingent of the Latin Kingdom of Jerusalem, the main Frankish state in the region, consisted only of some 700 knights, excluding the military orders. Henry was single-handedly offering to increase the number of their fighting elite by almost a third.[30]

The Templars were comfortable in exploiting guilt on behalf of the Holy Land – it all helped.

THE BURDEN IN THE EAST: 1154–1177

The Christian East was certainly in need of such help. From the very start of Henry's reign, the frontiers of the crusader states had come under intense pressure.

War in the Holy Land was being pushed to a level at which most of the local Frankish nobility were barely able to compete. Like it or not, the Templars (and their Hospitaller rivals) were often the only organisations able to step in and take up the slack.[31]

In the south, the last real opportunity to build a long-term future for the crusader states was gradually unfolding. During the 1160s there were sustained and increasingly desperate attempts by crusading armies to bring Egypt back under Christian control.[32]

The strategy was the correct one – the Franks needed Egypt's land and money if they were to have a long-term chance of survival. But it was also profoundly painful. Campaigning in Egypt left much of Palestine and the newly established crusader colonies poorly defended for long periods of time. As ever, the Templars were called upon to try to shore up the Christian armies, either directly, by contributing their troops to the campaigns across the southern frontiers, or indirectly, through increasingly forlorn attempts to fend off Muslim attacks further north.

The kings of Jerusalem had targeted Egypt, but at great cost in terms of casualties. This manpower drain was reflected in the flow of British Templar knights sent out to fill the order's depleted ranks in the East. It was not just the brothers who were prepared to sacrifice themselves, however – they were accompanied by their own small groups of retainers and by secular volunteers. These volunteers were often from families with close ties with the East and the order's other patrons and associates.

The surviving evidence does not allow us to identify the numbers involved. But anecdotal details show just how vital a role was played by western troops in the Holy Land, even when they were not part of an 'official' crusade or a full-time member of a military order.

The battle of Babayn in 1167 is the only major engagement in Egypt for which we have relatively detailed accounts – and it is no coincidence that all the named 'celebrity' casualties on the Frankish side were volunteers from Europe. These were probably men who had come in response to papal appeals made in 1165. Their prominence in the death toll certainly suggests a much higher level of participation from the European nobility than we might otherwise suppose. It is only through the accident, and tragedy, of their deaths that we know of the presence of western soldiers on the campaign.[33]

Closer to home, Henry's constable, Walter of Hereford, and his men had gone out to the East by 1160, probably to join the Templars. And there was occasional help with money. Both King Henry II of England and Louis VII of France raised taxes on behalf of the Holy Land in 1166. There was goodwill. There were volunteers from the West. But it was never quite enough.[34]

Many of the order's English patrons were similarly active volunteers and went on crusade to join the great struggle. Gilbert of Lacy, son of Roger of Lacy, was a particularly generous and prolific patron of the order. He gave the Templars major estates in Gloucestershire, including property in Winchecombe and Holeford and much of the land that later formed the Templar estate at Guiting. Gilbert went out to fight in the Latin East and, at some point after 1157–8, even became a brother knight himself.

Gilbert was a devout warrior, enthusiastic in the defence of the Holy Land. He clearly saw the Templars as being at the forefront of this fight and felt that joining the order was the best way in which he could help the cause. He rose quickly through the ranks. By 1160 he was in a position of authority and acted as one of the witnesses for the peace treaty between King Louis VII of France and Henry II. His distinguished career in the order culminated in him becoming the commander of the Templars in the county of Tripoli.

As a senior military leader, Gilbert commanded the army that heavily defeated the forces of Nur al-Din in 1163 'at a place commonly known as La Boquea [La Boquée]'. Even the normally critical William of Tyre described the English Templar in glowing terms. Gilbert was, he wrote, 'a nobleman of high rank, an experienced warrior and commander of the Knights Templar in these parts'. Nur al-Din himself was said to have been lucky to escape with his life. He fled, leaving his baggage train and personal goods behind.[35]

Gilbert was not the only English patron to join the Templars. We also know of another English brother knight in this period who gave lands to the order, presumably shortly before he joined. And there are records of a certain 'Richard the Templar' (*Ricardis templarii*), who is mentioned in the Inquest of 1185 as having donated 5 acres of land in Hertfordshire.[36]

Other patrons continued to do what they saw as their duty, even if circumstances prevented them from becoming brother knights themselves. Henry of Lacy, for instance, who gave the order property in Yorkshire, went on pilgrimage (and on campaign) to the Holy Land twice, firstly prior to 1159 and then again in 1177, when he joined the crusade of Philip, count of Flanders. Henry, presumably of a relatively mature age at this point, died during this second expedition. Henry was unlucky but not alone. Other determined English patrons who ventured out to defend the Holy Land included Reginald of St Valéry, who gave the Templars land in Gloucestershire, the church of Beckley in Oxfordshire and rents in Tarenteford, and Robert de Traci, who gave the order property in Yorkshire.[37]

The king might not have led a crusade in person, but the British Templars and their supporters sacrificed much to help the cause.

SALADIN: THE REMORSELESS THREAT

On 26 March 1169, Egypt acquired a new vizier, a governor ostensibly working in the service of the caliph al-Adid. The name of this vizier was Saladin.

The caliph was likeable and charming. He was described at the time by the Templar diplomat Geoffrey Fulcher and the Frankish envoy Lord Hugh of Caesarea as 'a young man of an extremely generous disposition whose first beard was just appearing'. Good grace and a charming nature were not enough to save him, however.[38]

The Egyptian courtiers and administrators over whom he presided were Shi'ite Muslims, unkindly described by outsiders (both Frankish and Turkic) as 'worthless and effeminate schemers'. Saladin came from a very different background. He was a Sunni Kurdish commander leading an army of hardened military slaves (mamluks) and mercenaries of nomadic-Turkic heritage. These Turks were characterised at the time by their predilection for extreme violence. Even Imad al-Din, Saladin's historian, later described them with the coy understatement of a courtier as 'rough companions'. There was inevitably tension between the two groups.[39]

That tension broke two years later.

Dawn raids took everyone by surprise. In June 1171, squads of Turkic soldiers surrounded the houses of the Fatimid Egyptian military commanders. They were killed immediately. At the same time, the young caliph, increasingly isolated, fell ill. There were rumours of poison. There were stories of a fall. Many believed the timing of this 'illness' was not coincidental.

A few weeks later, on 11 September, Saladin organised a massive propaganda display in Cairo. Almost 150 squadrons of cavalry marched through the city. This lavishly orchestrated event was calculated to intimidate the local populace and to impress the Byzantine and Frankish envoys who had been invited to watch the display. It succeeded on both counts.

Less than twenty-four hours later, the gracious young caliph, still only twenty years of age, died in mysterious circumstances.

A new era had begun.

8

❖

HENRY II – THE TEMPLARS IN IRELAND

Tellingly for those who took a cynical view about the depth of the king's enthusiasm for crusading, as soon as the Becket affair was concluded and he had rebuilt his relationship with the papacy, Henry decided . . . not to go on crusade.

Instead, in 1171, at almost the same time as Saladin's coup in Egypt was coming to a climax, he chose to take his army to Ireland. This move had some logic – in the short-term, the timing of the Irish campaign was probably dictated by Henry's desire to stop his Anglo-Norman marcher barons, some of whom had established themselves in Ireland, from becoming too independent.[1]

Regime change was also pleasing to the papacy, despite the way in which it distracted Henry from affairs in the East. The expedition got the full approval of Pope Alexander III, who was anxious to bring Ireland more fully into Catholic orthodoxy. Central to this approval was the pope's desire to force Ireland to adopt a more 'conventional' diocesan organisation – one in which the church was led by bishops (who were, not coincidentally, appointed more directly by the pope) rather than the existing structure in Ireland, which was largely dominated by the more independently minded local monastic communities.[2]

Henry's campaign succeeded. Hugh II of Lacy was installed as the king's vassal in control of Meath and made justiciar of Ireland. Tellingly, the new justiciar was also the son of a Templar knight, the devout Templar military commander Gilbert of Lacy.[3]

Perhaps not surprisingly under these circumstances, the Templars had a key part to play in Henry's 'pacification and modernisation' programme in Ireland. They were granted large estates to control; they were given an active policing role in managing some of the newly conquered territories; and they played a vital part in bringing Ireland's institutions more into line with the mainstream western practices of the time.

This new Irish Templar presence was nominally semi-autonomous, but reporting lines were blurred. There was a master of the Temple in Ireland, but he was appointed by the convent in the East, and the king of England generally expected to have a say in the appointment too. It was still part of the Templar province of England and was never entirely independent. They were subject to a degree of control from England.[4]

The order ran their interests in Ireland (and Scotland) as what were, in effect, subsidiaries of their headquarters in London. In this they have some-times been accused of being partisan and of favouring the 'English' invaders against the 'Irish' natives. The implication, of course, is that they were secretive, brutal operatives working for the English state, naturally cast as oppressors.

It is certainly true that there were clear parallels between the order's involvement in Ireland from the 1170s onwards and the path they had already helped take towards more centralisation in Scotland under King David I – and in helping the central authorities in England. In neither case were the order's actions accidental or a coincidence. But, as in Scotland, we need to be extremely careful how we interpret these actions.

Firstly, of course, nationalism was not what we think it was. For most medieval people, social class and religious preferences were far more impor-tant than 'nationalism'. It is often misleading, therefore, to talk of an 'English Templar' or an 'Irish Templar' – it is certainly true, for instance, that there were, as far as we know, no ethnic Irish Templar brothers.[5]

The fragmented native elite players in Ireland (many of whom were also, of course, ethnic Anglo-Norman or Welsh-Norman rather than Irish)

were primarily competing with each other and pursuing their own interests – they were not pursuing any abstract or romantic ideas about the
cause of Irish independence.

Similarly, the local 'English' barons, and many of the men Henry II
brought over to fight alongside them, were hardly Anglicised in any sense
that they would have understood. As their names and ancestry suggested,
these were, like many of the 'Irish' leaders they were fighting, largely
French-speaking Norman-heritage warriors. These were often men with
interests and landholdings spread across several 'countries'.[6]

Neither was religion the issue one might assume it to be. Everyone in the
contest, whether English, Irish, Anglo-Norman, Welsh-Norman or Scottish,
was, of course, more or less devoutly Catholic by faith. Even though the
pope tended to support the Norman brand of rule rather than the more
'Celtic' power structures of Ireland and Scotland, this was primarily because
of a desire to bring their religious hierarchies into line with more centralised
European norms. He was neither siding with one 'nation' over another, nor
specifically supporting the 'English' against the 'Irish' – the papacy had, after
all, similarly supported the Normans against the Anglo-Saxon state in 1066.

The Templars, like everyone else involved, had their own agenda, but it
was not a nationalistic one. They were there to help the papacy and, more
specifically, to try to herd the disjointed political powers of Europe towards
a coordinated defence of the Holy Land.

As we have seen, their instinct was usually to side with the central
authorities and to make themselves indispensable to them wherever
possible. But this was a pragmatic decision designed to further the cause of
the crusading movement, not a desire to oppress people in different parts
of the British Isles. They would not have seen their efforts to improve agricultural production in Ireland as being significantly different to their
building of new towns in East Anglia or chopping down woods in
Herefordshire. Templars did not play our nationalistic mind games.

As in the case of Scotland under King David I, the Templars were
comfortable in helping rulers of Norman heritage move into new lands.

They were happy to bring them closer to the mainstream model of a more centralised state. It was not what they necessarily wanted to do by choice but, if it was the next best alternative, they had the corporate experience and military muscle to help make it happen. Logic also dictated that the order should work very actively to rationalise the productivity of their estates in Ireland in much the same way as they had in England. And this doubtless upset many local interests.

Even so, some have been tempted to see Henry's interventions in Ireland as a cynical 'victory' for the Templars – it did, after all, significantly increase their wealth and influence in the British Isles. It was, however, second best. As with the Becket affair, it was not the outcome that they ideally wanted. They would have preferred Henry to have led his armies eastwards, to help the Holy Land, rather than westwards, to intimidate fellow Christians (and Catholic Christians at that) in Ireland. But that decision was ultimately out of their hands and, once it had been made, the order, as always, made the best of the situation they found themselves in.

The 'best' in this case was primarily financial. If Henry could not yet be persuaded to go on crusade, at least the Templars could help make his new lands (and their new Irish estates) more efficient – they could then shift some of that newly created wealth eastwards.

Henry certainly needed their help. The problems of administering Ireland soon became apparent and were never fully resolved.

Intervention from England had happened gradually. Anglo-Norman (and Welsh-Norman) mercenary-adventurers had been operating in Ireland since the 1160s, initially by invitation but increasingly on their own initiative. Henry was naturally suspicious of the growing independence of these Norman lords in Ireland and the effect this might have on their similarly unruly relatives in Wales and on the marches. He intervened directly in 1171 to re-establish order before things got too far out of hand.

Attempts to establish a more orderly administration were quickly put in place. The local Norman and Irish rulers both submitted to Henry and the process of assuming control from England got underway. By the treaty of Windsor, negotiated in 1175, the king of Connaught was recognised as High King of Ireland, and he was, in turn, required to offer his homage to Henry.[7]

This solution did not work as well as Henry had hoped, however. Ireland remained irritatingly localised and fragmented. The establishment of royal authority did not advance very far in his reign, and much of the colonisation of Ireland was driven by a number of the barons, such as Hugh II of Lacy, John de Courcy and others.

It was only in the reign of King John that the agents of royal government became a power in their own right. Direct interventions soon became the norm as he sought to establish a more centralised system of government. Settlers from England were encouraged to move to Ireland, and many structural aspects of English society were forcibly imposed. Ominously for the locals (and, ironically of course, also for the local 'Anglo-Norman' lords), many castles were built for the king and the Templars were introduced to help royal officials with the process of 'integration'.[8]

As organisations, the Templars and their rival military order the Hospitallers were well suited to the task – they were adept at improving agricultural productivity and experienced in creating new settlements wherever necessary, both in Britain and in the Holy Land.

Strangely for a monastic order, they also possessed the hard-nosed military skills needed to intimidate any local opposition. When the Templars were given an estate in County Sligo, for instance, the area was still a turbulent frontier zone. Perhaps not surprisingly, the gift, probably made by the Anglo-Norman Richard de Burgh I, the first lord of Connaught, seems to have had military connotations from the very outset. The order quickly moved to build a castle there in the late 1230s or 1240s, which later became known as Temple House Castle. It is clear that the Templars were expected to play a robust military role in return for their new landholdings.

Unusually for Templar houses in the West, the inventories of the order's Irish possessions also showed evidence of military activity. They included relatively large stocks of armour and weapons, including swords, helmets and lances. The Templars were generally precluded from fighting fellow Christians and doubtless hoped that the process of change would take place peacefully enough, but they were also prepared to enforce their will if necessary.[9]

We know from witness lists in charters that the Templars were in Ireland from at least 1177 onwards, but it is very likely that they came over to Ireland with Henry's entourage in 1171 or 1172. Certainly, the most important patron for the order in Ireland was the king himself. By 1185, Henry, perhaps rewarding their actions or looking to encourage their increased participation in his Irish project, had given the Templars mills and the church of Saint Alloch in Wexford, together with the estates of St Congol at Clontarf and Crooke and Kilbarry in the diocese of Waterford.[10]

As usual, where the king acted, his vassals, including the ever-generous Lacy family, followed. The more recently planted elements of the Anglo-Norman baronage were particularly lavish and gave the order extensive lands from their own holdings. These included estates in places such as Kilkenny and Louth. It is no coincidence that all Templar properties (with the exception of Temple House) are to be found clustered in the south and east of Ireland, in the areas most tightly controlled by the new generation of Anglo-Norman lords.[11]

The inventories of Templar properties in Ireland, gathered on 3 February 1308, are a valuable snapshot of the order's agricultural possessions and performance. The process of accelerating agricultural production and introducing new social structures had powered ahead on these Templar estates. Interestingly, their peasantry were generally not colonists – they were predominantly Irish rather than English settlers. But they were required to offer more services to their new lords than had previously been the case. Even more fundamentally, however, there is evidence that change on the Templar estates was not just restricted to social mores and manorial dues.

Pasture was turned into more productive (and more profitable) arable land. The old Irish traditions of cattle farming were transformed into a focus on more profitable cash crops. Wheat production increased to such an extent that by 1225 the Templars were given the right to transport and sell their excess cereal production anywhere in Ireland. There is also evidence that the order encouraged and participated in the growth of the Irish cloth industry. At the Templar house in Kilsaran (County Louth), for instance, a fourteenth-century inventory shows that there were robes of coloured wool and that six ells of white Irish cloth were in storage.

Higher productivity was turned into more money. Each Irish property was soon producing an average profit of £25 per annum, a figure comparable to the order's estates in Northumbria – a region with geographical similarities and, given the widespread cattle-rustling in the area and its proximity to Scotland, some similar security issues.[12]

There were relatively few Templars in each site, reflecting the very limited number of brothers on the ground in Ireland. Despite this, however, their estates seem to have been well run, with an emphasis, as one might expect, on income generation rather than subsistence.

It would be a mistake to exaggerate the level of innovation involved. The Templars behaved in a way that might be recognised as best practice across the Anglo-Norman community, rather than as cutting-edge innovators. But the order was certainly at the forefront of commerciality. It played an active role in developing Irish agricultural practices.[13]

It was not just the economic power of their own estates that the Templars wielded – they were also active participants in the royal administration.

As in England, the default mode of the Templars in Ireland was to promote stability. They tried to make effective diplomatic interventions when it seemed that internal squabbles were getting out of hand. Sometimes this worked. At other times it did not – and this was perhaps not too surprising given the volatile cast of characters involved.

One such failure took place in 1234. The Templars were trying to broker a truce, and hopefully a longer-lasting peace, between nobles loyal to the crown and the rebellious Richard Marshal, earl of Pembroke. Richard had been in open insurrection in England and had left for Ireland on 2 February. Unhelpfully, he brought his civil war with him.

During the siege of Richard's castle at Kildare by crown forces, the Templars organised an impromptu peace conference. They 'carried the messages from either party, [and] began to treat about a peace'. But the ill-tempered discussions started badly – and they quickly got worse. As words faltered, both sides turned to more direct forms of self-expression.

Richard Marshal was wounded in the ensuing fracas and died shortly afterwards, on 15 April 1234. This was not the outcome the Templars had looked for. They had wanted a peaceful resolution that would break the debilitating medieval cycle of feud and counter-feud. But they cannot have been entirely unhappy with the result, either – the rebellion was ended.[14]

In Ireland, the Templars' administrative roles went far beyond the normal tasks given to members of the order. They were not just almoners, mediators or legal advisers, but increasingly direct agents of the crown.

The English administration in Ireland was severely vulnerable to corruption and fraud – both were recurring features of long-distance administration in most medieval governments. The problem was systemic and impossible to fully eradicate. In the absence of a substantial bureaucracy, many officials took on roles in the administration largely because of the opportunities for personal gain. The king needed to be continually vigilant if he was to contain the worst excesses of this system.

The best way to do that, so the logic went, was to give power to men who were loyal and skilled financial administrators – and particularly to those without close (often too close) ties to the grand baronial families of Ireland. The Templars fitted that job description perfectly. Most of the brothers were from England and born into the middle ranks of society, rather than into the great dynasties of Ireland, and hence not too comfortably aligned with local interests. It also helped to be able to entrust authority to an institution such as the Templars, known for its loyalty to the crown.

Men with extended families had all the attendant predispositions towards venality and nepotism. The military orders, on the other hand, were members of a religious institution – they were, in theory at least, bound by strictures requiring them to have no children and to uphold a high moral code. Helpfully from a skill-set perspective, they were also corporations with financial sophistication and experience, developed in the course of their work for the crusading cause.[15]

A series of governmental jobs were passed to the Templars, initially focused (appropriately enough) on matters of financial security and the prevention of 'white collar crime'. By 1220, we find royal cash deposits in Ireland being put into the care of the brothers, who then also had the responsibility for transporting it securely back to England.

Cash-transfer responsibilities soon expanded to include the more fundamental issues of audit and governance. From the 1230s onwards, the Templars, and their counterparts in the Hospitallers, were tasked with overseeing the accounts of royal officials. The Templars were to provide administrative checks and balances and ensure that levels of fraud in this relatively distant province were kept to a minimum. Loyal and reliable officials in Ireland were in short supply and the military orders were able to help fill that gap.[16]

In 1234 Henry III issued orders that all the local Exchequer accounts should be reviewed not just by his justiciar and the Archbishop of Dublin, but also by the Irish master of the Templars. In a rare display of medieval audit project management, the three men were required to sign them off and send a copy of the finalised documents back to the king.

These responsibilities increased over time. In 1241–4 and again in 1250, we find Roger le Waleis, the Irish Templar master, acting as part of the auditing team for the treasury of Ireland. He oversaw the activities of the treasurer and was also one of the auditors for the Exchequer in 1253. Similarly, in 1270 Lord Edward (later Edward I) placed the Irish Templar master on the audit committee of Ireland, to help check the accounts of the treasurer.[17]

By 1278, the Templar master was required to help investigate and sign off the accounts of the previous royal justiciar of Ireland. This security operation, presumably designed to see how much the old incumbent had been skimming off, was repeated for good measure in 1280 and 1281. In

1301, the Templars were even made partially responsible for tax collection – they were given the job of gathering 'the new custom of Waterford'.[18]

Choosing the Templars as auditors and tax officials had its own logic. But even they were not entirely immune from corruption. The inevitable lack of close oversight did not help – financial power, both within the order itself and within the royal administration in Ireland, could lead anyone into temptation.

The Templars in Ireland, operating on the fringes of the order's British province, inevitably had more independence than those on estates near London. Human nature being what it is, power and semi-autonomous decision-making brought consequences with them. Two of the Irish Templar masters (or, more accurately, as none of them were Irish, Templar masters in Ireland) were disgraced and punished for their crimes.

The first was a Londoner named Brother Ralph of Southwark. Southwark, a notorious district in the south of London, was a byword for corruption and vice in medieval England. Much of the land was owned, inappropriately enough, by the bishop of Winchester and rented out to sex workers. With the characteristically robust medieval sense of humour, these young women were described as 'Winchester Geese', mockery aimed as much at the clergy as their tenants. Taking the joke even further, getting a dose of the clap became known as having 'been bitten by Winchester Geese'.

Perhaps not surprisingly, given the morals of his hometown, in 1234 Ralph went rogue. He abandoned his habit and absconded. Henry III instructed his justiciar to recognise Brother Roger le Waleis as his replacement. Just for good measure, he also ordered that Ralph of Southwark should be arrested if he ever showed his face in Ireland again.[19]

The behaviour of one of the last masters in Ireland was even more scandalous. Walter the Bachelor was the master of Ireland at the turn of the fourteenth century. He too succumbed to temptation. The corrupt master had been stealing from the order and was also found guilty of fraud. He was shipped back to London and died soon afterwards.[20]

There were times when you could not even trust a Templar.

9

HENRY II – PREPARING FOR WAR: 1177–1189

Saladin assumed power in Egypt in 1171. Within a few years he had also brought most of Syria under his control. His new empire stretched from North Africa up to Mesopotamia. For the crusaders, this represented a major deterioration of the military situation – always outnumbered, they were now surrounded as well.

By 1177 Saladin was ready. At last he felt confident enough to focus his attention in earnest on the crusader states. His armies invaded the southern frontiers of the Latin Kingdom of Jerusalem in overwhelming force. Lulled into complacency by their numerical superiority, however, Saladin's troops, in the words of the chronicler Ibn al-Athir, 'became over eager and relaxed, moving around the country secure and confident'. Overconfident, in fact.[1]

Sensing that the enemy had become overly dispersed, the small crusader forces ventured out to fight. Moving as quickly as they could, they tracked the Muslim armies down to a place called Mont Gisard and on 25 November they launched a desperate attempt to get to Saladin before his massive numerical advantages could be brought to bear.[2]

The Templars made up a significant part of the Frankish field army and added a degree of professionalism that was virtually unknown in the West. The master, Odo of Saint-Amand, gathered his local troops, including the nearby veteran garrison of Gaza. They were placed at the centre of the battle line. This was the position of greatest danger, but also where they could do most damage.

The brother knights spearheaded the Frankish attack. Significantly outnumbered and outflanked, the Franks had only one opportunity to charge – and that charge needed to succeed.

The Templar squadron, less than a hundred men, led the high-risk but potentially battle-winning assault. They deliberately focused on the person of Saladin and his family, who were protected by ranks of mounted body-guards. The attack was a triumph. An English chronicler, Ralph of Diceto, explicitly mentioned that it was this Templar charge into the Muslim battle lines that won the day. Ralph, writing in London and probably using information from one of the Templar newsletters that circulated in the West, confirmed that the master had led the charge in person, launching his company of brother knights into the heart of the Muslim army:

Odo the master of the Knighthood of the Temple . . . had eighty-four knights of his order with him in his personal company. He took himself into battle with his men, strengthened by the sign of the cross. Spurring all together, as one man, they made a charge, turning neither to the left nor to the right. Recognising the battalion in which Saladin commanded many knights, they manfully approached it, immediately penetrated it, incessantly knocked down, scattered, struck and crushed. Saladin was smitten with admiration, seeing his men dispersed everywhere, every-where turned in flight, everywhere given to the mouth of the sword. He took thought for himself and fled, throwing off his mail shirt for speed, mounted a racing camel and barely escaped with a few of his men.[3]

The headlong assault of the Templar heavy cavalry had a traumatic impact on the centre of the Muslim army. In the few mad minutes of the initial onslaught, one of the Templar knights nearly changed the course of history. He got within a few metres of Saladin himself but was eventually brought down by the sultan's bodyguards. As one Muslim chronicler wrote, the brother 'got close, almost reaching him, but the Frank was killed in front of him'. Visibly shaken, Saladin was hustled from the battlefield. He ran before any more of the Templars had a chance to get to him.[4]

In the aftermath of the battle, many of the fleeing Turks were butchered by their fellow Muslim Bedouin tribesmen, who often acted as auxiliaries and guides for the Templar cavalry units. Saladin, scared and humiliated in equal measure, spent the rest of his life trying to exact revenge on the Bedouin – and the Templars. Brother knights who had the misfortune to fall into his hands from this point onwards were almost invariably killed by their captors.[5]

Saladin's chance to take revenge on a grand scale came soon enough. Eighteen months later, in late August 1179, his armies struck at the construction site of what was to be the definitive Templar castle on the River Jordan – a magnificent fortification which they called Le Chastellet.

A siege was quickly put in place and mining began. When it became clear that a breach was imminent, the Templar garrison positioned wooden barricades behind the walls. As Saladin's men tried to push their way in, the knights set the barricades alight and formed up to make a last stand. There was a short pause in the fighting, with the Muslim assault squads understandably reticent about fighting their way across the flames. But there was no hurry. The fires eventually died down. The attackers poured through the breach. The fighting, partially obscured by smoke and dying flames, was brief but terrible.

Saladin personally interrogated all the prisoners to identify which of the mercenaries or local Arab Christians might be considered 'Muslim converts'. He had these killed first. The Templar prisoners were also executed immediately. This was an interesting, if unwelcome, compliment to their military effectiveness and the fear they had recently induced in Saladin at Mont Gisard. Most of the remaining European prisoners were butchered on the forced march back to Damascus.

But the damage to the order's fighting strength in the East had been traumatic. The fate of the garrison at Le Chastellet, combined with the loss of the master and the casualties sustained at the battle of Marj Ayun just a few months earlier, had once again decimated the front-line Templars in the Latin Kingdom of Jerusalem.[6]

The next few years saw the order desperately try to rebuild its strength and call on the help of its British brothers and volunteers.

FINESSE AND FUNDING: 1177–1185

The role of the Templars as Henry II's diplomats, advisers and trusted fixers continued with even greater intensity in the latter years of the king's reign. The order did everything it could to help prepare England to support the war effort and to send more men and money out to the East to fill the depleted ranks.[7]

Diplomacy was central to this effort. By acting as envoys for Henry the order sought to keep the peace – not for altruistic reasons, but to free up the king to fulfil his crusading vows.

This was no easy task. In 1173, Henry's sons and, even more humili-ating, his wife, all went into rebellion. The pope initially tried to patch things up by sending in a high-ranking Templar diplomat to reach a compromise. Geoffrey Fulcher, the same man who had helped negotia-tions with the ill-fated young Egyptian caliph al-Adid was despatched to act as an intermediary trusted by both sides.[8]

Despite Geoffrey's efforts, however, fighting continued into the following year. Henry had to raise troops to end the rebellion of Hugh Bigod, the earl of Norfolk and one of his more troublesome barons. When Hugh was forced to surrender, on 25 July 1174, the negotiations were largely led by the Templars' ex-master, Osto, ostensibly retired but actually working harder than ever. Embarrassingly for the order, a major distrac-tion occurred when Osto's horse, clearly not understanding the role it was expected to play in proceedings, kicked the king. Despite the bad omen, the negotiations came to a positive conclusion.[9]

Peace at home was helpful, but relations between the English crown and France were even more fundamental for the crusading cause. The French had been supporting Henry's rebel barons, and the order knew that it was only when peaceful relations existed between the two states that they could launch a crusade to help the Latin East.

As ever, the Templars, despite being famous for their warlike tendencies on Christendom's eastern front, were dedicated peace-mongers when it came to affairs of state within Europe. In pursuit of this elusive goal, for instance, the Yorkshire Templar diplomat Brother John of Rainville was sent to France by Henry to act as a messenger and envoy when a dispute arose about the dowry of King Louis VII's daughter.

A non-aggression pact between England and France, the Treaty of Ivry, was finally concluded on 21 September 1177. It settled the issue of the dowry, amongst other matters, and laid the foundations for what was hoped to be a future crusade. It was no coincidence that, once again, a Templar brother was involved in the delicate peace negotiations.[10]

As part of this long-standing diplomatic policy, another old Templar master, Richard of Hastings, continued to work symbiotically, both for the king and for the order, even after he had taken a step back. Richard had resigned in the late 1170s, to be succeeded as master in Britain by Brother Geoffrey Fitz Stephen (master c. 1180–95). Once again, connections were everything: two of Geoffrey's brothers, Ralph and Eustace Fitz Stephen, were trusted chamberlains of King Henry, so the order continued to have guaranteed access to the upper reaches of government when needed.[11]

Another prominent British Templar, Brother Roger the almoner, was also involved in diplomatic activity at this time in the French court. Between 1186 and 1187, there were continuing disputes between the increasingly elderly Henry and the new young French king, Philip II. Their armies met near Châteauroux in May 1187, but fighting was avoided by diplomacy and a two-year truce was called instead. Roger was the king's representative during much of the negotiations. War was (only very narrowly) averted, as the Templar diplomat and his comrades worked tirelessly for peace, alongside the papal legate.[12]

This outcome, partly engineered by the British Templars, was to have major consequences for the Middle East and the crusader states.

Unbeknownst to the men hammering out an agreement in France, in just a few weeks the forces of the Latin Kingdom of Jerusalem would be crushed by the huge cavalry armies of Saladin at the Horns of Hattin. Very soon, the Latin East would need all the help it could get – and with England and France at peace, the West was now much better placed to give it the military assistance it so desperately needed.[13]

In the meantime, and in the absence of a full-blown crusade, money was the most tangible way in which England could contribute to the defence of the Holy Land. The Templars stepped up to take an increasing role in the kingdom's financial administration, helping to raise money for the East and transporting it there as seamlessly as possible.[14]

Money might be unglamorous but crusading and finance were inextricably linked. The Becket affair had been hugely unhelpful. It distracted England from the crusading cause and set it at odds with much of the rest of Christendom. But the Templars did whatever they could to salvage something from the wreckage of that ugly collision between church and state. If they could not get an army from Henry, at least they could get money.

In such a time of religious and political isolation, Henry was desperate to rebuild his crusading credentials. From 1172 to 1184, he gave the military orders large sums of money to transport to the East, with instructions to keep it in safe storage until he arrived with his army.[15]

Driven by an unsavoury blend of guilt and the need for visible rehabilitation, Becket's death forced the king to be generous to the crusading cause. As we have seen, at Avranches in 1172 the king promised papal legates that he would go on crusade and pay for 200 knights to serve in the Holy Land for a year. And in his will (dated 2 February 1182), Henry promised to bequeath 20,000 marks to the Holy Land, including 5,000 marks each to be given to the Templars and the Hospitallers.[16]

But giving money was not without its own difficulties. In an age before online money transfers, treasure and cash needed to be moved securely – with extremely onerous implications for transport, logistics and security.

Once again, the Templars stepped in to manage the process and to ensure that the monies that had been promised arrived in the Holy Land intact.

The money that Henry provided in the immediate aftermath of the murder of Becket was just the beginning. Additional money was sent regularly to the East. When it arrived in Jerusalem, the Templars, along with the Hospitallers and the patriarch of Jerusalem, were entrusted with its safekeeping and ensuring that it was put to good use. As one chronicle put it:

> Henry II king of the English had accumulated a great deal of money with the Templars and Hospitallers. This money was usefully employed in the defence of Tyre and the rest of the kingdom's business. With pious and necessary forethought the magnificent king had sent this money to Jerusalem over a period of many years for the support of the Holy Land. It is said that the sum amounted to 30,000 marks [£20,000].[17]

Perhaps inevitably, given the nature of medieval sources, estimates of the actual sums involved varied. What all agreed, however, was that Henry's contribution, and the assistance of his British Templars, was considerable. The money flowed for many years, and the Templars played a central part in the process.[18]

Sometimes this money could take the form of lump sums. In 1177, for instance, the British Templar brother Robert of Pirou was sent to the East, along with William of Mandeville, with 500 silver marks to assist the crusade of the count of Flanders, which took place in 1177–8.[19]

Such gifts made excellent grand gestures. They were much appreciated. But, however helpful they might be, they could never provide the consistent funding that was so clearly needed. The real answer was taxation.

Taxation was never popular, particularly in a medieval society in which many people had little access to cash, but it was the only mechanism capable of providing sufficient help to the Latin East. Three main taxes for the Holy Land were levied in this period. One in 1166. Another in 1185.

And, as we shall see, most famously of all, the so-called Saladin Tithe of 1188.

The first two were wide ranging but did not hit the taxpayer too hard – the rates levied were relatively low. In response to a papal request in 1165 for a crusade, the English and French governments imposed what was, in effect, a tapered but combined income tax and wealth tax over the period 1166–70. As matters continued to deteriorate in the East, a further tax was levied in 1185. The Pipe Roll of 1187, for instance, records an example of 'alms' (presumably money raised by these tax returns) 'being granted for the eastern church' and transported to the Levant by royal ship from Southampton.

Both of these taxes were raised in a very public way and played an important part in the development of general taxation in England. Broad swathes of society, from the top down, were caught up in it. Taxation is never popular, but the fair and sustainable way in which it was levied kept opposition to a minimum.[20]

Exactly what happened to the money raised is hard to establish. Henry certainly had cash on deposit with the Templars to help fund military expenses in the Latin East. Money raised by the 1185 tax, for instance, could have been sent east with the English volunteers of 1186 and lodged with the king's other money deposits in Jerusalem. Similarly, the chronicler of Laon later wrote that Henry sent money back with the Templars and the patriarch of Jerusalem in 1185. These suggestions are not mutually contradictory, of course. Both versions are plausible. Both may be true.[21]

The Templars stepped up to help with these new taxes. From the late 1180s onwards, the New Temple in London was used to receive and hold revenues from the royal Exchequer. And these services were not just being made available to royal customers. The Templars made themselves increasingly attractive as the safe deposit storage facility of choice for other members of the government and leading citizens.[22]

The order became an important part of governmental financing. Templars acted as court officials with regard to financial matters, organising money transfers to the East – there is evidence of huge flows of money from England to the Holy Land via the Templars. The British Templars also made possible the non-physical transfer of cash for the crown by offering 'bills of exchange', thereby cutting down on the security problems associated with making bulky and difficult physical money transfers in an age with little or no police force.

The order's role as international bankers was gaining momentum. The necessary skill sets for crusade and finance merged seamlessly together. Military muscle was the most obvious ingredient for a successful expedition but logistics and money were vital, too. The Templars were highly motivated to make sure that all the different components were in place.[23]

The Templars had become skilled at handling large sums of money, and this inevitably affected the order's reputation, for good and bad. But almost none of this money was for the enrichment of the Templars themselves. Any surplus they produced, whether by agriculture, trade or professional services, was destined to be sent to the Holy Land – cash was always needed to build their castles and maintain their troops on the battlefields of the Middle East. The Templars were adept at dealing with money (other people's as well as their own) but they were handling it for a higher cause than their own greed.

They were the 'poor knights' who dealt with complex financial deals. They collected more or less unpopular taxes and held vast sums of money in their treasure houses. And they were the hugely ferocious warriors who desperately sought peace to further the cause of a pacifistic religion.

There was a dangerous fragility in that tension.

But as the Christian world in the East faced imminent collapse, their polarised talents were soon to be needed more than ever.

THE WORLD TURNED UPSIDE DOWN

The year was 1185. A time of extremes.

One of the British Templars serving in the East went rogue. He became an apostate and was recruited by Saladin to become a commander in the armies of Islam.[24]

His story is an extraordinary one. The chronicler Roger of Howden records that he was an English knight from St Albans (*Robertus de Sancto Albanus*) who had joined the Templars. But his career in the order had come to an explosive end. He had a massive falling out with his comrades.

The reasons for this are no longer clear. Roger did not say what they were, so presumably he did not know either. Perhaps Robert found the life too tough and the discipline of the Templars too harsh. Perhaps he was passed over for promotion once too often. Or perhaps he had a nervous breakdown of some kind. But while the cause remains unclear, the outcome was undeniable: Robert snapped. And in the most emotionally and physically violent way.

He fled towards Muslim-held territory – if he was based in one of the Templars' many border castles, this would have made his escape all the easier. Once beyond Christian control, he volunteered his services to the Ayyubid authorities. This must have been something of a coup for Saladin, and Robert eventually ingratiated himself sufficiently to be given a wife – a wife, it was even said, who was one of the sultan's nieces.

The 1180s were characterised by constant warfare in the Holy Land. Saladin's armies invaded the crusader states, and particularly the Latin Kingdom of Jerusalem, on an almost annual basis. From July to September 1185, Muslim troops rampaged across Galilee and Transjordan in enormous strength.

According to Roger of Howden, Robert was given command of a large cavalry force – one which had been dispatched to destroy the lands around Jerusalem. It was suggested that Robert had personally lobbied Saladin for the mission and had promised that he could even recover the Holy City, if only he were given sufficient men for the job.

The apostate Templar launched himself enthusiastically into the task. The city's garrison had been stripped down to create a field army with which to meet Saladin and the main Muslim army down on the southern borders at Kerak. Unlikely though it seems with hindsight, it is possible that Robert really thought that Jerusalem, with few defenders and the element of surprise on his side, might be captured.

In the event, it was all over-egged – a massive anticlimax. Robert led his men raiding around the outskirts of Jerusalem. Killing civilians in the surrounding villages was easy but when he arrived outside the walls of the city itself, things began to unravel. In a high-risk but bold move, the local militia and what remained of the garrison of Jerusalem gathered around the crusaders' secret weapon – the True Cross (that is, the remnants of the cross believed to have been used at the crucifixion of Jesus). They rushed out of one of the city's concealed gates, carrying the Cross before them, and defeated the renegade's army. Robert himself barely escaped with his life.[25]

What became of the British Templar is not known. But the hollow boastfulness exposed, his stock with Saladin presumably plummeted.

MISSION IMPOSSIBLE?

Robert of St Albans had failed that time. But by the mid-1180s the crusader states were being invaded on an almost continual basis. The only things keeping the Christian East alive were state-of-the-art castles, large numbers of mercenaries and a hefty dose of good luck.

It was in this context of desperation that the most important crusading diplomatic mission of the twelfth century arrived to speak to Henry II and his court. The ambassadors were led by the patriarch of Jerusalem, Eraclius.

As the dramatic centrepiece of the visit to England, on 10 February Eraclius consecrated the British Templars' headquarters at what they called the New Temple, just off Fleet Street. He was, from their perspective, probably the most senior Catholic in the world other than the pope himself.

Eraclius was in England as part of a diplomatic offensive and fund-raising mission. In an irony that the patriarch could not have been aware of, he was gathering money in England with which to fend off attacks exactly like that launched by 'Robertus', the renegade English Templar.

King Henry II was in the audience. He had recently started using the New Temple as an integrated part of his financial affairs. And, in a massive endorsement of the order's role, he had let it be known that he planned to be buried there. The affairs of the order were inextricably linked with those of his administration. If anyone had ever doubted it, recognition that the Templars were now operating at the centre of government was complete.[26]

The consecration of the order's new British headquarters in London was an important part of the theatre of the visit. The ceremony was attended by many of the most powerful men and women in England, including the king himself. Spiritual rewards were showered on the Templars' church – those who visited it at least once a year were granted an indulgence of sixty days. But the real business was far more tangible – and far more serious.[27]

No one could be any in any doubt about the growing problems in the East. The gravity of the military situation was reflected in the seniority of those asking for help. The mission did not start well. The Templar master was part of the original delegation but died shortly after arriving back in Europe, thereby diminishing its diplomatic power. This setback was followed by disappointing discussions at the French court with King Philip II, a man never greatly enthused by the crusades.

The frustrated mission headed off to London and the court of Henry II. Here, perhaps, they had greater expectations of help. Henry, a monarch with close family links to the Holy Land, had, in theory at least, a very personal stake in the safety of the crusader states – and, as we have seen, he and his people had been generous to the cause.

Matters started well. An initial, emotionally charged meeting at Reading was extremely encouraging. Henry convened a week-long conference in Clerkenwell to discuss how best to help the Latin East. Everything was going well. But the lobbying stalled. Eraclius did everything he could to move Henry to action, but made little progress. Frustrated, angry and desperately aware of the consequences of failure, the patriarch overplayed his hand. He became openly critical of the king.

This was not a strategy calculated to achieve success. By the time Eraclius set off on his way back to the East, he had completely thrown diplomatic niceties to the wind. What could have been a productive final discussion between Henry and the patriarch at Dover ended up as a late-night shouting match, with insults and anger ending the mission to England.

Some claimed that the patriarch had even offered the crown of Jerusalem to the king. If it was true, it was probably just a final, desperate rhetorical flourish. Henry had his own empire to worry about. He was, at best, being asked to come and shoulder long-term responsibility for the well-being of the crusader states, but without the accompanying material upside that any medieval ruler would have expected.[28]

In these circumstances a full-blown crusade could not be organised under the direct military leadership of Henry II. The king did make the effort, however, in conjunction with the patriarch and the French king, to put plans in place for the new tax of 1185. He also authorised, and probably encouraged, some crusade preaching to take place, in order to generate English volunteers for the cause.

The pleas of patriarch Eraclius may have failed to sufficiently rouse the enthusiasm of the king, but they did have an effect on some of those around him. Many pious English nobles took their contingents and personal retinues out to help in the East. There had been precedents throughout Henry's reign. The king's constable, for instance, took his own small army to the Latin Kingdom of Jerusalem in 1160 and, while on campaign, kept in close contact with his fellow Englishmen in the Templars who were stationed there, including Gilbert of Lacy.[29]

Men of all ages, including elderly veterans of the Second Crusade, followed the call. Some even remained in the Holy Land long enough to participate in the disastrous Hattin campaign two years later.[30]

As we have seen, Roger I of Mowbray was captured as the climactic battle ground to its grim conclusion. Hugh of Beauchamp, one of the Beauchamps of Eaton, was not so lucky, however – he died on the field of battle at Hattin. Hugh had long been a Templar patron, as well as an enthusiastic crusader, and had given the order one virgate (approximately 30 acres) of land in Bedfordshire. Another patron, Hugh II of Malebisse, who had given the order lands in Great Broughton and Scawton in Yorkshire, was probably also on the crusade.[31]

Crusading heroism continued to enter the family history of the knightly classes through the actions of such men and their followers. Memories and stories tumbled through the generations – Stephen of Mandeville, for instance, was proudly celebrated by his family as having died 'in an engagement on the road to Jerusalem'. Other nobles such as William of Mandeville also made the journey to the crusader states and offered their services with varying degrees of success. Some, like Hugh of Braimuster, who disposed of all his lands before he left England, seem to have had no intention of ever returning and dedicated the rest of their lives to the crusading cause.

There were problems involved, however, in sustaining the flow of volunteers in this period. Communications between Europe and the Levant were painfully slow and deeply unconducive to implementing a coherent strategy.

Unknown to the patriarch, since he had been away, talks had been conducted with Saladin. Entirely sensibly under the circumstances, a four-year truce had been agreed in Eraclius's absence. Most of the putative crusaders inspired by the 1185 mission turned up in the Latin East only to find that their military services were not needed. Many fulfilled their religious devotions and caught the next boat back to Europe.[32]

The illustrious knight William Marshal was a good example of the difficulties involved in this period. He was a long-standing Templar supporter and patron who had given the order lands in Herefordshire. William had been at the deathbed of Henry the Young King (Henry II's eldest son) in the summer of 1183. Henry junior had previously vowed to go on crusade and his failure to fulfil that vow weighed heavily upon him.

As he lay dying, the Young King handed his pilgrim cross of cloth and the cloak onto which it was woven to his companion William, a man described as Henry's *carissimus* – the man most dear to him. 'Marshal, Marshal', the writer of *The History of William Marshal* made him say, 'I leave you my cross, so that on my behalf you can take it to the Holy Sepulchre and with it pay my debt to God.' Deeply moved by his lord's distress, William promised that he would go to the Holy Land in his stead.

After Henry had been buried at Rouen in July 1183, William, already at the relatively mature age of thirty-six or thirty-seven, sought permission from King Henry to go to the East on his son's behalf. Henry agreed and gave him 100 Angevin pounds 'to assist him on his journey'. This was a useful gesture of financial support and endorsement, although, as one contemporary biography rather ungratefully commented, the sum involved would barely pay for one of his horses.[33]

Like his late lord, William was a committed crusader. He may even have thought about permanently emigrating to the East – he certainly put his affairs in suspiciously good order before he set off. But, in a military context, his trip was less significant. The pious William seems to have seen it as a personal pilgrimage rather than a full-scale expedition. He took only a small contingent with him, including his squire, Eustace Betrimont.

William travelled to the East on the autumn sea passage, arriving in October or very early November 1183, just before the shipping lanes closed until the weather improved again in the spring. William spent about two years in the Latin East, and we know that he was back in France at the end of 1185 or early 1186.

With his military experience and warlike nature, William would almost certainly have seen as much action as possible during this period. Although there was less fighting than usual in 1184–5, he and his men may well have seen some service. Perhaps they were with the army of Jerusalem in the successful campaign of manoeuvre in the summer of 1184 to fend off Saladin's attacks on the key castles of Kerak and Belvoir.

William's military exploits in the Latin East were inevitably curtailed soon afterwards, however. The four-year truce that was subsequently negotiated with Saladin started in the spring of 1185. The enforced peace of a ceasefire probably accounts for the strangely unspecific rhetoric of William's biographer when describing his activities in the East. In two years, he wrote, William 'performed more feats of prowess, more acts of daring and largesse, more fine deeds than anyone else had achieved in seven' – all of which was fine, but there was a noticeable (and deeply suspicious) reticence to specify what those deeds actually were.

Everyone knew that this was just a lull in the fighting, however. Far worse was still to come. William's biographer was probably being all too accurate when he wrote that the Templars 'loved him dearly for the great qualities they had found in him: they were very upset to see him go'. The admiration of the Templars was fully reciprocated. William built up an even closer relationship with the brothers and seems to have become a Templar associate himself – before he left Jerusalem, he made a binding commitment to end his life within the order.[34]

The timing of his arrival in the Holy Land was unfortunate. But the Templars on the front line would soon be in grave need of men like William Marshal.

DEFIANCE AND DESTRUCTION: 1187

The British Templars did everything they could to salvage something of value from Eraclius's disappointing diplomatic mission to the West. They helped ensure that he at least brought money and some men back with him. The retired British Templar master, Richard of Hastings, left England with his retinue to accompany the patriarch on his journey back to the crusader states.

Richard's Templar comrades in the Latin East were trying in vain to defend the eastern frontiers. In the spring of 1187, the precarious truce collapsed. Saladin launched yet another series of coordinated assaults on the crusader states.

One of his armies carried out a massive cavalry foray deep into the heart of the kingdom of Jerusalem, 'to plunder and destroy' the villages around Acre. This detachment was chased by a Frankish column, some 110–140 cavalrymen in total, mostly Templars, who had set off in pursuit of the Turkic raiders earlier in the day. The tiny crusader force eventually intercepted them near the Spring of the Cresson.

Having found them, however, the Templars realised the enormity of the situation – the 'raiding party' they were chasing was in fact a group of some 6,000–7,000 cavalry. The numbers involved were huge, dwarfing their Frankish opponents. Despite its size, a force like this did not even qualify as an 'army' in the Muslim sources. One Muslim commentator merely described it as 'a good-sized detachment'. But it was a profound example of just how outnumbered the Christian defenders were. This Muslim cavalry 'detachment' was significantly bigger than the mounted arm of all three crusader states combined.

Gerard of Ridefort, the Templar master, was in command. He insisted that his men try to charge their way through rather than go back to wait for reinforcements. The outcome was predictable. The knights fought as best they could but the end came with shocking speed. Within minutes the entire crusader forces, with the ironic exception of Gerard of Ridefort himself and a couple of other knights, were either dead or taken prisoner, awaiting death or captivity. Many of the Templar knights were killed or wounded in the charge. The survivors were bound and forced to kneel, before being beheaded by their captors.[35]

The catastrophe at Cresson was just a foretaste of what was to come, however. A few weeks later, Saladin managed to goad the entire Christian army into a similarly foolhardy manoeuvre. As a provocation, he put the Christian castle of Tiberias under siege. The weak and vacillating King Guy of Lusignan was persuaded to take his troops to the rescue.

On 4 July 1187, the army continued to trudge eastwards, dehydrated to the point of incapacity. When it had almost arrived at the approaches to the hills known as the 'Horns of Hattin', it was brought to a standstill. Rather than stay on the defensive, the ever-aggressive Templars launched a desperate charge to buy some time and to relieve the mounting pressure on the army. Their attack had some initial success. But eventually, heavily outnumbered, the Templar cavalry were badly cut up and repulsed.[36]

The Templar rearguard was increasingly pushed back as the Muslim weight of numbers began to tell. A series of increasingly forlorn charges took place by the Franks towards the end of the battle, but the survivors were finally forced to surrender. The Templar prisoners were gathered together by Saladin. They were then hacked to death in an amateur but triumphalist way by his religious scholars and sufis.[37]

The Frankish army that was fought to a standstill and destroyed at the battle of Hattin in 1187 was in large part the creation of Henry II and the British Templars. Together, they had arranged for large sums of money to be sent east and stored in Jerusalem. The master of the Templars, Gerard of Ridefort, had advised Guy of Lusignan, king of Jerusalem, to announce that all those who would join them would be well paid, as he would release the money deposited with the Temple by Henry. This treasure allowed Guy to assemble a formidable army of his own, which he, a weak man in an even weaker position, then proceeded to squander.[38]

But the exact fate of the British Templars in those doomed ranks remains largely unknown. The old British Templar master, Richard of Hastings, for instance, had left England in 1185 with his men to accompany the patriarch of Jerusalem on his journey home. It would be good to hope that Richard died quickly in the forlorn but heroic charge at the Spring of the Cresson. Or perhaps that he was brought down by archery in the last moments of the desperate fighting at Hattin. Like many of his fellow brothers, however, it is all too likely that he was executed alongside the other prisoners from the military orders.

A LAND OF RUINS

The Templars were amongst the first to send the appalling news of the Frankish collapse to the West. Most of the brothers in the Holy Land were dead. But, just a few days after the battle, Brother Terricus, now the most senior surviving Templar in the East, wrote back to his comrades in England and the other provinces of Europe. His letter, preserved by the chronicler Roger of Howden, begged for urgent help.

The Templar order, according to Terricus, had been 'almost annihilated'. There were a few stunned survivors, but the Templars in the East had ceased to exist as a fighting force. Terricus's hurried letter ended with a poignant, desperate plea for his fellow brothers in the western preceptories 'to come with all haste to our aid and that of eastern Christendom which is, at present, totally lost'. He was not exaggerating.[39]

A few months later, in January 1188, Terricus had recovered sufficiently to write a more measured assessment of the situation, this time to Henry II. He gave the king an update on military progress in the East and reminded him that some Christian garrisons, including the Templars at Safad, were, against all logic, still holding out against Saladin's armies. More optimistically, and doubtless to emphasise that the Latin East could still be saved if aid arrived in time, he informed Henry that the Templars and their Hospitaller comrades had helped to get aid to the Frankish holdouts in the coastal city of Tyre and had inflicted a naval reverse on Saladin's fleet.[40]

The damage had been severe. The Latin East had been almost swept away. But with help from the kings of England, the British Templars and others, all might not be lost.

PREPARING FOR THE FIGHT-BACK

The pace at which Christendom responded to the disaster was depressingly slow. The response was piecemeal, delayed by poor communications, internal wrangling and a fragmented political landscape.

King Henry II, for all that he was unwilling or unable to lead a crusade in person, was quicker than most European rulers in his response to the crisis – and in this he was helped by the efficiency of his Angevin bureaucracy. He and his agents continued to raise money for another crusade. Detailed planning was put in place for the expected counter-offensive.

By the autumn of 1188, money and supplies were being gathered in the south of England. The Templars were naturally involved in the process. There were several different ways of raising money. Men who had vowed to take the cross but who later thought better of it, perhaps through fear or infirmity, could be leant on to pay for the privilege of forgetting their promise – 'redemption money', as it was called. For the wealthy, this fine could be substantial. The bishop of Norwich, for example, was expected to pay 1,000 marks in compensation for his broken vow, and the money was, very appropriately, collected by the Templars.[41]

But the main source of crusading revenue was the new Saladin Tithe. The tithe of 1188 was different to its predecessors of 1166 and 1185. Rather than being a sliding scale of taxation run out over several years, the 1188 version was sharper but more limited in time – it was fixed for one year only. This was an emergency measure designed to kick-start a crusade, rather than a more sustained attempt to provide finance for frontier defence in the Latin East.

And that was the correct approach. Those threatened frontiers were under threat no more – in most cases they had simply ceased to exist.

Henry occasionally used the crusading movement in a cynical way, but he was careful to enforce the Saladin Tithe of 1188 in England. This was, after all, other people's money. We do not know how much money was raised, but its success was probably in inverse proportion to its popularity – if we use that as our guide, the tax was a great success indeed.

The Saladin Tithe was widely hated, partly because of its severity, and partly because of the dangerous precedent it created – at least from a taxpayer's perspective. So deep was the opposition in France that King Philip was forced to give up the attempt to impose it. In England, however, regardless of unpopularity, tax collection continued.[42]

To help ensure that the promised sums materialised, the Templars helped the process along. They were inevitably highly motivated to help where revenues for the Holy Land were concerned. The Saladin Tithe was unusual but logical. It was an early form of 'hypothecated' tax (that is, a specific tax allocated for a particular purpose) and the Templars were, given their clear corporate objectives, an appropriately 'hypothecated' organisation.[43]

The sums involved were huge. A Templar chaplain, writing a few years after the event, in 1191–2, estimated that the money sent by Henry II to the Holy Land amounted to some 30,000 marks. There are suggestions in the chronicles that it was spent on soldiers, military equipment and fortifications, and this seems entirely feasible – but no registers of specific military expenses in the Latin Kingdom of Jerusalem from this period have survived. The chronicle of Ernoul, for instance, says that the money provided by Henry (presumably from the 1185 taxation) funded a contingent of 4,000 infantry. These men fought, all too briefly, under the English royal standard at Hattin in 1187.[44]

Very embarrassingly, however, it was also a British Templar who most visibly hindered this process. The order was deeply involved in the fund-raising, but human frailties were all too apparent, even in this time of emergency. In 1188, Gilbert of Hogestan, a senior Templar brother, was found to be embezzling funds that had been earmarked to help the Latin East. Gilbert might have got away with it if he had not been so greedy. He skimmed so much money off the top of the tax receipts that his fellow Templars noticed that their cash levels were steadily going down, rather than up – an unsubtle clue that even the least numerate of the brothers could not overlook.

Henry did not exact punishment himself, probably out of respect for the jurisdiction of the Templars. Instead, the thief was handed over to the order. He was dealt with in London by Geoffrey Fitz Stephen, the order's master. Presumably Gilbert spent a lengthy time in prison for his crimes. Roger of Howden was disappointed and appropriately judgemental – he thought that Gilbert deserved to be hanged for the outrage and castigated him suitably in his 'Gesta'.[45]

Even more unhelpfully, mustering for the coming crusade was hindered by the fact that King Henry was still at war with his surviving sons. The distraction of a war in France, and the prospect of treachery at home, inevitably delayed any expedition to the East. It is ironic that Richard the Lionheart, given his later reputation as Britain's highest-achieving crusader, had held back preparations by waging war on his father in concert with King Philip of France.

But Henry died on 6 July 1189, freeing up the throne for his rebellious elder son. Now was the time for Richard to redeem himself. He was invested as duke of Normandy a few days later, on 20 July, and crowned king in Westminster Abbey on Sunday 13 September 1189. The fight-back could begin in earnest.[46]

10

❖

RICHARD THE LIONHEART – THE VANGUARD OF CHRISTENDOM: 1189-1199

In Richard the Lionheart the British Templars found their ideal partner.

The new king was a gifted general, a talented tactician, and a man who shared the Templars' enthusiasm for defending the Latin East. Working with the Templars, Richard was the perfect conduit for moving military resources to the East and using them to best effect against the man who had become the nemesis of the crusader states – Saladin.

The reign of Richard I (r.1189–99) gave the British Templars a ruler who was militarily at the heart of the crusading movement. He was self-assured and ambitious, someone who would take England beyond merely offering financial help. Instead, he moved enthusiastically into the realms of direct and very personal military intervention.

Richard was a warrior by temperament and experience. And he was dedicated to the cause of crusading. This dedication was personal as well as political. He had been present when patriarch Eraclius of Jerusalem helped consecrate the New Temple in London in 1185 and was aware of the offers, perhaps even of the crown itself, that the desperate royal administration in Jerusalem had made to his father Henry.

For Richard, the defence of the Holy Land was about family as well as faith. As a proud Angevin, Richard had claims to the throne of Jerusalem in his own right, through his great-grandfather Fulk, count of Anjou and king of Jerusalem. Most of the twelfth century kings of Jerusalem were his relatives – cadet members of the Angevin line, cousins or uncles of the kings of England. When he later arbitrated in disputes about the succession to the throne of Jerusalem, he was acting as a senior family member as much as a crusader. Richard may have seen the Third Crusade and the rescue of the Holy Land at least partially as the restoration of what was (and could become again) a prestigious part of his own patrimony.[1]

But, regardless of Richard's motivation, the British Templars rose to the challenge in any way they could. In this period the order took on an even more important role in preparing the English state for crusading. They played an active part in all aspects of that preparation – financial, logistical, strategic planning, tactical deployment and naval warfare.

They, and England, were now focused on war.

FINANCING THE FIGHT-BACK

Armies and heroic charges take pride of place in the history books, but Richard understood all too well that he needed far less glamorous things too. If his campaign in the distant lands of the eastern Mediterranean was to have any realistic chance of success he knew that he had to have an efficient supply chain, together with plenty of shipping and a detailed logistical plan.

Only money could make these things happen.

The cost of the Third Crusade was huge. Everything was up for sale, and every effort was made to raise money quickly for the expedition. The almost seamless success of the preparations was a testament to the Angevin governmental machine, to Richard's focus on his goal and to the help of others, such as the Templars, in bringing this intricate plan to fruition.[2]

He did everything he could to raise money quickly. It is likely that much of what was collected from the Saladin Tithe was still in England in 1189 and used by Richard to part fund his crusade. Roger of Howden, who is normally well informed about such things, records that there were 90,000 marks in the treasury at Winchester in August 1189. Such a vast sum could not have been collected from ordinary royal revenues.[3]

But Richard ratcheted up the fundraising even more. He increased taxes and emptied the treasury. He extracted penalties from corrupt office-holders. He sold positions and lands. He even considered pawning the crown jewels. Almost everything was up for sale. He was reported to have said, possibly apocryphally but with an underlying kernel of truth, that 'if I could have found a buyer I would have sold London itself'.[4]

Enemies and rivals, particularly great men who had grown rich in public office, were told to pay large financial penalties. But no one was exempt. Even trusted companions were expected to pay up. William Longchamp, bishop of Ely, was once tartly described as 'a remarkable person who made up for the shortness of his stature by his arrogance'. Richard left him in charge while he was on crusade, but he was told to contribute £3,000 to the cause, nominally at least, as 'payment' for taking on the office of chancellor. He also had to give up some of his lands as part of his contribution towards the war effort. Everyone had to do their part.[5]

Further down the social hierarchy, the overriding need for crusading cash could lead to some instances in which the normal conventions of the age were upended. We know, for instance, that William FitzAldelin was forced to borrow money for his participation in the Third Crusade, even from his own men. In 1190, he gave his sergeant, Durand, son of Drew, lands in Yorkshire, partly, as one might expect, in return for 'his homage and service', but also, far more surprisingly, he acknowledged that the transaction was in payment 'for the ten marks which the aforesaid Durand gave to me for my journey to Jerusalem'.[6]

The British Templars' main energies were inevitably focused on the military aspects of the campaign. Crusading as an enterprise was, of course, at the heart of their corporate purpose. The Third Crusade represented the culmination of many years of preparation and behind-the-scenes lobbying. But, like Richard, the Templars knew that wars are won just as much by finance and logistics as by soldiers on battlefields. Without money there was no army and, even if there was an army, no way of transporting it to what little remained of the Christian East.

Richard of Devizes displayed a dry medieval wit when he summarised the ruthless progress of those fundraising efforts: 'The king,' he wrote, 'most obligingly unburdened all those whose money was a burden to them.'[7]

NEW KNIGHTHOOD, NEW TACTICS

Money was vital but training was the other, far less visible, area where preparation was needed – and for crusading warfare there was much to learn.

Richard's army arrived in the Holy Land able to operate as a coherent and professional force. It had every appearance of knowing how to fight and manoeuvre in the face of massed Muslim horse archers. This seems simple enough. It is easy to take it for granted.

But this style of fighting was something the vast majority of the men, including Richard himself, would never have encountered before their arrival in the East. The prior training and counsel provided by Richard's many British Templar companions and advisers undoubtedly played a major part in shaping their battlefield performance.

This was far more significant than one might imagine. Warfare in the East was profoundly different. No matter how experienced a British contingent or a band of mercenaries might be, the style of warfare they found when they arrived in Palestine was alien to everything they had encountered in the West.

The Templar knights sometimes had a (not entirely unwarranted) reputation for arrogance and fanaticism. And their overconfidence in battle, such as at the battles of the Spring of the Cresson and Hattin in 1187, could lead to disaster. But their troops in the Middle East were far more cohesive than their counterparts in Europe. They were more disciplined, partly because they had the experience and training to ensure that they could be, but also because they knew that they *had* to be.

The military orders, and particularly the British Templars, almost certainly briefed and trained Richard and his men on the difficult art of enacting the famous crusader 'fighting march'. This extremely delicate manoeuvre involved forming a huge 'moving-box' shape in order to deprive the highly flexible Turkic light cavalry of any opportunity to attack flanks or rear. It was this was formation that Richard later used to such good effect as he led his army down the coast of Palestine.

The king was an excellent pupil and a talented general. But he also had the masters of Middle Eastern warfare as his teachers.

KING AND COMMANDER: RICHARD AND THE TEMPLAR LEADERSHIP

There were never many British Templars.

As they were always so small in numbers, quality had to substitute for quantity – high-level influence and good relationships were central to the role of the order.

In the case of kings who had particular significance within the crusading movement, such as Richard I, the Templar order went to great lengths to ensure that their leadership and connections were closely aligned.

Templar leadership within the British province was given due consideration. Geoffrey Fitz Stephen seems to have made an effective transition between the administrations of Henry and Richard – he remained head of the order in Britain for several years. William of Newsham, one of the British order's inner circle, eventually took over from Geoffrey Fitz Stephen as master in 1195 and remained in office until 1200.

William's elevation to this critical position was carefully planned. There were many close links between the secular nobility and the new Templar master. He came from Yorkshire, for instance, near Temple Newsham, which, as we have seen, had been founded by the Lacy family during Henry II's reign. Close connections and good relationships were the key to making things happen in a medieval society – and the order was adept at working the system.[8]

Far more importantly, however, even the grand master of the Templars, the leader of the entire order, was changed to accommodate the needs of the relationship with King Richard.[9]

Richard was vital to the crusading cause on many different levels. He was an enthusiastic participant and a gifted soldier, but, even more practically, he had a powerful fleet with which to transport a crusading army. Both main military orders, the Templars and the Hospitallers, changed their senior leadership to allow them better access to Richard. Garnier of Nablus, a former English prior, was made grand master of the Hospitallers in 1190. And the Templars, not to be outdone, appointed Robert IV, lord of Sablé, as their grand master in June 1191.[10]

Once again, this was no random choice. In Robert they had selected one of King Richard's admirals and close friends, a man with good connections at the English court and with proven naval skills.

Sea power was particularly important on this expedition. The Third Crusade was dominated by the English and this was largely made possible by the fact that Richard had a substantial fleet. This allowed him to project naval power into the eastern Mediterranean aided, at least in part, by the efforts of the British Templars. Having access to these ships allowed Richard's army to retain strategic flexibility, to arrive in the East relatively quickly and, barring disasters at sea, in good shape.[11]

The British Templars played a very significant role in the administration of the navy. They were employed extensively in the transport of men and horses by sea. Not surprisingly, they used the order's logistical experience and shipping assets, which had been developed to help supply the Latin East, to good effect.

The order knew that these naval skills were sorely needed. Negotiating the land route to the Holy Land was extremely dangerous. The only viable alternative (and this was the option chosen by both the French and English kings) was to build a fleet and sail down to the eastern Mediterranean. This would also ideally involve setting up supply bases on the Christian-held islands along the way. Sicily and Cyprus both became important in this regard.

Everyone made their own preparations as best they could. Ships, some of which were supplied by the Templars and the Hospitallers, were painstakingly gathered from across northern Europe. By the time the English fleet eventually left Sicily in the spring of 1191 it consisted of no less than 219 vessels of different types and sizes.

Men were the obvious cargo, but so too were large quantities of supplies. Horses were essential and took up far more room than humans. The transportation of animals inevitably caused problems – taking large quantities of precious but fragile horseflesh on rudimentary ships from northern Europe down the Atlantic coast of France and Spain, across the Mediterranean and into the Middle East was never easy.[12]

King Richard was complicit in bringing the order even closer into his government. He had grown up with Templars at court and always had a close relationship with the brothers. It was this relationship of trust that eventually made possible the appointment of one of his naval commanders as master of the entire organisation. The papacy was similarly pleased to see the ties of trust between the English crown and this papal order confirmed, and for the Templars themselves it ensured that their influence was strong at the highest levels.

Perhaps not surprisingly, given his role as admiral, military adviser and political fixer, Robert of Sablé had a less than conventional monastic background. The Templars were warrior monks and Robert, like so many of his comrades, was more comfortable with the former role, as a warrior, than the latter. Importantly, Robert was already a direct vassal of King Richard, holding lands in the valley of the River Sarthe, which constituted one of the main lordships in northern Anjou. Theirs was a close relationship based on loyalty and trust.[13]

Richard had relied on Robert over many years and placed him in a series of important positions. In the first half of 1190, Robert was made a commander (or 'justiciar') of the royal fleet. Later that year, in the winter of 1190–1, while the royal fleet was in Sicily, Robert was given responsibility for Richard's delicate negotiations with their host, King Tancred of

Sicily – a man also called by some, much less flatteringly, 'The Monkey King', because of his small stature and unprepossessing looks.[14]

Robert and his colleague in the discussions were clearly very highly respected within the army. They were described by one participant as 'men of renown, men of high lineage and great nobility, men of great importance, the men who would deal with this business'. Robert himself was referred to as 'a noble man of high birth and great affability'.

Throughout the campaign, Robert and the other British Templars acted as mediators between the kings of England and France. Richard and Philip were both highly competitive and antagonistic. They had initially agreed to share the booty taken on crusade and both tried to push the point to its furthest extreme.

The Templars played a major role in the commission set up to resolve these issues. They worked hard to keep the fragile unity of the armies of the Third Crusade intact for as long as possible. Tense and irritable negotiations eventually culminated in the Treaty of Messina, agreed in October 1190. This finally settled the fate of the possessions of crusaders who died on their way to the Holy Land.

Robert was already of mature years when he became grand master of the Templars. He may have seen membership of the order as the most fitting way to end his career and an appropriate way for a military man to gain remission of his sins. He was a widower with few ties and joined the order as soon as he arrived in Acre. He showed every sign of dedicating himself fully to the crusading movement. With no wife and of advancing age, Robert probably wanted a fresh start to the final chapter of his life.

Like many of his class, he had had a chequered past. The crusade, and a life of military religious devotion, was a way of atoning for things he now regretted. He had been part of the unsuccessful revolt by Henry the Young King against his father, Henry II, in 1173. Perhaps even more tellingly, in his younger years Robert had not always shown the church the level of respect that was expected of a medieval lord – in several cases he seems to have encroached on their rights and revenues.

Robert accordingly made elaborate preparations for his new life. He founded a monastery. He confirmed religious donations and made new ones. Most importantly, he made a very public point of trying to make personal amends for his previous wrongdoings. Just before setting off, Robert invited the Abbot of Evron to join him in the castle keep of Codoingel. Together they reviewed the estate they could see stretching before them. Then, highly symbolically, Robert had wine brought up to them. Kneeling, he refused to get up until the Abbot had served him, thus publicly forgiving him for his past behaviour.

Robert could leave for the East with his affairs in order and was prepared to finish his life in the defence of the Holy Land. He did indeed die soon afterwards, on 28 September 1193, having served his lord and Christendom well – and hopefully at peace with his God.[15]

MILITES CHRISTI - 'AS PROUD AS LUCIFER HIMSELF'

Richard left for Normandy with the first contingents of the army in December 1189. He was not to return to England for almost five years.

By the standards of the time, his forces were huge. As always, the nobility attracted most of the attention of the chronicles, but the vast majority of the men were ordinary people – and they were not all there for the reasons one might expect.

Some of the English and Welsh crusaders were criminals serving to pay for their sins and as punishment for their crimes. A number of infamous criminals from Usk ('the most notorious murderers, thieves, and robbers of the neighbourhood') were sent to fight in the crusader states. So too were a group of murderers from St Clear's. But most of the army were well-supplied and fully equipped soldiers – men who had extensive military experience. The poor and unarmed might be keen to go on a pilgrimage to the East, but they were very little use in a fight with the world's finest horse archers.[16]

The army, and its naval components, were so big that it had to split up for logistical ease. But the cumulative numbers were impressive. One of the English crusaders, Roger of Howden, later wrote that there were eighty Londoners in just one contingent – the full complement of the kind of cargo vessel known as a *buss*.

The trauma of the loss of Jerusalem had been reflected in the number of men volunteering for a new crusade. In Wales alone, a preaching tour by the archbishop of Canterbury in March and April of 1188 gathered no less than 3,000 enthusiastic soldiers for the expedition. Gerald of Wales, perhaps rather uncharitably, wrote that, although these archers were the best that Wales had to offer, their bows were not terribly good. They could not, he suggested, shoot very far. They were, however (and here it sounds as though he was damning with faint praise), 'powerful enough to inflict wounds in a close fight'.[17]

Just as tartly, and with more foreboding for the future of the order, Gerald also referred to the supposed arrogance of the British Templars. He purported to quote King Richard (himself no shrinking violet) as saying that when he died he would 'bequeath [his] pride to the high-minded Templars and Hospitallers, which are as proud as Lucifer himself'.[18]

Another chronicler, Richard of Devizes, estimated that the fleet that sailed round Spain and Portugal carried nearly 9,000 men on it, including sailors. This was in addition to King Richard's army, which set off from Marseille. And there was also an advance party, which had gone on ahead under the command of Baldwin, the archbishop of Canterbury. This group sailed straight to Palestine to provide timely reinforcements for the Christian cause, arriving in Tyre on 16 September 1190. But, even so, Richard's troops still left with him in Marseille accounted for an additional 2,500–3,000 men, sailing in some thirty vessels of their own.

By the time Richard reached the eastern Mediterranean, he may have had as many as 17,000 men with him, in addition to the advance party sent to Palestine and those other English crusaders (including the enthusiastic Londoners) who had sailed on earlier to help the king of Portugal.[19]

A German army had been the first to set off. Its progress showed the wisdom of travelling by sea. In 1189, it marched across Europe and on into Cilicia. It fell apart quickly, however, when their leader, the Emperor Barbarossa, drowned on 10 June 1190 in the River Saleph. Only about a third of the original army made it through to the Holy Land.

The French and English contingents, led by King Philip II and King Richard I respectively, set off in July 1190. This was a full three years after the catastrophe at Hattin. In the meantime, the remnants of the Latin East had been holding on by their fingertips.

Richard did not arrive in the East until June 1191. He had over-wintered in Sicily and conquered Cyprus en route, taking it from a Byzantine usurper, the 'Emperor of Cyprus'. Cyprus was just a stepping-stone and a huge in-region supply base, however. The king, with his continuing need for ready cash with which to pay his troops, almost imme-diately sold the island to the Templars. The order, eager to help, promised Richard a down payment of 40,000 gold besants, with a further 60,000 to be paid over time from their new Cypriot revenues.[20]

As at the Spring of the Cresson, however, the Templars' legendary over-confidence led them into trouble. Despite being excellent estate managers and expert warriors, the order found itself vastly overextended in Cyprus. The huge casualties of the late 1180s and the demands of the continual fighting in Palestine and Syria meant that they were already stretched far too thinly. Absurdly, they could spare only twenty brothers to administer the entire island – in itself a shocking indicator of the Franks' broader manpower problems.

A rebellion broke out in Nicosia on 5 April 1192. The untenable nature of the order's Rule quickly became clear. Although they retained a few properties in Cyprus, they had to give the island to Guy of Lusignan soon after.[21]

The French army had arrived at the siegeworks of Acre in May 1191, and the main English contingent arrived on 8 June. With the presence of the western armies, the seemingly interminable siege, which had been the main focus of the Christian counter-offensive, finally ground to a conclu-sion: the city surrendered on 12 July 1191.[22]

Ironically, given their modern reputation as religious fanatics, the Templars were broadly trusted by the Muslims. They were respected as people you could do business with – men accustomed to the way things operated in the East. The terms for the surrender of Acre and the conditions for the capitulation of the garrison were thrashed out in the Templars' tent, just outside the city. The order negotiated with Saladin on Richard's behalf. They warned the sultan, all too presciently, of the bloody consequences that would ensue if he deliberately delayed the peace process.[23]

Sulking and overshadowed, King Philip II returned to France just a couple of weeks later, on 3 August. This left King Richard (more or less) in charge and struggling to lead a continued Christian recovery in Palestine. Richard, understandably bitter, later wrote that 'within fifteen days, the king of France left us to return home. But we place the love and honour of God before our own or the acquisition of many kingdoms.'[24]

The full extent of what Richard's army had learnt from the Templars was soon to be tested to the full.

A few weeks after the fall of Acre, the king and his troops began a march down the coast, starting out on 25 August 1191. This expedition was partly a demonstration to project Christian power once again. But, more tangibly, it was also a chance to reclaim some of the vital ports of Palestine. It was a textbook example of how to carry out a 'fighting-march' – a march, moreover, largely conducted by men who had only been in the Latin East for a few weeks and who were thus ostensibly unaccustomed to the deadly nuances of warfare in the East.[25]

On 3 September 1191, the army crossed the inauspiciously named Dead River. Under the tightening pressure of Saladin's cavalry, the army began to instinctively bunch up together. This forced the column to move in a 'closer order than it would ever again'. The Templars, because of their reputation for discipline and experience of battle in the East, were placed in the most dangerous position on this bitterly hard day's march. As the chronicler Ambroise wrote, 'The rearguard was taken by the Templars, who [medieval pun alert] furrowed their temples in the evening because they had lost so many horses during the day that they nearly despaired.' The army then camped and regrouped for two days.[26]

Ambroise might joke, but the skirmishing as they set off from the river-banks was far from funny – it had nearly ended in disaster for the English. King Richard, always eager to see action in person, was almost killed. As he later wrote back home, 'A lance caused us a wound in the left side, but thanks to God's grace it has already healed [as of 1 October 1191].' Ambroise corroborated the royal version of the same incident and wrote that 'the king of England, who went after the Turks closely, was injured in the side by a javelin from a Turk whom he had attacked. However, he was not seriously hurt and quickly turned on them.'[27]

The column marched slowly on. On 7 September 1191, the army approached the old Christian castle of Arsuf and battle was joined with Saladin's armies.

The Templars had been given the vanguard of the column, though the more delicate rearguard position was still only entrusted to another military order, this time the Hospitallers. Even so, after the battle, many in the army regretted that the Templars were not in the more dangerous place. There was much criticism of the Hospitallers' performance (probably rather harshly). Accusations were made about their lack of discipline – it was said that they had charged too soon, thereby triggering the battle and diminishing the scale of the eventual English victory.[28]

The Hospitallers in the rearguard had certainly been provoked into making a somewhat premature charge. Richard had his hand forced and, with the Templars, the English and his Breton, Angevin and Poitevin troops, joined them in charging towards the Muslim army. The Turkic horsemen were routed as the attacks rippled down the line and, as Saladin's cavalry fled, his Egyptian infantry were ridden down and massacred.[29]

The Templars and the English knights had done their job well. Two further charges culminated in what Saladin's biographer Baha al-Din (who was on the battlefield) described as 'a complete rout' of the Muslim army.

Christian casualties were relatively light. It seems that only one European prisoner was taken that day; Saladin had him beheaded later that evening, as a form of desultory consolation for the embarrassment to which he had just been subjected.[30]

However unfair the criticism of the Hospitallers, it is significant that, when the Christian army set off again, on 9 September 1191, the Templars were back in their usual position: 'the Templars protected the rearguard that day, where they were positioned, for it is a common saying that he who is prepared cannot be mocked. But in vain were they prepared, for they did not see a Turk that day'.[31]

Even the Templars were by no means invincible, however. A group of brother knights were dispatched on 6 November 1191 to guard a party of English squires who were out foraging. The men were ambushed by several squadrons of Saladin's cavalry and what should have been a simple task nearly turned into a massacre. The Templars became involved in a bitter dismounted struggle, fighting back to back, as the Muslim mounted archers closed in on all sides.

The Templars were rescued and extracted from the fighting with the loss of just three men. But it had been a close thing. The brother knights serving alongside the English army had once more been given the more dangerous tasks. Even under the most trying of circumstances, the mounted brothers did not desert their foragers, who were presumably working on foot. Most of the English squires and their Templar guards got back to camp safely.[32]

The 'fighting-march' had been impressive. It had shown that Richard's army was a force to be reckoned with. It had given him the opportunity to inflict a tactical defeat on his opponent – Arsuf was Saladin's first major battlefield defeat since 1177. And it had re-established Christian control over much of the coast of Palestine. Beyond this, however, the fighting developed into a stalemate.

The question of strategic objectives, and particularly the fate of Jerusalem, inevitably arose at the King's Council. The Templars were a key part of this Council meeting, as they had the most detailed local knowledge and insight. Controversially, but entirely correctly, they persuaded Richard not to try to recapture the Holy City.[33] Retaking Jerusalem would have been emotionally satisfying. The Templars also knew, however, that the attempt to do so, in the face of the enemy and along difficult supply lines, would be highly dangerous.[34]

Just as importantly, even the famously aggressive brothers did not believe that the city, inland and underpopulated as it was, could be held for long if it were recaptured. Instead, the Templars argued that it would only be the beginning of much greater problems ahead. Keeping it, they pointed out, 'would still be a perilous undertaking, if it were not quickly peopled with such men as would stay, for all the travellers . . . would have made their pilgrimage and would return to their own land from which they had come and the land would be lost again when the people scattered.'[35]

A three-year truce was agreed in September 1192. Richard and his men returned home in October. They were frustrated but had, with the help of the Templars, achieved more than many might have expected at the outset.[36]

BROTHERS IN ARMS

For the British Templars and their many patrons, English leadership of the Third Crusade was a perfect opportunity to give further proof of their commitment to the cause.

Richard himself was an active patron, giving them power and influence. Within a few weeks of becoming king, he had confirmed all their previous grants and privileges. Despite having put the country onto a war footing, he encouraged the order to continue their local agricultural efficiency drive, allowing them to convert woods into arable land in several places, including Herefordshire and Oxfordshire. He may also have found time to give them additional lands in Warwickshire, Pembroke, Suffolk and Lundy Island.[37]

Donors to the Templars were also fighting in the front ranks, often guided by long-standing family traditions of patronage. William of Mowbray, son of Roger I of Mowbray, for instance, was both a generous patron and a crusader on the expedition. Other supporters included Gilbert Malet and Robert III of Stafford, who had given the order lands in Warwickshire and Lincolnshire. Similarly, Hugh of Neville, who fought with Richard at the battle of Jaffa, was a patron and had given them the estate of Lokeswood.[38]

Fatality rates amongst these patrons were inevitably high – a stark reminder of the sacrifices that crusading demanded. The earl of Leicester, Robert III 'Blanchmains', was a Templar donor who went on the crusade alongside the brother knights. He had given the order rents in Warwickshire and a mill in Wiltshire. Robert III died in Dyrrachium, in modern-day Albania, while he was trying to make his way to the Holy Land.[39]

There were others, too. Ranulf d'Aubigny, who had given the order lands in Lincolnshire, died at Acre in 1191. And the constable of Chester, John Fitz Eustace of Lacy, who gave the Templars the church of Marnham in Nottinghamshire, died at Tyre on 11 October 1190, while Acre was still under siege. Men were prepared to give more than just land.[40]

But some, at least, got home to tell tales of their adventures.

There were even beneficiaries amongst the brave men who had served alongside Richard in the East. Battlefield performance was often reflected in advancement on their return to England. Hubert Walter, for instance, the astute leader of the advance party after Archbishop Baldwin's death, had a meteoric career: he eventually became archbishop of Canterbury (in 1193), chief justiciar of England (1193–8) and chancellor (1199–1205).

Hugh of Neville was rewarded for his outstanding service on the crusade. He eventually became chief forester (an office that sounds obscure but was in fact highly lucrative) in 1198, after having been given a valuable wardship and a series of appointments as sheriff of Oxfordshire, Essex and Hertfordshire. The bonding of warfare, and the trust it engendered, was an enduring route to the king's favour.[41]

There were many losers, however, and the end of the crusade did not mean the end of the hugely unpopular taxation that sustained it.

Richard, like the Templars, was a great warrior and admired by many. But he was also a man whose pride and fierce competitiveness made enemies – and that was to make his long journey home from the Holy Land even longer and more difficult than it should have been. The king had opponents in Europe, as well as in the Middle East. When he left Palestine in 1192, Richard had his personal security in mind. He was disguised, appropriately enough, as a Templar knight and travelled in the company of four genuine Templar brothers who acted as his bodyguards.[42]

This was an excellent idea – but it was not enough.

Being larger than life was to the king's detriment on this occasion. Richard was recognised while in the territory of Duke Leopold of Austria, one of the many people he had offended whilst on crusade. He was arrested and imprisoned at Durnstein. Later he was transferred to Trifels Castle, where he was held by Henry VI, the Holy Roman Emperor. At least one patron of the British Templars was with him. William of Mowbray, who had made generous donations in the past, was a hostage for Richard's ransom in Germany. He had probably left Palestine as part of the king's retinue in 1191 and, like his master, got waylaid.

A ransom of 150,000 marks was raised in England for his release, adding a further financial burden to that already imposed by the Saladin Tithe. The money was gathered by a levy on all properties, including those owned by the (normally exempt) Templars. There is no specific evidence about the order's role in raising money for the ransom of King Richard, but as loyal servants and allies of a devoted crusader king, they would have done everything possible to see him freed as quickly as possible.[43]

Richard was released on 4 February 1194 and returned to find a double betrayal – his erstwhile crusading colleague, King Philip of France, had taken advantage of his absence to invade Normandy. And his brother John had treacherously gone into revolt.[44]

Paying money to support a winning team is rarely popular, but paying extortion money for a kidnapping at the end of a crusade that failed to free Jerusalem was doubly galling. It was a petty end to a glorious attempt.

With hindsight, the Third Crusade achieved a great deal. Much of the Palestinian and Syrian coastline, with its all-important (and highly defensible) maritime cities, had been recaptured. The crusader states, which were on the verge of being snuffed out, had been rescued and would continue, albeit in an increasingly unviable state of decay, for another century. And it had proved that Saladin, however big his armies, was not invincible.

All of which was impressive. But the interior of Palestine had been substantially lost and could not be recovered. It no longer had a Christian population capable of self-defence. And, even more importantly, the city of Jerusalem, which was militarily negligible but of huge significance to the crusading movement, remained in enemy hands. The decision not to besiege it had been correct – the logic was impeccable. But on an emotional level it was a huge anticlimax.

England had expended many lives and huge quantities of treasure to make the crusade possible. But the high-profile prize remained elusive. And any perceived failure reflected particularly poorly on the movement's standard-bearers – the Templars.[45]

Basking in the glow of success, the order's undoubted faults, foremost amongst which were its occasional pride and arrogance, could be forgiven. When crusades ended in failure, however, the brother knights increasingly looked like expensive and out-of-touch prima donnas.

It did not bode well for the future.

11

❖

JOHN – STRANGE TIMES, STRANGE PARTNERS: 1199–1216

A popular ruler with charm and charisma can be forgiven much. He commands reserves of loyalty. He is given the benefit of the doubt. One like John, however, was neither trusted nor trusting. Instead, his personality was dominated by irritability, anger and poor behaviour. All kings have problems thrust upon them, but John also had an outstanding track record of creating his own.

As an underemployed younger son, John was known as 'Lackland' in his early years. He continued to be lacklustre throughout his reign. He was not always lucky – but he brought much of his bad luck with him. Short-tempered and ungrateful, John fell out with far too many people, far too often.

John needed talented partners who would be able to help him by taking a longer-term and more unemotional view of the world – men such as the British Templars.

The king was a man to whom trust did not come easily. He made an exception with the Templars, however, and he relied on them increasingly during his reign. This even extended to a close friendship with some of the individual brother knights, and with three men in particular – Aimery of Saint-Maur, the master of the Templars in England for most of his reign, Brother Alan Martel (later master in 1222–8) and Brother Roger, John's almoner.

Aimery of Saint-Maur was a constant presence with King John in the latter years of his reign. He was by his side throughout much of the fighting with his barons. In line with the interests of both the realm and the order, he was one of the advisers who helped persuade John to issue Magna Carta in June 1215. Aimery was present at John's deathbed in October 1216 and was one of the men tasked by the king with enacting his last will and testament.[1]

Alan Martel also played an important part at the heart of government, even at the very end of John's administration. His service was recognised and well rewarded. In October 1214, the village of Tolleshunt was given by the normally unemotional John 'to our beloved and faithful Alan Martel to sustain him in our service', and another grant of land to the order in 1215 specifically mentioned the high regard in which he was held by the king.

Similarly, Brother Roger the almoner helped John extensively as a military specialist and project manager, both on land and at sea. The Templars were amongst John's most trusted advisers. In a rare and personal sign of his affection for the order, John gave the brothers an annual gift of ten male fallow deer each year, to be eaten at the chapter meeting in London during their Pentecostal dinner.[2]

King John needed the British Templars and, whether with venison or not, they welcomed the opportunity to take a place at his top table.[3]

The Templars' business was war in the East. Anything that distracted western leaders and their countries from the defence of the Holy Land was profoundly unhelpful.

Richard I was a highly skilled warrior, famous for his exploits on crusade. Under his rule, however, England itself remained relatively peaceful. For most of his reign, Richard was absent and his lands (as they belonged to someone who was on crusade) were placed under papal protection. Even more ironically, having survived years of campaigning and personal combat in the Holy Land, Richard was wounded by a French crossbow bolt in a minor siege at an even more minor castle. He died on 6 April 1199, in the arms of his mother, Eleanor of Aquitaine.

Perhaps surprisingly, it was in the reign of his brother John, a monarch who had little intrinsic interest in the crusades or the Latin East, that the order came into its own in Britain. This may seem strange but was not without its own internal logic.

King John's reign was very different to that of Richard's. Unlike his brother, he had no intention of leading a crusade to the Middle East in person. But England nonetheless often found itself in a state of war. John's England existed in a series of crises, either at home or abroad. Conflict after conflict erupted, partly because of bad luck, partly because of circumstances but also partly because of John's sly and prickly personality. England under his rule was on a semi-permanent war footing.

His administration was in continual need of bureaucrats and clerks to keep his finances and military logistics working – these were the unglamorous building blocks that sustained his armies and his increasingly large navy. John's political situation and personal shortcomings meant that he needed help from people who had professional skills, but were not partisan. The Templars were an obvious choice.

When looking at the past, it is tempting to take a contrarian stance. It makes for a more interesting read – to argue, for instance, that Nero was not as bad as everyone said, or to suggest that Caligula was just terribly misunderstood. King John bucks this trend.

Contemporary chronicles were almost universally damning of his government and his 'foreign' advisers. They criticised his policies – losing Normandy was never going to be popular. They criticised his actions – kings were not expected to be sexually abstinent, but sleeping with the wives and daughters of the men you rely on is rarely sensible. The chronicles criticised his personality. And, fair or not, they criticised his lack of moral compass and religious devotion.[4]

From the Templars' perspective, John was similarly unimpressive. He was not interested in the crusader states and would never lead a crusading army. He was not adept at running a stable and peaceful country which could provide financial resources for the East. And he was no more (sometimes far less) than conventionally pious.[5]

King John was not ideal material with which to work. But with Richard gone, the order needed to move on. King John was all that was on offer – he was the man they had to deal with. Taking the long-term view, as only an international corporation can, the Templars realised that their best option was to help him stabilise the realm. When the infighting had passed, so their strategic logic went, John or his successors would be better placed to help the crusading movement once more.

The logic was correct, but desperately uninspiring. These were hard times for the British Templars. The crusading movement was at a low ebb. After the exertions of the Third Crusade and the bitter aftermath of King Richard's ransom money, England was exhausted. The Fourth Crusade (1202–4) was preached in England but failed to attract much support, even before it controversially became subverted into an attack on Christian Byzantium. Templar patrons – men who were usually amongst the most enthusiastic supporters of the crusading cause – were no exception.[6]

There is proof of only two participating patrons. One of them, William of Say, confirmed their ownership of the manor of Saddlescombe. The other, Robert of Ros, founded the order's preceptory at Ribston (Yorkshire), explicitly writing that the gift was made to help support the Holy Land – *ad sustentionem Sanctae Terrea*. But, across the country, enthusiasm was in short supply, for the moment at least.[7]

The Templars made all the usual polite obeisances to their new king. They gave John a beautiful riding horse as a coronation gift. Doubtless this was well received. But, even more practically, given that John had inherited a treasury emptied by the Third Crusade and Richard's ransom payments, the order also ingratiated themselves financially with the new regime: they gave the king £1,000 as a sweetener for receiving a wide-ranging royal confirmation of their assets and privileges.[8]

Their gestures of loyalty were reciprocated. In 1199, as soon as he was crowned, John made extremely generous grants to the Templars. He understood the key role they had played in maintaining the peace in previous reigns – and particularly in guaranteeing peace treaties with the French in the 1190s. John may have suspected, all too presciently, that he would soon be needing their services.[9]

DIPLOMATS FOR THE UNDIPLOMATIC

Most obviously, a man who is not naturally gifted with social skills needs to outsource his problems to people who are. The diplomatic history of the Templars in John's service is accordingly a mirror and a metaphor for the entire troubled period.

John's reign began as it went on – in a cycle of conflict. He had access to significant military resources and was not completely inept as a strategist. But his lack of emotional intelligence meant that he often alienated those he most needed to influence. John's inability to behave with empathy contributed significantly to his unerring ability to snatch defeat from the jaws of victory.

The way John dealt with his young nephew was characteristic of this not entirely irrational but ultimately counterproductive style of leadership. Arthur I, duke of Brittany and earl of Richmond, the son of John's late elder brother Geoffrey, had gone into revolt with French support. Arthur had been King Richard's appointed heir at one point and was irritatingly close to the French king – he was disloyal and clearly represented a threat to John's interests.

From 1199 to 1202, John fought a desultory war against the recalcitrant teenager. He eventually managed to bring overwhelming force to bear against Arthur and his allies, and captured him at Mirebeau in August 1202.

So far, so good. John had won. He had shown his military skill. He had flaunted his power. And he had the leverage of a prisoner. All he needed to do now was to be magnanimous.

Instead, he let his inner self, vicious, paranoid and petulant, come to the fore. Arthur was taken to one of John's dungeons in Rouen. There, perhaps on the night of 3 April 1203, the prisoner was rumoured to have been killed in a drunken frenzy by his uncle. He was still only fifteen or sixteen years old. Some said that he had been mutilated first, perhaps castrated and blinded. The young man was never seen again.

Not surprisingly, John's subjects in Brittany were outraged. They never forgave him. Many others, traitors and loyalists alike, were similarly unimpressed. John had revealed what he was capable of and people did not like what they saw. What he envisaged as a show of strength, others saw merely as a weak display of cruelty and self-indulgence.[10]

This cycle was repeated throughout John's reign. He had a lot going for him. He ruled over prosperous lands and had a substantial army. He was an anointed monarch in a deeply pious age. With these advantages, he could achieve a lot. But whatever he achieved he often managed to throw away at the last moment. His lack of emotional connection with those around him undermined his ability to trust or be trusted.

He was at war with France for most of his reign. This was no abstract matter. Most of the leading nobles in England also held large estates in France and, for many, the king of France was also a liege lord. Losing Normandy and the other continental possessions was not just a problem of national pride or foreign policy. It was a deeply personal matter for almost all the great families. So personal, in fact, that military failure in France could quickly trigger civil war in England.

Unlike his brother Richard, John was not a natural general. Instead, over a few short months in 1202–4, he lost Normandy and, arguably, much of the respect he had amongst his leading vassals.

In the spring of 1203, the war with France took a massive turn for the worse. King Philip of France and his army first attacked Anjou, the heart of John's family empire, and then Normandy. Castle after castle fell into French hands. In the summer, Philip invaded again, capturing the castle of Radepont in a siege that lasted just over a fortnight.

John's response to the French offensive was characteristic. In the autumn of 1203, with Normandy under siege and his empire facing collapse, he made an extraordinary decision – he left his men and went back to England. This was ostensibly to raise reinforcements. But the king, unpopular and suspicious, was too insecure and too preoccupied with the possibility of rebellion to come back. When strong military leadership was most needed, John was nowhere to be seen.[11]

Templar envoys and mediators were used to limit the damage. They struggled to put a diplomatic settlement in place. The master of the British Templars, Aimery of Saint-Maur, was employed by the king from February 1204 onwards in negotiations with the French. His mission was ostensibly to negotiate ransoms and prisoner of war exchanges, but Aimery's real objective was to try to broker a truce, no matter how humiliating, before Normandy collapsed altogether.[12]

John was getting desperate. Château Gaillard, the heart of John's regional defences, was under siege. Despite a fierce defence, the castle fell on 6 March 1204. In the wake of this defeat, it quickly became apparent that loyalty to John was thin. He sent Hugh of Wells, his chief clerk, to lead a peace mission alongside Aimery. Not surprisingly, the French were having none of it. Continued peace overtures were made in April and May 1204, but King Philip wisely ignored them, maintaining his military momentum. Instead, he pushed on to complete the conquest of Normandy – resistance collapsed as soon as people felt that it was safe to change sides.[13]

In August 1205 another Templar diplomat, this time a certain Brother Geoffrey, was sent by John on a mission to the French court. Again, this was presumably an attempt to broker a peace treaty. Two years later, in 1207, we find the Templars still keeping diplomatic channels open and working for John in organising the release of important prisoners, such as Gerard of Athée. Gerard was one of John's most valued mercenary captains, and had been ransomed with the aid of Templar money – a loan for his release was arranged by them for this purpose in 1206. The Templar brothers in France even went so far as to escort Gerard and his family to the coast, so that their safety could be guaranteed on the way back to England.

John continued to use the Templars in his attempts to recover his lost empire in France. In 1211–12, the order's financiers and diplomats at the New Temple in London were engaged to provide money subsidies for the forces of the German emperor, Otto IV, in order to buy his support against the French. At least one British Templar emissary accompanied the emperor's envoys back to Germany to help organise the transactions. John also reached out to the papacy at this time of crisis to try to get support from the church. Once again, British Templar diplomats, including Alan Martel, were dispatched on his behalf, reaching the papal court in early 1213.[14]

By April 1213, war with France took on an even more active footing – King Philip declared his intention to invade England. King John hurried down to the south coast to meet the threat. A conference was convened at the Templar house in Ewell, near Dover. There, with the brothers and other military advisers, he hurriedly organised defence plans with which to counter an amphibious invasion. In May, he had a British Templar envoy carry a letter from the English barons to King Philip, expressing their loyalty and support for John – hopefully ensuring that Philip had no illusions about the level of baronial support he might find for an invasion of England or, after the intervention by Brother Alan Martel earlier in the year, the stance of the papacy.[15]

By 1214, King John was confident enough to go back onto the offensive, in a last concerted attempt to recover Normandy. Inevitably, his confidante, the ubiquitous Brother Alan Martel, accompanied the king on campaign in Poitou. Other Templar brothers took a very active role in funding the expedition, writing back to England to get more money sent out and guarding some of his vital war chests. Things went well at first. Anjou was recovered by the end of June.[16]

As ever with King John, however, initial hope turned to disappointment. The French victory at the battle of Bouvines on 27 July 1214 was a disastrous turning point – the German emperor was almost killed and his army routed. John's expensively subsidised German allies were knocked out of the war.

John was forced to make a humiliating peace with King Philip and return the Angevin lands he had recaptured. Alan Martel and other Templar brothers were present at the discussions and were probably instrumental in agreeing the truce and final treaty. Even the depressing job of transporting the defeated expeditionary force back to England was partly dependent on the Templars. Embarrassingly, the British master, Aimery of Saint-Maur, and the Templar master in Poitou, Gerard Brochard, had to lend John the money to get his men home.[17]

In October 1214, John arrived back in England. But a debilitating and unsuccessful war with the French was just one of his problems. The king had a raft of unhelpful issues to address with his own vassals. Expensive military failures abroad helped destabilise men who were already deeply suspicious of their king. Simmering disputes and resentments from earlier in the reign tipped over into open rebellion.

The Templars did what they could to maintain peace in England. On 6 January 1215, as relations between the crown and much of the nobility went into terminal decline, the order hosted a conference at the New Temple. The objective was to agree reforms which might avert open warfare. John and his nobility both saw the Templars' headquarters as safe and neutral ground.[18]

The meeting delayed outright war for a while, but, although the Templars were trusted as middlemen, John and the barons were (quite rightly as it transpired) suspicious of each other's intentions, and war crept ever closer.

While going through the motions of negotiating with his discontented barons, John was in fact playing for time. He made concessions to the church and, most importantly, wrote to Pope Innocent III to say that he would take the cross and join a crusade to the Holy Land. As ever, this ostensibly clever move was ultimately counterproductive. John managed to combine short-term political astuteness with longer-term emotional ineptitude. Peace had been in his grasp, but he could not resist the chance to outflank his opponents and start the conflict up again.

King John's status as crusader was a fraud. It was cynically calculated to gather political support for his cause. But, tactically at least, the ploy worked. The pope could be a powerful ally and, as was intended, announcing a crusade elicited a Pavlovian response in the Vatican. In July 1215, after John had asked for 'crusader' status once more, Pope Innocent started to excommunicate John's domestic opponents. Exactly as the king had planned, the pope took an unashamedly partisan viewpoint. He accused John's enemies of being 'worse than Saracens, for they are trying to depose a king who would help the Holy Land'.

Innocent went far beyond mere disapproval, however. He strayed into areas of direct military intervention. According to the chronicler Ralph of Coggeshall, Hugh of Boves, one of John's mercenary captains, was given papal letters with which he was able to recruit troops from Flanders and Brabant for the royalist cause. Papal indulgences were offered to those who fought for John. And, just a few months later, in January 1216, the pope went even further and encouraged the archbishop of Bourges to raise troops to fight on John's behalf.[19]

This attitude goes a long way towards explaining the behaviour of the Templars. As ever, they were agents of the papacy. The central authorities, however imperfect they might be, were the chief vehicle for launching substantive crusades to help the Latin East – so, despite their misgivings, the order's default response was to help the king.

But, all too predictably, John's military plans were inwardly focused. He soon began to recruit mercenaries, but these were to fight against his English barons, rather than against the Turks in Egypt and Syria. He turned once more to the Templars (and specifically his almoner, Brother Roger) to help raise an army with which to fight this new civil war. Roger was ordered to prepare ships for the fleet to bring the king's mercenaries over from the Continent.[20]

John's barons were increasingly pushed into open conflict. Facing excommunication by the pope and dealing with a deeply untrustworthy monarch, they now had almost no choice. By May 1215, war was inevitable. The Templars were definitively forced into their customary mode of supporting the central government, an administration which, however distasteful, had promised to give active support to the crusading movement if it survived.

The Templars continued to offer their good offices throughout the war. They generally acted for John, but were sufficiently trusted by both sides to be able to act as peace negotiators whenever they could. The order played their role as diplomats and military advisers, even at the short-lived peace agreement that was thrashed out at Runnymede on 15 June 1215 – the historic day when all parties signed the Magna Carta. 'Almeric the master of the knights-Templar' was one of the nobles present when the document was signed.[21]

Similarly, when negotiations for truces or safe conducts took place, the Templars were at the centre of discussions. And in particularly sensitive situations, such as the exchange of hostages or prisoners of war, the order was often there to guarantee safety and security for all. During the siege of Rochester, for instance, a castle that was then in baronial hands, the Templars helped bring out the garrison under promise of safe conduct.

On many other occasions they accompanied both parties during negotiations in order to ensure personal safety. At the end of June 1216, for instance, John called on Master Aimery of Saint-Maur to undertake an important prisoner exchange in person. Aimery accompanied four of John's knights from the dungeon of Rochester Castle, where they had been held, this time by the French, in an exchange for Roger of St Andrews, one of John's prisoners.[22]

Walking a line that maintained the respect of all parties was difficult. The Templars were, of course, not allowed to take part in fighting between Christians. But they did everything else they could to support the royal war effort. On a day-to-day basis, they were certainly at the command of

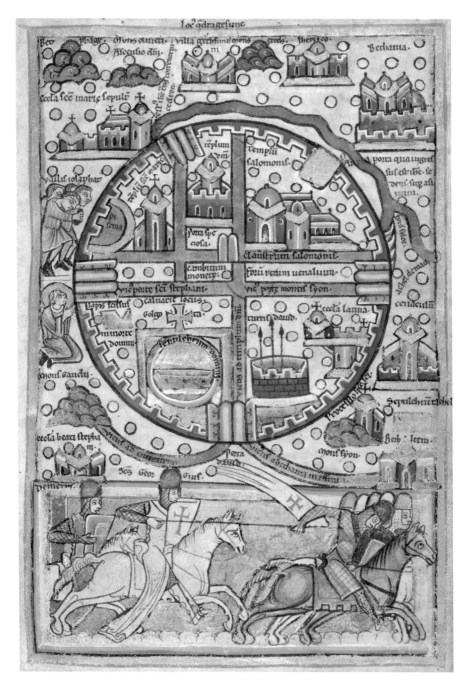

1. Jerusalem was back in Christian hands, but this just created a new problem. The defence of the Holy Land could not be adequately undertaken by the tiny number of crusaders left behind after the survivors of the First Crusade went home – ultimately it would require the full assistance and support of those left behind in Europe. There needed to be a mechanism by which the seemingly contradictory drivers of spiritual devotion and military muscle could be brought together to help defend the newly recovered lands. The Templars were that mechanism.

2. In 1187, at the end of the battle of Hattin, the remaining Templar cavalry and their comrades formed up in a thin, fragile line of some 200 men. Wounded, dehydrated and surrounded, they launched two final charges until, with no horses left to carry them, they were forced to fight on foot. The Templar survivors were executed on the battlefield by Saladin.

3. In 1310, at York, a very different story unfolded. Witnesses testified that the Templars habitually indulged in homosexual orgies, spat on the crucifix and, most vividly of all, kissed a calf's anus. How, in the space of a little over a hundred years, did the British Templars make the journey from heroic warriors to satanists and devil worshippers?

4. It was King Baldwin II of Jerusalem who moved the Templars into the iconic al-Aqsa mosque, giving them a substantial base and, coincidentally, their name. He was the man with the imagination and vision to see that they could be a unique (and desperately needed) way of bringing the resources of the West to the aid of the East.

5. King Stephen and Queen Mathilda of Boulogne had deep connections with the crusading movement. After Stephen's capture at the battle of Lincoln in 1141 it was even suggested that if Stephen were released, he might promise to immediately leave the country and, like his father, fight in the crusader states instead. Queen Mathilda and her husband played a crucial part in kickstarting the order's estate network in large parts of England.

6. King Stephen's Angevin opponents, the Empress Mathilda and her son Henry, also had close ties to the crusading movement. The order made efforts to remain on good terms with them whenever possible – Templar interests, after all, transcended those of local family issues in the West. The king of Jerusalem, for instance, Fulk of Anjou (r. 1131–42), was both a Templar associate and Henry's grandfather; not coincidentally, mother and son made significant grants to the Templars during the civil war.

7. Bisham, founded before 1139 by Robert de Ferrers, earl of Derby, was an important Templar manor house and an early indication of the Templars' growing popularity in Britain.

8 & 9. Queen Mathilda was a driving force in establishing the Templar order in England and a major donor in her own right. She gave the Templars the large estate and church at Cressing in 1136/7, the magnificent barns of which still survive today. It soon became one of their most important commanderies. Perhaps significantly, the grant of Cressing was made for the benefit of the soul of her crusader father, as well as those of herself and Stephen.

10 & 11. In 1161 the British Templars established their permanent headquarters: the New Temple in London. Significantly, the Templar church in Paris, capital of the arch-rival of the English crown, was of a far simpler design and much less ornate than its equivalent in London. The New Temple seems to have been designed by an architect from northern France with a mandate to create a state-of-the-art building which would make a visual statement – and Henry II was intimately involved in the initiative to create a new Templar base in his capital city.

12. Henry II took a particular interest in the order's preceptory in Garway, perhaps because of its frontier location on the Welsh borders – landlords on the marches tended to be tough, and with good reason. Over time, the Templars became an ever more important force in the region. Given their proven loyalty to the crown, the order was probably acting as a check to the often wayward ambitions of the frontier lords who were their neighbours, as well as to the Welsh.

13 & 14. The Becket affair encapsulates much of the British Templars' strategy. The order's mission was to transform the energy of Europe into the resources needed to defend the Latin East. In pursuit of that goal, they strived for good relations to be re-established between Becket and the king, and between church and state. When that became impossible, after Becket's murder – commemorated in relics and stained glass – they pursued the next best thing; they helped make peace between Henry and the papacy; and they used the moral outrage generated by the incident to extract as much money as possible from the English crown for the use of the crusading movement.

15. Miniature in four compartments with portraits of English kings: Henry II and Richard I, in the upper register, and John and Henry III, in the lower register. Each had different attitudes to crusading and to the British Templars – each man required an extremely sensitive, and very different, approach from the brothers.

16. Hugely outnumbered, a squadron of eighty-five Templar knights saved the Latin Kingdom of Jerusalem: they charged into the centre of the Muslim army at Mont Gisard, almost killing Saladin and routing his men. Visibly shaken, Saladin was hustled from the battlefield before any more of the Templars had a chance to get to him. The manuscript dutifully shows King Baldwin IV leading the combat, but the monarch, despite being a brave and respected leader of his people, was a sixteen-year-old leper. The Templars were his strong right arm on the day.

17. The rivalry of Richard I and Philip II of France was deeply unhelpful to the crusading movement. Fighting broke out between them in 1194 and continued until Richard's death in April 1199. The battle of Gisors was a victory for the outnumbered Anglo-Norman army, but Richard was dead within six months, leaving the defence of Normandy to someone far less effective: his brother John.

18. A popular ruler with charm and charisma can be forgiven much. He commands reserves of loyalty. He is given the benefit of the doubt. One like John, however, was neither trusted nor trusting. Instead, his personality was dominated by irritability, anger and poor behaviour. John needed talented partners who would be able to help him by taking a longer-term and more unemotional view of the world – men such as the British Templars.

19. Château Gaillard was at the heart of John's regional defences in Normandy. Despite fierce resistance, the castle fell on 6 March 1204. In the wake of this defeat, it quickly became apparent that loyalty to John was thin. He sent Hugh of Wells, his chief clerk, to lead a peace mission alongside Aimery, master of the British Templars. Not surprisingly, the French were having none of it. Continued peace overtures were made in April and May 1204, but King Philip wisely ignored them, maintaining his military momentum. Instead, he pushed on to complete the conquest of Normandy – resistance collapsed as soon as people felt that it was safe to change sides.

20. Friendless even in death, John's body was escorted south by mercenaries, before being buried in Worcester Cathedral. Despite John's unsuitability as a crusading king, however, the Templars remained faithful – they celebrated mass regularly for his immortal soul at the New Temple in London. For them, loyalty extended beyond the grave.

21. William Marshal was a long-term ally of the order and on his deathbed he formally became a Templar. Most effigies portray the deceased in their prime – that is, at the ideal age when their resurrection would occur. But William was famed for his longevity. He had remained active in the affairs of state into his seventies – and so, unusually, the effigy portrays an old man with deeply etched lines on either side of his nose and a heavily wrinkled brow. Here was the aged but towering figure that everyone remembered and respected. The famous old soldier had found a suitably militant home in death as well as life.

22. Gold's international credibility had a value in crusading logistics which surpassed other forms of currency; its reputational strength had a major impact on Henry III's currency policy. There was no English gold coinage in this period, but he built up a substantial bullion store in the New Temple at certain times, driven partly by the demands of campaigning on the continent but also by the possibility that he might one day want to raise an army and travel east – indeed, Henry's assiduous gathering of stores of gold is one of the main indicators that his commitment to the crusading cause was genuine.

23. Temple Balsall provides a good case study of how the Templars made the best of their agricultural possessions. The manor, in Warwickshire, was given to the Templars by the devout crusader Roger I of Mowbray in the period 1145–8. As Balsall was in the middle of the Forest of Arden, it was a form of 'pioneer' settlement. The estate was literally being carved out from the woods by the gruelling and labour-intensive process of land clearance by deforestation (assarting). Balsall was an asset that was being actively developed.

24. The excavation of Philip d'Aubigny's grave and ledger stone in front of the Holy Sepulchre in 1925. Philip d'Aubigny provides an extreme example of the way in which English family crusading traditions resonated across the generations. Philip's father had died on the Third Crusade, and Philip himself was an enthusiastic participant on the Fifth Crusade. Undeterred, Philip took the cross again in 1228, and once more in 1234–5. He died on crusade and, as he wished, was buried at the very epicentre of Christianity, in the Holy Sepulchre at Jerusalem. His tomb slab still survives. The short message carved on it simply says: 'Here lies Philip d'Aubigny. May his soul rest in peace. Amen.'

25. Like his ancestor Richard the Lionheart, Edward I was exactly what the order needed. In him England had a leader who was a dedicated warrior and personally brave – he had an enthusiasm for war which was combined with a pious and deeply personal devotion to the crusading cause. In Edward I the British Templars once more had a crusader king – a true *Rex Crucesignatus*.

26. Sultan Baybars was impressed by Edward when he was on crusade. He did not want Edward coming back with a bigger army to finish what he had started. In June 1272 a night-time attack was launched to kill the prince while he was in his bedroom at Acre. But, despite being wounded, he 'caught up a dagger from the table which was in the chamber, and stabbed the Saracen in the head and killed him'. Edward's wife, Eleanor of Castile, was in the room when the attack took place. She had gone to the Holy Land with Edward and gave birth to their daughter, Joan of Acre, while out there; in keeping with the family tradition, Joan would herself vow to go on crusade, back to her birthplace, in July 1290.

27. Towards the end of the thirteenth century there were few Templars left in Britain, and many of these were elderly, broken men. The Templar care home at Denney in Cambridgeshire was, apart from the headquarters in London, the largest concentration of Templars in Britain – but it was full of men who could no longer serve. One was described as insane, perhaps suffering from severe PTSD, and most of the rest were too old and frail to fight. With all available combat troops being called to the crusader states, the order in Britain was fast becoming a shell.

28. October 1307. Friday the thirteenth. Shocking dawn raids took place in Paris and across the rest of France. The French Templars were arrested en masse, in what almost amounted to an internal coup d'état. There was no warning of the suppression. Many of the brothers were on royal service, helping the king of France's officials, when the order for the suppression was issued. Some Templars had to be escorted back to Paris, under arrest, by the very people they were working with. The face of the central figure shows the incredulity felt even by some of Philip's own arresting officers.

29. James of Molay had his faults as a leader. He had not always shown good judgement. But in his final hours he tried to make up for his mistakes. He and Geoffrey of Charney, the master of Normandy, were burned alive by the French king on the Île-des-Javiaux, still refusing to admit the trumped-up charges. All 'who saw them [had] much admiration and surprise for the constancy of their death and final denial'. Personal bravery was their last substitute for hope.

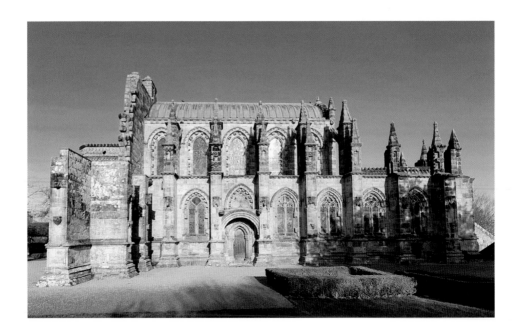

30 & 31. Rosslyn chapel can be seen as a metaphor for the broader, and unnecessary, plethora of Templar conspiracy theories. The chapel supposedly has close connections to the Templars and has 'associations' (whatever that means) with the Holy Grail. None of this is true. The chapel has no obvious links with the Templars at all. Work on the building did not begin until 1446 and continued until 1484: Rosslyn was indisputably built some 140–180 years after the order ceased to exist. But the beauty and artistry of the chapel is extraordinary in itself: like the Templar order, it is unnecessary to encumber it with fake legends.

King John. He was at the helm of the legitimate government and was now, in theory at least, a committed crusader.

The order inevitably had very few men on the ground in England but they did what they could to help John's preparations. Their military tasks were wide ranging and important.

John's use of the Templars to transport money to pay for troops and munitions became commonplace during the baronial revolt. And the order carried out castle inspections for the king, making sure that his fortifications were fully provisioned and ready for war. On 14 May, for instance, Alan Martel was instructed to send longbows, lances and square-headed bolts (presumably for ballistae) to John's castle at Marlborough. A couple of weeks later, they were also using their men to transport money on the king's behalf to his fortress at Devizes.

The order helped John organise shipping for his mercenaries, transporting them from the Continent in October and November 1215. And they held large parts of the royal war chest in trust. The Templars were tough and untouchable, just the men to do such difficult but vital work.[23]

Behind the scenes, the British Templars' military expertise was certainly exploited to the full, even if the brothers could not actually be deployed as frontline troops. Most of this expertise and advice was imparted in person, of course, or in documents that are now lost. One surviving example of their military counsel, however, is particularly telling.

Devizes Castle was always vital for the royalist cause, but it assumed even greater importance after French troops started landing in England in the spring of 1216 to help the rebels. The Templars, famous for their expertise in building some of the Holy Land's most impressive castles, were naturally sought after for their advice.

After French troops took Winchester on 14 June 1216, John dispatched his trusted Templar agent Alan Martel to Devizes. The Templars were already very familiar with the castle and its defences as they had been intimately involved in paying and resupplying the garrison. Alan was now tasked with making sure that last-minute improvements to the fortifications were made and that troop dispositions were equally effective. Interestingly, most of his efforts were focused on improving the defences of the weakest points of any castle – the gates.

Martel issued specific instructions that the 'Great Gate' of Devizes Castle should be defended by Oliver and Geoffrey of Buteville and their Poitevin contingent. The defence of the gate called 'Casteletti', on the other hand, was to be the responsibility of Thomas of Sanford (the castle's constable) and Richard of Rivers. We know little of the underlying logic that lay behind such orders – perhaps there was some tension between the mercenary leaders and the castle's garrison that needed defusing. But it is clear that the Templars had good tactical knowledge of the situation and were using their experience to help the king's cause.[24]

A couple of months earlier, in March 1216, we find another example of how deeply integrated the British Templars were into John's war effort. The king sent three letters to his financial centre in Corfe Castle, with instructions for vital money transfers. Tellingly, all three involved the Templars.

One letter gave instructions that certain (unspecified) sums of money should be given to Alan Martel and that Martel should also be given an account of how much was left afterwards. A second letter set out a more detailed version of the transaction and specified that, while some money should be given to Alan Martel, a further sum should also be given to a different Templar, Brother Geoffrey. A third letter, emphasising the importance of the Templars still further, was an instruction to John's men in the castle – it ordered them to obey Alan Martel and stressed that further instructions would be given in person by Templar Brother Aimery (presumably the master, Aimery of Saint-Maur).[25]

Even in the dying months of John's reign, the Templars were still intervening in military affairs on John's behalf. The important castle of Bristol, controlling the vital western port, needed a stronger garrison to ensure its continued security in the face of a possible French siege. A mercenary force commanded by Savaric of Mauléon was dispatched to bolster its defences. In July 1216, the Templars, led by Brother Roger the almoner, were sent in to ensure that the command structure of the castle's garrison was clarified and that both parties worked well together. Again, they were perhaps aware of some underlying animosity or rivalry between Savaric and Philip d'Albini, John's constable at Bristol.[26]

However distasteful they found the job, the Templars were there to the last.

THE TEMPLARS AND THE NAVY

The Templars' military support extended beyond castles, prisoner exchanges and financing. They were instrumental in creating a new navy.

Richard I's fleet, which had been developed at least partly with assistance from the Templars, had been a significant success. But the fleet was a single-use weapon, a specific vehicle for a specific expedition. Wooden ships rotted and had a very limited life. It was no more a 'standing navy' than most medieval states had a 'standing army'.

John, with his huge and ultimately disastrous commitments on the Continent, was soon in need of his own fleet, however. The shock of losing Normandy had made organising the navy both more necessary and more difficult. The collapse of much of the old continental Angevin empire meant the loss of vital ports – and, just as importantly, the loss of access to local soldiers. Troops that would usually have been recruited in France now needed to be shipped in from England or elsewhere. This was compounded by the fact that the coast of northern France was now enemy territory – it had become far easier for the French to launch an invasion of England.[27]

Naval matters were increasingly important. A threatened French invasion of England in 1213 was thwarted by aggressive naval action, as an English fleet, partly funded by the order, took the fight to the enemy before they were fully prepared.

On 30–31 May, Philip's navy was at anchor at Damme, the port of Bruges, while the king and his army besieged Ghent. The English ships arrived unexpectedly. They created havoc amongst the mostly unmanned and moored French shipping. They 'cut the cables of three hundred of their ships loaded with corn, wine, flour, meat, arms, and other stores, and sent them to sea to make for England; besides these they set fire to and burned a hundred or more which were aground, after taking all the stores from them'.

Hundreds of French ships were captured, and the remainder were destroyed. The brothers of the New Temple had been instrumental in financing the English fleet which destroyed Philip's navy and, arguably, won England's first major naval victory against France.[28]

But that was the high point. In the last two years of John's reign, there were continuing efforts to ward off a French naval invasion in support of the baronial revolt, but with much less success.

The Templars were called upon to help the navy in different ways. Most obviously, they could provide ships – they were, after all, experienced shipowners in their own right. In June 1213, for instance, shortly after the battle of Damme, we know that Templar ships under the command of Brother Gilbert, who was based in Dieppe, were instructed to join the royal fleet. In return for their service, the order was given valuable trading rights, particularly with regard to bringing wine and other goods into England.[29]

Less obviously, but probably more usefully for King John, they could also offer their administrative and logistical skills to help build up a navy in short order.

As was often the case in the medieval world, there was surprisingly little distinction between military and civilian vessels or between naval operations and commerce – the skillsets and infrastructure needed were almost identical. The same vessels could be used, with minimal adaptation, to fight battles or to transport pilgrims, money and trading goods. The Templars owned ships that were indeed military vessels, but they were also flexible.[30]

The order had made long-standing attempts to improve its access to shipping in England. London and the ports of the south-east were an obvious focus for Templar shipping, but conscious efforts took place to expand their maritime interests into the west of England, particularly Bristol.

Bristol in the twelfth century was the second largest city in England. It had, like London, a thriving trade with France, importing luxury goods, food and wine. At some point before 1147, the order began to acquire lands in Redcliffe, a suburb of the medieval walled city (the area eventually became known as Temple Fee).[31]

As usual, the Templars sought to improve their holdings. They diverted the Avon to improve its navigability and, not coincidentally, its commercial value. They also built a stone bridge over the river. The Bristol commandery eventually became the centre of a large agricultural estate, with lands stretching down towards Cornwall, but it was primarily a shipping hub for the order.

As well as the two major cities of London and Bristol, we know that the British Templars had many other maritime facilities which could be used for a range of commercial and military activities. The order had licences to use the ports of Winchelsea, Portsmouth and Rye, but they also had naval resources in places such as Shoreham in Sussex and Dunwich in Suffolk. Dover was another centre for the order and the royal constable of the castle was expected to provide a ship at his port for Templar diplomats whenever they were working on the king's business.

As one would expect from an international organisation that needed to maintain a strong logistical capability between western Europe and the Levant, the British Templars had close shipping links with the Continent. The order had naval facilities at Marseille, but their fleet was based at La Rochelle, on the French Atlantic coast. This was their main maritime link between Britain and France. Because of the survival of some contemporary licensing records, we even know the names of two of these Templar ships: one, a galley, was unimaginatively named *La Templere*; the other, normally used as a merchant ship, was called *La Buzard*.[32]

As well as being shipowners, the Templars were also able to provide the means for others to acquire ships, particularly when they felt it would further the interests of the order to do so. In 1214, for instance, they lent King John £133 so that he could buy one of their Spanish vessels. Like any good second-hand car dealer, they not only provided credit and financing facilities, but also promised to give him his money back if the reconditioned ship proved not to be to his liking.[33]

The order's involvement with the English navy increased still further in the summer of 1215. William of Wrotham, one of John's admirals and the royal official in charge of naval administration, deserted the royal cause. John immediately drafted in a Templar, Brother Roger the almoner, to take over his duties.

Roger was already trusted and close to the king. He quickly took command of the royal harbours and fleet. Combining other Templar skills with his maritime responsibilities, William also became involved in handling naval finances, paying the wages of sailors and mercenaries. He organised freight transfers and was responsible for the collection of duties (the *frettum*). Later, he even made the arrangements for ships to carry the king's messengers and envoys on their business.

Roger was soon organising the transportation of horses and troops from France to England to help sustain John's war effort. He sourced twelve ships in July 1215 and paid the sailors' wages on the king's behalf. By September 1215, Roger was involved in arranging passage to England for mercenaries, both infantry and cavalry, led by the mercenary commander Geoffrey of Martiny. In March 1216, just before French troops landed in England, Roger was once again instructed to find money for a ship to bring another mercenary contingent over, this time commanded by Robert of Betun.[34]

The Templars' skills in helping to build and manage military shipping for others meant that they remained in demand in this capacity even after John's death. By the 1220s a Templar brother became one of the leading administrators of the new royal fleet. This man, a certain Brother Thomas, was referred to as 'the keeper [*custos*] of the Great Ship' – he was retained to project manage a vital naval construction and refurbishment project for the crown at Portsmouth.

The commander of the nearby castle at Porchester was instructed to provide Thomas with the on-board artillery (*ballistae*) and other weapons that he and his team needed to complete the fitting out of this major warship, and we know that the Templars also received money to pay the wages of the carpenters and other ship-workers.

Brother Thomas's success was rewarded with more work. Soon afterwards, a ship named *La Cardinale* arrived from Portugal. The vessel, together with its cargo, was also bought by the crown and it too was put under Brother Thomas's command.[35]

Brother Thomas became deeply involved in Henry III's campaigns to retain control of Gascony. These actions went way beyond the Templars' more normal 'consultative' role when it came to military action between warring Christian states. He was given the task of organising the muster of the royal ships at Portsmouth, including assembling 200 vessels there for the king in 1226. Another flotilla was gathered under his supervision the following year.

When Thomas sailed to Gascony, later in 1226, he was in joint command of substantial elements of the royal fleet. The king wanted no ambiguity. He explicitly ordered that the English and Welsh ships, together with their seamen and bailiffs, should obey the orders of 'our beloved' Brother Thomas. Those orders were far reaching. Brother Thomas and his fleet were engaged in active combat duties, capturing ships thought to be trading with the enemy, and transporting soldiers and military equipment into Gascony. Thomas and his Templar comrades were naval experts and accordingly in high demand.

Thomas seems to have had a darker side, too. There are indications that the hard-working Templar may have liked to play hard too – some said that he enjoyed other aspects of his job rather too much.

We know that he had a substantial interest in the cross-Channel wine trade. In the summer of 1225 he was commissioned to buy 200 tuns of wine from Bordeaux on behalf of the king. As part of this trade, one of Thomas's less onerous duties in port was to supervise the inspection and sealing of wine casks as they were brought on and off the ships. And it was in this capacity that he was accused of taking some of the king's wine for his own use. Thomas was arrested.

Guilty or not (and such crimes were by no means uncommon in what passed for the bureaucracies of the medieval world), Thomas was soon freed. The arrest was probably just a warning – he was far too useful to be left languishing in a royal dungeon for long. And the goodwill of the Templar order was an asset to be nurtured.

Strangely, there are other signs that the warrior monk had unusual character flaws that may have contributed to his edgy reputation. While on his naval campaign in Gascony in June 1226, Thomas's brother Richard (who was not a Templar) served under his command. Soon afterwards, in circumstances that are now unclear, Thomas had his brother arrested and imprisoned for mutiny. Richard was eventually freed but, significantly, not at Brother Thomas's request. The king released him, but only after lobbying from the citizens of Bayonne.[36]

We do not know what became of the flawed but talented Brother Thomas. Mysterious and elusive, he disappears from history. But the influence of the Templars on the early years of the English navy continued to resonate.

GOD'S BANKERS: THE TEMPLARS
AND ENGLAND'S FINANCES

It was Richard the Lionheart who became known as the warrior king. But his brother John also presided over a perpetual 'war economy'. He was always looking for loans and new sources of income.

The Templars' experience in this field was eagerly exploited by John. But the skills of the order in organising war finance could also be turned to broader uses. The political and military instability at the end of John's reign meant that he had to decentralise his finances – and in these fragmented circumstances he had to put a very careful guard on his money.

Security issues meant that he needed to create a series of localised 'treasuries' in his major castles. The New Temple became similar to one of these castle treasuries but, because of its proximity and the wide-reaching political help given by the order to John's administration, its role was particularly important.[37]

This was the usual symbiotic relationship between the king and the Templars. John used the order's financial skills to help keep his government afloat, and the Templars used those same skills as a way of increasing their power and influence. The New Temple became a major financial centre and the order was even, on occasion, given responsibility for John's war chest.[38]

Contrary to the theories of some modern conspiracists, the Templars' financial skills had been developed to help in their military role, rather than out of greed or a desire for power. Their financial interests, like all the order's other functions, were primarily focused on the wars that raged intermittently over the twelfth and thirteenth centuries in the Holy Land.

This clear strategic priority was naturally reflected in the way they handled their finances in Britain and in the other provinces of the West. Monies were gathered from around Britain and collected every year at the provincial chapter meeting. They were then transferred to Paris, the headquarters of the order in the West. From there the funds were sent to the East, where they could be deployed to support the brother knights and sergeants, fund castle building and repairs and hire mercenaries.

The necessity for such regular money transfers encouraged the order to develop some of the most sophisticated international banking processes known in western Europe at that time. Crucially, this meant that the Templars were able to move money, whether on their own behalf or on behalf of others, to third parties without actually transferring the physical bullion or other assets.

The unique blend of military excellence, ecclesiastical objectivity and financial knowledge led to the order being trusted for sensitive tasks. The Templars were sometimes called upon to safeguard the interests of widows, a practice that had begun in Henry II's reign. The king had made arrangements for Margaret, the widow of his eldest son, Young Henry, to be given £2,750 per annum in payment of her marriage portion. He had the money stored in Templar houses, to be disbursed in two payments each year – one in the spring and one in the winter.[39]

The Templars' services to widows continued into the thirteenth century. Berengaria of Navarre, Richard I's widow, was supposed to receive a regular pension from the New Temple, partially in recognition of the dowry that she had brought with her. King John, true to form, failed to live up to his side of the agreement – she was not given the sums to which she was entitled.

Eventually, in September 1216, John made a secret agreement with Berengaria regarding her dowry and the future payments owed to her. The documentation for this revised deal was held in the New Temple, and the Templar Brother Alan Martel was one of the witnesses. After John's death just a few weeks later, Berengaria's agents, one of them a Templar brother, came to the New Temple to collect the first instalment of the money owed to her.

During the difficult years of Henry III's minority which followed, however, the substantial size of the sums involved caused problems. A further treaty was required. It was agreed that Berengaria was to come to the New Temple in person, or send a Templar messenger in her stead, to receive 2,000 marks each year. The money would be paid in two instalments – one on All Saints' Day and the other on Ascension Day. In November 1221, for instance, the Templar Brother Simon was given 1,000 marks, which he was to hold on Berengaria's behalf. By 1223, payments to her were taken directly from the king's treasure, also held in the New Temple.[40]

Taking on financial responsibilities for dowries was a similar service regularly provided by the Templars. In 1228, King Alexander II of Scotland paid the dowry of his sister through the New Temple. The order also paid the final instalment of the dowry required for Henry III's sister Isabella in 1257, and for King John's daughter Eleanor when she married Simon de Montfort.[41]

The New Temple was used as a place of safekeeping for valuables of all kinds. King John began to store documents and charters in the order's care, and the New Temple became, at least in part, a secure royal store house.[42]

Unsurprisingly, the storage of documents (and particularly those documents relating to financial transactions or land ownership) began in tandem with the storage of more obvious valuables. The Templars were not in charge of collecting the crusading tax of 1201 (a fortieth of the king's revenues, alongside those of his barons, knights and freemen), but its documentation was stored in the New Temple. So too were the funds raised by that tax – funds presumably ready for shipment to the East by the brothers themselves. The key requirements of storage, security and finance all converged easily in one location.[43]

Under John, the New Temple was increasingly used for the storage of chancellery records too, particularly with regard to sensitive documents of state. In March 1215, for instance, when John needed surety for Walter of Lacy's payment of fines, he had all of Walter's charters and title deeds put into safekeeping with the Templars until the money had been handed over.[44]

This was all entirely rational. But, more emotionally, it is the little things that often say so much. The Templars were trusted enough to be put in charge of the royal jewels and regalia. John was famous for his love of jewels. This hobby, like so many of his private activities, did little to endear him to those who had to pay for it – his subjects. We know that the Templars had the crown jewels in their care at least by 1204, because in December of that year the king asked for them back. He was eager to show them off at his Christmas celebrations in Tewkesbury. Brother Alan and Brother Roger, the royal almoner, duly delivered them to the king.

The winter of 1204–5 was one of the worst in living memory. Normandy had just been lost. The government was in tatters. With his characteristic emotional intelligence, John decided to focus on other essential affairs of state – his jewellery collection. The list of gems and jewels he gathered in front of him screamed outrageous luxury and sumptuousness.

What his lucky subjects in Tewkesbury felt about the show is not recorded – and it is probably just as well. Were they impressed with the vast array of brooches, encrusted with rubies and emeralds? Did they enjoy looking at the seven ebony staffs of office, weighed down with diamonds and gemstones? Even his clothes were over the top. John's robe was worked in gold with additional gemstones. His white gloves were adorned with sapphires and amethysts. The effect was flamboyant but hardly regal. This was a costume from the dressing-up box of someone entitled and out of touch, not the aura of quiet authority that he presumably thought it achieved.[45]

The Templars were still looking after the royal jewels in the New Temple in 1215 when John took back the regalia from their safekeeping. There were no more fashion shows but he was worried that the baronial rebels would take control of London. As his world fell apart, John wanted his precious jewels close to hand.[46]

Items in secure storage often required secure transit. This is a perennial problem. Crime lords in 1970s New York, for instance, employed local police to act as couriers for money and other shipments. Law enforcement officers were highly skilled third parties, almost untouchable by other drug barons. They were uniquely well suited to handle sensitive logistics issues. While it is extremely unlikely that the idea was borrowed from thirteenth-century British governmental practices, it was an excellent plan – and King John, with his very different baronial problems, had beaten them to it by over 700 years.

The Templars had a unique combination of military skills and financial expertise. They were trusted to move money within and between different countries on behalf of governments, nobles and merchants. In a time of crisis, and in a fragmented world where few could be trusted, John did not have the luxury of a centralised treasure store. As a result, his dispersed treasure created significant problems for the transportation of bullion.

Once more, the Templars' muscular qualities as security guards, trusted third parties and financial-logistics specialists made them ideally suited to help. In May 1213, for instance, 10,000 marks, which John had on deposit at the New Temple, were brought to his chamber in Wingham by a Templar retinue led by Alan Martel. The order had clearly been responsible for both the safekeeping and the secure transportation of this very significant sum.[47]

Financial structures became ever more difficult towards the end of John's reign. By early 1215, much of the country was in rebel hands. John became more reliant on the war chests held in his major strongholds, such as Corfe Castle and Nottingham Castle. This naturally created transportation problems, as it was only from these widely dispersed military locations that money could be distributed.

Within months, the traditional royal system of money transportation from these sites was replaced by a series of Templar security units, usually led by a senior brother such as Alan Martel or Master Aimery. Travelling round the country with the money, these Templar groups were able to ensure secure transport and, as military advisers, were also able to improve military preparedness at the sites they moved the money to.[48]

It was just another small step from transporting money to gathering it. For John, the Templars could become debt collectors. Cash flow was problematic. Nobody wants to give money to a regime that is in serious trouble – there is, after all, a major chance that the government will collapse and the debt will be written off altogether.

In 1214, for instance, when King John was in particularly desperate straits, he sent a 'commission', including the Templar Brother Hugh of Swaby, to Ghent and Ypres to call in local debts. The plan was that the commissioners would then pass on the monies collected to yet another Templar, Brother William Cadel. He would then organise expedited shipping back to England, perhaps on board one of the Templar ships carrying wine from Gascony, or perhaps arranging a money transfer using a bill of exchange. The delegation seems to have been only partially successful, but the Templars did everything they could to help.[49]

When cash flow failed, credit was required too. The Templars helped John with a series of crucial loans to allow his government to stagger on. The first of these were in the period 1204–6, when the king tried (and failed) to recover Normandy. Even more loans were needed in the period 1214–16. The Templars helped keep the king's administration afloat after his continental military adventures had failed, particularly after the disastrous defeat of his allies at the battle of Bouvines in 1214.[50]

What was useful for the king also applied to others – and particularly those who were involved in the crusading movement. Pious donors wanted to send money, goods and men to the help of the Holy Land and the Templars were highly motivated to help them do so.

Larger loans to potential crusaders were usually arranged by the provincial headquarters in London. Occasionally, however, smaller sums could be raised in the order's rural houses. Some of these micro-loans might be secured against the prospect of future crops, or, more poignantly, even using second-hand clothing as collateral. But generally there was a clear distinction between the respective roles of the rural and urban houses. The provincial centre at New Temple dealt with financing and other professional services; the rural houses dealt primarily with agricultural production and logistics.[51]

In the short term, the Templars' expertise in dealing with such large and relatively complex financial transactions was useful. It worked both for the order and for their patrons. Over the longer term, however, it brought dangers with it. As the Jewish community also found out to its cost, being associated with financial expertise in a volatile medieval society was a dangerously double-edged asset. Killing those you owe money to is a time-honoured way of writing off loans.

And having a reputation as clever financiers is only a short step from jealous accusations of greed and avarice.

Such a reputation was a long way from the truth.

The Templars have provided the backdrop for a thousand different stories of hidden treasure and mysterious riches. The truth was far more prosaic.

When the order was finally closed down, the king's administration was naturally anxious to ensure that money owed to the Templars was paid to the crown, rather than just being written off. So, at the end of 1308, local sheriffs were tasked with tracking down records of what was owed and collecting the debts.

Disappointingly for the sheriffs, almost no cash was found outside London and what little there was seems mainly to have been earmarked as wages for the order's workers. The paltry sums they eventually recovered show just how little the rural houses were involved in financial matters. In the whole of Herefordshire, for instance, there were just two cash loans to be called in, one for 10 shillings and the other for 20 shillings and 8 pence. The other debts owing in the county were merely the consequence of agricultural transactions that had been interrupted in progress – money that was still due from customers for purchases of cloth and oxen, and rents that were unpaid but still pending. This was not the kind of treasure that the royal bureaucrats had been looking for.[52]

Even in the New Temple, there were no huge sums of 'Templar treasure'. The money was not kept by the order – most of it belonged to other people or it was just passing through, on its way to help the cause in the East. The money, and the blood of the Templar knights themselves, was spent in the defence of the Holy Land.

But cynics did not always want to see it that way.

12

HENRY III – REBUILDING BRITAIN: 1216–1269

Even nature turned on a tyrant – or at least that was how many chose to see it.

September 1216. John was still campaigning against his disillusioned barons. Taking his spite out on those least able to defend themselves, the king and his soldiers spent their time 'committing terrible ravages in the counties of Suffolk and Norfolk'.

He then took his army on a march 'towards the north, but in crossing the river Wellester, he lost all his carts, wagons, and baggage horses, together with his money, costly vessels, and everything which he had a particular regard for; for the land opened in the middle of the water and caused whirlpools which sucked in [all his treasure], as well as men and horses, so that no one escaped to tell the king of the misfortune.'[1]

This was an exaggerated account, one of many that railed against the unpopular monarch. But it was also a metaphor of sorts. John was on the verge of bankruptcy. A Scottish army was invading in the north. French troops were on English soil in the south. Many of his barons were in open revolt and controlled large parts of England. Now, the chroniclers implied, God showed His contempt for the tyrant, too – destroying his baggage train and pulling his money down into the sands. John's ramshackle government was still undefeated but rapidly running out of road.

The misery that crippled the country ended unexpectedly quickly. Just a few weeks later, on the night of 18 October, John died of dysentery. As some unkind commentators at the time reflected, his soul, like his treasure, was sucked down into hell. Friendless even in death, the king's body was escorted south by mercenaries, before being buried in Worcester Cathedral.

The Templars remained faithful, however – they celebrated mass regularly for John's immortal soul at the New Temple in London. For them, loyalty extended beyond the grave.[2]

There were, if one cared to look for them, disturbing parallels between the slow train crash of John's reign and the deteriorating situation in the Holy Land. For much of the thirteenth century, and particularly from 1250 onwards, the Franks were little more than bit-part players in a landscape dominated by huge Mamluk armies and the other new entrants in an already dangerous region – the fearsome Mongols.

Despite this unstoppable strategic shift, however, the British Templars did their best to support the terminally failing (and terminally fractious) Frankish colonies.

They did this, once more, in a symbiotic military partnership with the English crown. As this period saw the growing need for men and money to be shifted to the East, so the British Templars played an increasingly desperate role in helping the cause – by continuing to improve financial, logistical and agricultural efficiency in Britain.

THE CHURCH MILITANT

It was a slow and dangerous start.

John was dead. But the conflicts that had scarred England during his reign refused to die with him. War with the rebel barons rumbled on – on Henry's accession (when he was just nine years old) they still held most of England. And fighting with France continued intermittently until 1226.[3]

The British Templars and, more broadly, their ultimate masters in the papal curia, did everything they could to support Henry and his fragile administration during his minority (1216–27). They continued their role in affairs of state, propping up a series of governments until Henry III could come of age. The order was able to offer financial support during these troubled years and worked closely with the young king's loyal counsellors and the papal legates to ensure that his authority was strengthened. They helped to ensure that he had the necessary military and diplomatic resources to establish a viable government.

The New Temple in London was at the forefront of that effort. The order's headquarters were frequently used as the venue in which vital governmental decisions were decided – in 1223, for instance, terms were hammered out by the contending parties in the Temple precinct to help stave off another debilitating bout of civil war. And the Temple acted as an important part of the financial administration for much of Henry's reign.[4]

The supportive role of the Templars during his father's reign and the fragile, formative years of his minority had a major influence on how Henry viewed the order. John's relationship with the Templars had been close but it was fundamentally transactional in nature – a relationship driven by need rather than affection.

Henry III's ties with the Templars, however, were both deeper and more emotional. He had been brought up in a household in which the Templars played a central part, particularly in times of emergency. His father had a good relationship with the order. But perhaps even more importantly, Henry's regent, William Marshal, the man he relied on for protection and who served him faithfully throughout the dangerous early years of his reign, was closely associated with the Templars.

The regent was, not coincidentally, close friends with Aimery of Saint-Maur, the master of the British Templars. The two men were old and exhausted their last energies in the service of the young king. But together they made a huge difference in keeping the ship of state afloat.[5]

William Marshal and his family had been deeply committed to the Templars for decades. This devotion went far beyond mere talk. William gave the order the very substantial estate of Upleadon in Herefordshire – it was estimated to be worth £28 12s in 1338. Even more personally, while in the Holy Land in the 1180s, William had built up a close relationship with the brothers and seems to have become an associate of the order. When he was on his deathbed, the regent formally became a Templar.

His body was carried in procession and temporarily laid to rest at Reading Abbey, then taken to Staines and on to Westminster Abbey. There a mass and night-time vigil was held to celebrate the life and devotion of the old soldier. His funeral was held at the New Temple, probably on 20 May 1219, in a service led by the archbishop of Canterbury. His body was laid to rest next to that of his comrade Aimery. Although present at William's deathbed, Aimery had, with poignant symmetry, preceded his friend in death just a few days earlier.

His tomb can still be seen in the New Temple in London, alongside the memorials to his fellow warriors. By a strange chance, we have a little detail about what his burial service in the New Temple church looked like. When he was in Jerusalem, death and the Templars being uppermost in his mind, he bought two expensive lengths of silken cloth, which he wanted to be used as a shroud for his corpse, and had them transported back to England. Perhaps he is still dressed in what little is left of them.[6]

Despite the best efforts of well-meaning Victorian restorers and the less well-meaning attention of the Luftwaffe, we even have a good idea of which effigy belongs to him. In the nave of the New Temple there is an imposing and extremely unusual effigy. A grizzled warrior, confident and serene, lies in chain mail armour and shield. Under his mailed feet lies a lion whose head is pierced by the knight's sword.

On the face of it, this is not too unusual. Many knights have similar memorials. This one is subtly different, however. Most effigies portray the deceased in their prime – that is, at the ideal age when their resurrection would occur. But William Marshal was famed for his longevity – he had remained active in the affairs of state into his seventies. This rare feature of his political and military life was reflected in the features of his face – unusually, the effigy portrays an old man with deeply etched lines on either

161

side of his nose and a heavily wrinkled brow. Here was the aged but towering figure that everyone remembered and respected.[7]

The famous old soldier had found a suitably militant home in death as well as life.

A RELATIONSHIP OF TRUST

The Marshals were a family with close ties to the Templars. His sons, William II (d. 1231) and Gilbert (d. 1241), continued this tradition of devotion and were also buried in the New Temple, alongside their father.[8]

King Henry very nearly followed their example. He had been particularly close friends with William II and was deeply distressed by his death. Shortly afterwards, in July 1231, he announced that he too wanted to be buried in the Templars' London precincts. Shortly afterwards a document noted that 'the king has entrusted his body for burial [there] after his mortal end'. He even went so far as to put the finances in place to make sure that it happened. Henry gave the brothers an estate as part payment for his plot and granted the New Temple an annual sum of £8 to support three chaplains in saying daily prayers – one for his immortal soul, one for the faithful departed and one for all the Christian people.[9]

It was probably also at this time that Henry commissioned the remodelling of the choir at the New Temple church in London. The elaborate new structure was suitably impressive. It had three aisles and, most importantly, space for a king's tomb as well as three altars. Work on the elaborate rebuilding project was completed by 1240, when it was consecrated anew in a service attended by Henry himself and many of his magnates.[10]

The king confirmed his decision to be buried there in 1235, while the building work was still underway. Henry, it was announced, 'of his free will from his especial love towards the order and brethren of the Temple has given his body after his death to the Temple of London there to be buried'. There were even explicit instructions (vital, given the litigious tendencies of religious institutions) to ensure that 'no other religious house even if founded by the king [was] to oppose it'.

Circumstances changed during his exceptionally long reign. Henry was eventually buried in the far grander and more conventionally appropriate setting of the newly redesigned Westminster Abbey, but his commitment to the order was undoubted.[11]

Henry's complex duties as king meant that he was never able to go on crusade in person. He had to contend with multiple civil wars, rebellions and conflicts with all his neighbours – but support for the crusading movement and the Templars was a constant feature of his long reign. Under his rule, many Englishmen ventured out to the crusader states and monies were regularly gathered and sent east. His commitment was a personal one, clearly dating back to his earliest years.

It is not always easy to discern the full emotional context of the relationship through the dry prism of the surviving documents – these are often little more than lists of tax returns or formulaic legal confirmations of land transactions. But it is perhaps no coincidence to find reference to the Templars giving presents (presumably for the Christmas season) to the young king at the time he was making elaborate preparations for his eventual burial in the New Temple.

What to get the man who has everything was clearly a medieval problem, just as much as a modern one. A surviving list of royal presents received between November 1234 and June 1235 includes reference to no fewer than twelve belts given to Henry. But the Templars' gift was the grandest – the showiest item in an already crowded field. It was also the heaviest belt (about 7 troy ounces) and was described as being crafted from gold and silk thread, with a silver attachment. It was given to Henry by the Templar master in person.[12]

In the Templars, Henry III knew he had devoted advisers that he could trust and fixers he could depend on.

He would need them.

PATRONS OF THE CAUSE

King Henry III took the cross no less than three times – in 1216 (when he was still a child and clearly incapable of leading an army), again in 1250 and finally in 1271. On two of these occasions the reasons were clearly political – the usual ploy to get papal support and protection at a time when his administration needed it most. But his vows in 1250 were deeply puzzling, for contemporary commentators just as much as for modern historians.

Henry had made all the right noises with regard to crusading in the past. But, tellingly, words had never manifested themselves in action. On the contrary, in 1245 he had even refused to allow the bishop of Beirut to come to England to preach for a new crusade and, shortly after taking the cross in 1250, we find the king, perversely but driven by reasons of self-interest, trying to stop other English crusaders from setting off.

But Henry was genuinely pious. There is some evidence from the period 1252–3 to suggest that he was expecting to go on crusade in the summer of 1256. Serious and detailed planning took place. Marseille was to be the main embarkation point from Europe. Supply depots were to be established in the East. Discussions took place with the British Templars to get them to provide shipping and accommodation for the vanguard of the English expeditionary force.

Preparations seemed robust. But nothing happened.

Before the expedition could set off, Henry was distracted by equally expensive military and political problems far closer to home, particularly in Gascony. Supporting the crusading cause was always on the agenda, but so were many other things.[13]

Throughout his reign, there were continuing efforts to help the Holy Land. Henry was a solid, if not spectacular, financial patron of the Templars. He gave 500 marks to the British Templars in 1238, to help them with the costs of ransoming their surviving brothers after the battle of Darbsak the previous year. Henry also gave 2,000 marks to help prop up the defences of the crusader states in May 1264. The grant was made 'to keep in the Holy Land as many knights yearly as can be maintained by it and this in part ransom of the king's vow if by any unexpected chance he cannot go in person to the Holy Land'. Promises were still being acknowledged.[14]

There were also regular payments to the order, the so-called 'Templars' mark', which were taken from each English shire after 1156. The master of the British Templars received in addition an annual sum of 50 marks from Henry III and later too from his son Edward I to maintain a knight in the Holy Land on their behalf.[15]

Royal patronage towards the Templars continued to be important, both in its own right and as a tangible expression of the crown's support for the crusading cause. Sometimes this support could be very practical. Henry gave them two estates, for instance, one at Rockley in Wiltshire and another at Lillestone in 1234–5. As a useful addition to their London properties, he also gave them two forges in Fleet Street, close to the New Temple.[16]

But the support could also be intensely personal. In 1237, for instance, as part of a story of which we know tantalisingly little, Henry III gave a certain Peter of Burton money to buy a robe when he became a Templar.[17]

This patronage naturally found echoes further down the social hierarchy. Some of this generosity was triggered by the experience of fighting alongside the Templar brothers on campaign. The close ties of comradeship that this created often lasted a lifetime. Two of the wills drawn up at the siege of Damietta in 1249, during the Seventh Crusade, show the devotion and generosity of crusaders to their comrades in the British Templars. While they were fighting in Egypt, over 3,000 miles away from England, these men still found time to make generous donations to the order – a heightened sense of mortality doubtless helped focus the minds of both men.[18]

Similarly, while he was on campaign in the East in 1241, William Peverel confirmed the gift of the manor of Sandford, which his uncle

Thomas had previously made over to the Templars. The agreement was made on 2 May 1241, the day before he set sail from Acre back to England with Henry III's brother Richard of Cornwall. It seems likely that William's decision was influenced by the dangers of the trip which lay ahead – he was trying to make his peace with God, and God's warrior representatives on earth, before he entrusted his life to the lottery of a voyage on the unpredictable Mediterranean Sea.[19]

In Henry's reign, people were still prepared to sacrifice their financial security to help the cause. In 1247, Hugh FitzHenry wanted to join the British Templars and go on crusade. As part of this process, he put his lands in Abingdon up for sale. This precipitated an unsightly rush of offers and gazumping counteroffers amongst the other local landowners. Eventually the monks of Abingdon won out, largely because of the expertise of their wily property expert, a certain Nicholas of Headington. His deft manoeuvring is an early but sadly still rare example of an effective estate agent. But at least Hugh raised money to help him fight in the East.[20]

As in previous reigns, female support remained important. Richard of Cornwall confirmed a charter in 1233/4, in which a certain Matilda, daughter of Ranulf, gave the Templars land at Stoke Talmage in Oxfordshire.[21] The Templars acquired the estate of Cranford, on the Bath Road leading out of London, from Joan Hakepit in 1240. John le Chapeler and his wife added lands and a house to the estate in 1242 in return for food and a lifetime pension from the brothers.[22]

Victory in the East was increasingly elusive, but people on the home front could still show their commitment.

THE TEMPLAR DIPLOMATS

Master Aimery died a few days before his comrade William Marshal (May 1219) and was succeeded by Brother Alan Martel. Alan remained in the post until he too died in 1228. His selection as master was astute. The new leader of the British Templars was known and respected by the leading English political figures of the day.

Alan came from a family with a long tradition of service in English government – William Martel, for instance, had served as a steward (or *dapifer*) for King Stephen during the civil war against Empress Mathilda in the twelfth century. More to the point, Alan had represented Henry's father, King John, in many highly sensitive political and diplomatic capacities, including travelling to Europe to help with negotiations for Henry's marriage.

Once again, the Templars had astutely reorganised their leadership to ensure that they were at the heart of government.

Diplomatic activity conducted by the Templars in this period tended to focus on two main areas: the relationship of the English crown with other parts of Britain and interventions to help save the last remaining possessions in Gascony.

In the British Isles, as we have seen, the Templars were used extensively in the administration of Ireland by the English authorities. They were frequently employed as diplomats and envoys in dealings with the Scottish crown during the minority of King Alexander III (1249–62). The Templar Brother John Le Large, an important member of Henry's entourage, was sent on the king's business up to Scotland in 1268. In an intimate, almost homely aside, the expenses necessary for the trip (some 6 marks) were ordered to be paid out to John as quickly as possible, to ensure that the mission was not delayed.[23]

The order was also called on to mediate with the Welsh when things went badly. In 1262 a truce between Wales and England ran out. Henry III, still recovering from a major illness, was confronted with invasion in the west. In November, Welsh troops attacked and occupied large parts of Roger Mortimer's estates. A Templar brother, the commander of the order's marcher house in Garway, was sent by Henry in January 1263 to act as a mediator. He tried hard but his mission was unsuccessful. The muster of the English troops in Herefordshire was delayed and Prince Llewellyn, the Welsh leader, took the opportunity to side with the English rebels, led by Simon de Montfort.[24]

The Templar diplomatic missions to France and other parts of the Continent were arguably even more sensitive. For much of the 1220s, relations between England and France were tense, often descending into war. In 1224 the French invaded the English possessions of Gascony and Poitou. Poitou was permanently lost, but royal troops were mustered, and Gascony was recovered later in the year. The Templars were used by Henry in this campaign to mediate and negotiate as appropriate.[25]

A peace treaty was patched up with the French in May 1227 by Richard of Cornwall, Henry's brother, but, as so often with frontier disputes, the peace was fragile. By August the master of the British Templars, Alan Martel, and other brothers were back in France for further negotiations, trying to clarify fine details or perhaps to renegotiate certain terms.

Even so, the truce was broken on the English side in 1228 by an attack on the town of Saint-Émilion. Henry was forced to pay financial restitution for breaching the treaty. The money, appropriately enough, given the level of trust they commanded on all sides, was to be guaranteed by the Templars and paid to the French from royal funds taken from their coffers in the New Temple. This was Alan Martel's last major job for the English crown. He died later in the year, in September 1228, soon after he had patched over these diplomatic cracks.[26]

THE TEMPLAR FINANCIERS: BANK
MANAGERS TO THE GENTRY

Financial support from the order went alongside diplomatic activity, particularly in the fragile years of Henry's minority (1216–27). This support ranged from help with paying household bills through to international money transfers and the funding of armies.

Control of the king's personal finances was entrusted to the Templars. Trivial though it may seem to us, in the Middle Ages the king's personal finances, and those of his household, were extremely sensitive and inextricably linked with the finances of the state.

One of the king's treasuries, known as the 'wardrobe' (*garderoba*), moved with the king, and he had much easier access to its contents. The Templar Brother Robert of Melksham was made almoner early in Henry's reign. During this time the traditional role of the job (which had been primarily focused on dispensing money for charitable causes) was expanded. During the crises of Henry's minority it included at least some control over the king's wardrobe and hence the finances necessary for the upkeep of his household. This was a responsible job, given the king's poverty at that time, and we know that Henry kept what was in effect a current account with the order at the New Temple throughout his reign.[27]

In 1225, King Henry III moved this wardrobe treasury to a permanent location – the Templar's London headquarters at the New Temple. This change improved security, as the money was in one place, guarded by the Templar brothers, and made it easier for the king to get to this store of money.

The New Temple, and thus the wardrobe, also acted as a safe deposit house for treasure both for the monarchy (who sometimes kept the crown jewels there) and for the more prosperous citizens of London – the jewellery of Queen Eleanor, Henry III's wife, was stored at the New Temple, for instance.[28] The Templar's international network also allowed them to undertake foreign exchange transactions more easily than was possible through the cumbersome and less well-connected Exchequer.[29]

Other financial roles were less personal, but even more demanding. In the aftermath of John's wars and the continuing conflicts, there was an overriding need for money to keep the administration running. At the beginning of Henry's minority, the lack of money was a continual problem and the Templars played an active role in re-establishing financial stability. The vice chancellor of England, for instance, was instructed to leave the royal seal and any money he had been given with the Templar master whenever he left London.[30]

For much of this period, the New Temple provided a convenient treasury store in London and operated in parallel with more traditional financial structures when needed. It even had the personnel and facilities to allow it to take over in emergencies, such as when the death of the regent William Marshal in 1219 caused a power struggle in the minority government. It operated as part of the state's financial system and some of the government's money was stored there. The Templar headquarters received taxes and other crown revenues from Ireland, for instance, in addition to holding the king's personal 'bank account'.[31]

Beyond England, the international financial and logistical network the Templars had established across Europe and the Middle East made them extremely attractive partners for Henry. Even in the earliest days of his minority, a Templar preceptor named Brother Gerard Brochard was actively involved in gathering royal rents in Bordeaux. Gerald also used them in September 1217, perhaps more selfishly, to pay off the debts that King John had run up with the order.[32]

As in King John's day, the Templars were often used to physically move money to English troops and mercenaries during Henry's campaigns on the Continent. They also took on equally sensitive tasks such as acting as couriers, negotiating ransoms and truces and transporting horses and men.

In the period 1254–5, for instance, a Templar brother named Alan of Kent seems to have developed something of a specialism in this line of work. He organised and conducted a series of cash-carrying expeditions on behalf of Henry to Paris, Gascony and Toulouse. The sums involved were huge. It has been estimated that Alan and his Templar bodyguards cumulatively carried money equivalent to over a third of Henry's annual revenues on these trips.[33]

Helping the king was fine but ultimately, of course, the Templars saw financing as a tactical means to a far more strategic end. They wanted to help the Latin East and it was in gold that the interests of the king and crusading coincided.

Gold's international credibility had a value in crusading logistics that surpassed other forms of currency. This made it the most widely trusted means of exchange. In 1267, while the English crusader Hugh of Neville was in the East, he paid his own troops (who had no choice but to trust him) in silver. But it was significant that he paid the local merchants and tradesmen of Acre in gold. Men who had more leverage in a commercial deal were able to demand the strongest international currency for their transactions.[34]

The reputational strength of gold had a major impact on Henry's currency policy. There was no English gold coinage in this period, but he built up a substantial bullion store in the New Temple at certain times, driven partly by the demands of campaigning on the Continent but also by the possibility that he might one day want to raise an army and travel east. Indeed, Henry's assiduous gathering of stores of gold is one of the main indicators that his commitment to the crusading cause was genuine.[35]

The king seems to have started to accumulate gold in 1243 and some of this treasure was kept with the Templars. We know from references dating to around July 1245 that he issued instructions as to how the gold was to be weighed and that at least part of it was to be stored safely in the New Temple. Much of this gold was spent during Henry's Gascon campaign of 1253-4, but another gold collection was amassed from 1254 onwards as planning for a possible crusade became more detailed, only to be sold in 1260-1.[36]

'THE PROMISES MADE TO HIM'

Not surprisingly, the Templars were also at the heart of more general efforts to raise money for the defence of the Holy Land. In June 1222, a Great Council was convened in Westminster to raise taxes for the aid of the Holy Land. All property owners were called upon to contribute. A sliding scale of financial contributions was fixed, ranging from a penny for small freeholders up to 3 marks for an earl.

Specific instructions were issued to ensure that the money raised would be entrusted to the taxpayers' local Templar house or to other nearby monasteries. The taxes would then be gathered and stored at the New Temple in London by 1 November 1222, before being sent out to Palestine.

At around the same time, and not coincidentally, John of Brienne, the king of Jerusalem, came to Britain. He had been fighting on the Fifth Crusade (1217–21) alongside some of the more eminent English crusaders. They had assured him, perhaps over-optimistically, that he would receive a warm and generous welcome in Britain.

Philip d'Aubigny, an English crusader who had been tutor to the young King Henry, wrote back home shortly after the evacuation of Damietta in 1221, saying, 'I have also to tell you that [John] the lord king of Jerusalem is about to come to your part of the world; therefore, I ask you to provide him with aid in accordance with the promises made to him and to other magnates, for his debts are so great that it is a wonder to describe them.'

Indeed, it seems likely that it was these unspecified promises, made by English crusaders as the wine flowed all too freely around the comradely siege campfires of Egypt, that sparked off John's interest in coming to England. Drunken conversations and big talk were cheap, but they became the catalyst for the taxation imposed by the Great Council in the summer of 1222.[37]

In the autumn of 1223, John of Brienne arrived in England. He expected to collect the promised riches and gather military support. He was to be disappointed.

The English chroniclers put a partisan face on their version of events. One wrote that, when John went home, he was 'loaded [down] with gold and silver, donated with the greatest largesse by the archbishops, bishops, earls and barons'. But these seem to have been gifts and individual presents – the promised, and very substantial, lump sum did not materialise. John's trip lasted less than a month. He was unable to get promises of armies to go on crusade. The king returned to France, complaining of the 'English foxes [*vulpines*] on the other side of the Channel'.[38]

King John of Jerusalem was bitter, but perhaps unreasonably so. Shortfalls in raising the funds were not the fault of the king or the Templars.

Inevitably, attempting to raise money through special taxation did not go entirely smoothly. On 12 April 1224, for instance, royal sheriffs were still making efforts to ensure that the local Templars and other monastic orders got the money that was due. It was clear that the New Temple had not received the funds it had been expecting and, at the end of 1224, the king had to issue yet another edict, requiring payments to be made in full by January 1225.[39]

The Templars could lobby and cajole but, as John of Brienne found out to his chagrin, they were rarely fully in control.

A REPUTATION FOR MONEY

If relying on other people's largesse could be frustrating, the Templars were all too aware that they sometimes had to step up to bridge the financial shortfalls themselves.

Lending money to those who needed additional financing to go on crusade was a service the Templars provided. But having established lending as a service, it was natural to occasionally extend it for non-crusading purposes. Even the king needed help – Henry borrowed money from the Templars when necessary, particularly in the 1230s and '40s.

During Henry's reign, the New Temple became more fully involved in what was, literally, merchant banking. In 1260 and 1267, records show instances in which debts were incurred by third parties. It is significant that both borrowers and lenders (who were not necessarily based in London) stipulated that repayments were to be made at the Templar head-quarters. The inconvenience and risks of travel were felt to be outweighed by the advantages provided by the trusted and well-guarded Templar location – the New Temple was a place where merchants' transactions could be verified and witnessed.[40]

Even more helpfully, the order began to extend the use of the New Temple and its experience in international credit transfers to help promote long-distance trade. This allowed money to be lodged at a local Templar preceptory for commercial transactions and then drawn down elsewhere. Funds could be given to the order in England and then withdrawn, say, at the Templar headquarters in Paris.[41]

Over the course of the thirteenth century, it is estimated that in excess of 1 million marks passed through the strongrooms of the New Temple. The Templars were extremely well integrated into the finances of the English state. At least two Templars were also royal Treasurers, in addition to their other financial duties at the order's headquarters. Logically, this all made perfect sense.

The British Templars were just doing their job. They needed to cultivate their political influence and leverage their ability to undertake large, complex financial transactions – both skills-sets were essential if they were to pursue their ultimate corporate objective of generating and moving resources from the European provinces out to the Latin East.

Only the tiniest fraction of those million-plus marks belonged to the order itself or was hoarded by them for self-aggrandisement. The truth behind their vows of poverty quickly became apparent when the order was suppressed in 1308: there was no hidden treasure, no bloated, rich brothers.[42]

But, on an emotional level, it did not always smell right. Privileged religious institutions that dabbled in power politics and high finance risked being seen as venal and exploitative. If they were good at such things, as the Templars usually were, they inevitably aroused deep-seated jealousies.

Matthew Paris, the famous English chronicler, was a case in point. As an individual, he was a manager's worst nightmare. He disliked everyone who had any kind of authority over him. And he could not help but show it when he wrote his histories.

Matthew was a complex man. He was a proud Englishman (or at least he loudly disliked foreigners – not quite the same thing, obviously). But, ironically, he disapproved of the English king because of his power and authority. Similarly, he was an ostensibly devout Catholic monk but he disapproved of the pope – again, because of the authority he wielded. The

Templars were in the middle of this petulant Venn diagram – he disliked them because they were, for much of the time, heavily involved in finance (which for him meant 'rich', or at least richer than him) and because they were favourites of both Henry III and the pope.[43]

One of the British Templars, Brother Geoffrey, was appointed as almoner for the king in 1229 (significantly succeeding yet another Templar in the role). He later became keeper of the royal wardrobe. These were both sensitive financial positions, dealing with important aspects of Henry's personal finances and accounting.

For reasons that are not entirely clear, but which undoubtedly relate to Matthew Paris's difficult personality and his distrust of anyone with access to power, Geoffrey was soundly castigated in his chronicle. Geoffrey's retirement from his post in 1240 was described by Matthew as being brought on by his uncontrollable arrogance and pride – a characterisation that was in many ways just a distillation of the chronicler's broader distaste for the Templars.[44]

In fact, quite the opposite was true. As far as we can tell from other sources, Brother Geoffrey the almoner was a hardworking and respected servant of the crown. Before he was made almoner he had already been employed as a diplomatic envoy by Henry and was responsible for significant aspects of the royal finances. He even had far-reaching military-logistical responsibilities – he purchased a catapult and stones for the siege of Bedford, for instance, and helped equip other military expeditions for the king. Most significantly, after Geoffrey's retirement King Henry continued to send his favoured servant presents – so much for his dismissal in disgrace. Far from being fired for dereliction of his duties, Geoffrey retired in entirely honourable circumstances, having served his order and his king well.[45]

Geoffrey was just following a long tradition of financial service by the Templars to the English crown. But being clever, successful and good with money is not an easy route to popularity. There were problems associated with being gifted financiers – problems that could come back to bite.

FARMING FOR THE FAITH

Although it was not always apparent at the time, the crusader states were entering a period of terminal decline.

There were increasingly few military situations in which the Templars, or indeed anyone else, could make a definitively positive contribution. But there was one area they could control and one unequivocal way in which they could help – they could increase the efficiency of their farms and estates back in the West, thereby generating more money to help bolster the defences of the Holy Land.

And that was what they proceeded to do.

Templar estate management normally centred around a base known as a preceptory (or commandery). Each was managed by a preceptor (or commander). But it is perhaps more realistic to envisage each preceptory as a collection of assets, rather than as a single grand manor. The commandery at Garway, on the Welsh borders, for instance, also had rents from properties in the city of Hereford, income from its three watermills and rent from the nearby villages of St Wulstan, Harewood, Great Corras and Llanrothal. And all this was in addition to the rent from Garway itself and the offerings from the beautiful local church.[46]

Despite their increasingly acute manpower problems, however, which inevitably limited their ability to innovate, the Templars were at the forefront of best practice in terms of how best to exploit these assets. They correctly identified the most profitable crops to focus on – generally wool and wheat. And, belying later rumours of greed, they seem to have been good employers, paying their workers in cash when appropriate and offering them other forms of payment in kind as well, such as food or items of clothing.[47]

By the time the order was closed down, the Templars in England and Wales had no fewer than 141 estates, the vast majority of which were in England. They were arguably, apart from the king himself, the richest landowners in Britain. Estimates suggest that the Templars owned approximately 35,000 acres of land under cultivation in Britain, alongside a similar amount of permanent pasture and woodland. These were massive holdings.[48]

The productivity of these estates was impressive. Arable farming alone on their lands in 1309 produced marketable seed crops valued at more than £2,000 – a figure that few others could match. These revenues were the culmination of almost 200 years of generous patronage, compounded by the efficient estate management practices consistently pursued by the order.[49]

The Templars preferred to grow wheat on their estates wherever possible. Lands that were unsuitable for wheat, such as those they had been given in Devon and Cornwall, were leased out as soon as possible rather than being managed directly. In this, as in so many other things, the order was just being rational. Wheat was not easy to grow but it was valuable. For an organisation trying to generate as much money as possible to support the war effort in the eastern Mediterranean, it was an ideal cash crop.

Making alcohol was another profitable activity, as well as presumably being much welcomed by the brothers themselves. Then as now, cider-making was common in Herefordshire and the Templars' estate at Upleadon was a big producer. Beautiful cider apple orchards are still there today. We know that the Templars at Bulstrode also had their own breweries – 50 gallons of cider were seized at the commandery when the king's men raided it in 1308. Other English houses, including Swanton, Keele, Warpsgrove, Merton, Bisham and Roydon, also made cider and sold apples. The more adventurous estates, such as Gislingham and Strood, even branched out into wine production.[50]

Arable farming was the backbone of the English Templar estates, but livestock farming was also important. Quite apart from their horses and other working animals, the order in 1308 had some 30,000 sheep in England and Wales, producing almost 40,000 pounds of wool every year. Appropriately enough for such an international organisation, the main buyers of Templar wool were the foremost Italian wool merchants, attracted by the fine quality of the order's product. Interestingly, it seems that superior Templar estate management practices meant that they also produced higher wool yields than average.[51]

Templar flocks had relatively large numbers of wethers – sheep that produce heavier wool than ewes but which, as they are neutered, cannot reproduce. To counteract this deficiency, the order seems to have developed specialised breeding stations such as that in Eagle, their preceptory in Lincolnshire, in order to replenish the flocks. These relatively advanced techniques allowed the brothers to increase wool production to the point where it accounted for approximately half of all their livestock activity.[52]

At the more exotic end of the agricultural spectrum, even unconventional animals could prove profitable under the right conditions. The preceptories at Cressing in Essex and Temple Guiting in Gloucestershire both had flocks of peacocks. And irritable but regal looking swans were kept at the Templar houses in Balsall and Sandford.[53]

Levels of mechanisation were inevitably primitive. But, when it was possible, we once again find the British Templars at the forefront of progress. Mills, whether powered by water or by the wind, were the main available technology at this time, and they were widely adopted by the order. The British Templars were also leaders in the development of fulling mills, which allowed the large-scale finishing of wool cloth to be carried out more efficiently. Early progress was apparent. Even the Inquest of 1185 showed that the order had built fulling mills at Newsham in Yorkshire and Temple Guiting in Gloucestershire with which to produce large volumes of woollen cloth. By doing so they were able to capture much more of the margins in the wool industry for themselves, rather than letting the merchants and their downstream customers take a bigger cut of the profits.[54]

Other ways of maximising agricultural returns included running markets and fairs, either on their own behalf or on behalf of their tenants. As well as benefiting from the broader economic advantages that these offered, the order was also able to exploit their rights to exact customs dues or tolls, producing yet another income stream. In Hertfordshire alone, for instance, they organised three very profitable markets and fairs at Baldock, Lannock and Buntingford.[55]

Temple Balsall provides a good case study of how the Templars made the best of their agricultural possessions. The manor, in Warwickshire, was given to the Templars by Roger I of Mowbray. Roger had been on crusade in 1146–7. Inspired by taking his vows, he gave the manor to the order at some point in the period 1145–8. He also donated the church of Hampton-in-Arden in the early 1160s. As we have seen, the aged but indefatigable Roger went on crusade again in 1185. Captured at the battle of Hattin, he was ransomed but died soon after. He was buried, as he wanted, in his beloved Holy Land.[56]

Roger was not alone in his desire to help the Holy Land – it was clear that the crusader states needed all the financial help they could get. The 'Inquest of 1185', a survey of Templar assets in England, was drawn up on the orders of the master, Geoffrey Fitz Stephen, as part of the order's drive to maximise the support it could offer at that critical time.[57]

Luckily for us, this 'Inquest', completed when Roger was setting off for the East, has survived. It gives a fascinating snapshot of what had happened in Temple Balsall in the previous forty years.

In all, there were sixty-seven tenants on the site, farming some 640 acres of arable land. The Templars also owned half of the neighbouring manor of Barston, but it is perhaps significant that there were far fewer peasants working far more land there. In the demographics at play at Balsall in 1185, we see the attraction of a new, developing site, acting as a magnet for peasants who were either landless or trying to better their situation by hard work and more intensive farming.[58]

As Balsall was in the middle of the Forest of Arden, it was a form of 'pioneer' settlement. The estate was literally being carved out from the woods by the gruelling and labour-intensive process of land clearance by deforestation (*assarting*). These were industrious people who were making new lives (and even new names) for themselves. Many of them had come from what were, by medieval standards, relatively distant places to grasp the opportunity – some from Nuneaton to the north-east, others from Wardle in Cheshire.

The hard-won name of one tenant, 'Henry of the Clearings' (or 'Henricus de Sartis'), speaks to the frontier nature of the settlement. Other tenants' names similarly suggestive of this back-breaking clearance process include 'Ralph at the Grove' and 'Wluric the charcoal-burner'.[59]

As a new settlement, rather than one with longer established and more traditional dues, the Templars were able to ratchet up the money produced by the land. The rents at Balsall were double those paid by tenants at Barston. And, as well as the rent, there were other ways to raise money from their tenants. On top of the usual array of labour dues which they had to provide, the Templars' tenants were liable for death duties and had to pay for the privilege of marrying off their daughters or selling any male foals born on the land. Popular or not, efforts were being made to maximise every possible source of income from the land.

The manor was still 'work in progress' when the Inquest of 1185 was completed. Mill land had been allocated, but the mill itself had still not been built. Some of the woods had yet to be cleared. The central demesne lands of the home farm, which would have provided food for the Templars and their full-time staff and labourers, were still being let out to third parties. But Balsall was an asset that was being actively developed.[60]

Lincolnshire provides another interesting case study. The same 'Inquest' showed that the Templars there were, if not innovators, certainly 'early adopters' in terms of medieval agriculture. The move towards horse plough teams (as opposed to using teams of oxen) was pushed forward. Logistics were modernised and haulage by horses, which provided greater speed and efficiency, was introduced.[61]

Production was similarly streamlined. Commercial crops such as wheat and barley were maximised for the cash they could generate, while less valuable crops such as rye and oats were retained for consumption on the order's estates. Manuring and weeding were practised extensively, and multiple ploughing was put in place to improve productivity. And a system of three-course rotation on a two-field system was introduced to significantly increase the intensity of cropping. Estate management was increasingly regularised, with a preceptor (who was a Templar) in overall charge of operations, but with a sergeant and a reeve managing everyday tasks.[62]

The Templars were not radicals in terms of agricultural matters. But they did the best they could within the limits of their resources. They made sure their estates were productive, delivering exceptional quantities of livestock and crops. This enhanced productivity did not happen by accident – it was generated by long-term planning and putting efficient new managerial practices into place.[63]

But it is important to remember that the Templars were an order focused on the defence of the Holy Land. Even when dealing with agricultural issues, there was a military subtext to everything they did. Modern armies, with all the resources of industrialised societies behind them, have a huge logistical tail supporting a relatively small number of soldiers fighting in the front line. The Templars, however, reversed this pattern. With more simple structures and far more limited resources at their disposal, they needed to make everything count.

By the latter years of the twelfth century, there were perhaps some 300–400 Templar knights in the Latin East, most of whom lost their lives during the pitched battles of the 1170s and 1180s or were executed in captivity by their Muslim opponents. These men were just the tip of the Templar war machine in the region, however.

They were supported by up to 1,000 brother sergeants, who were in turn supplemented by mercenaries hired from across Europe and the eastern Mediterranean. There were also local volunteers and other soldiers recruited from amongst the native Christians of the Holy Land. These included the famous Turcopole horse archers who made up perhaps half of the Christian cavalry and were such a vital ingredient of the Frankish battle line.

By contrast, when the order collapsed in Britain in 1308, the number of men at home was tiny and, despite the increasingly desperate efforts to produce 'witnesses' of wrongdoing and generate incriminating evidence, only 108 men were available to be called to testify, with perhaps another 35 or 40 being too old or frail to be subjected to the ordeal.

This was reflected throughout the Templar properties in Britain. By the beginning of the fourteenth century, many of the Templar estates had no Templars resident in them at all – they were run by leaseholders, managers or bailiffs. And of the forty-two residences theoretically inhabited by Templar brothers in 1308, ten had only one brother living there and seven had none. Only four houses had more than four brothers in residence.[64]

Even the provincial headquarters, the New Temple in London, had only eight Templar brothers in residence. Likewise, the important Lincolnshire commandery of Bruer had just four brothers on site when the arrests took place.

This does not mean they were empty. There were other people in all these places, of course. Many of them were closely associated with the order. There were guests, servants and other employees (female and male), pensioners (again women as well as men), lay brothers and local members of confraternities – but the core number of Templars in Britain, as in all the western provinces, was surprisingly small. This goes a long way towards explaining why there was so little active resistance when the order was suppressed.

British Templars who were capable of military service were overwhelmingly to be found where they were needed most – at the sharp end of the crusading movement, fighting and dying in the castles of the Holy Land.[65]

13

◇

MELTDOWN ON THE EASTERN FRONT: 1216–1269

The deteriorating military situation in the East had a dramatic effect on the way the order operated in Britain.

The British Templars had been at the heart of the royal administration's financial affairs in the early and middle years of Henry's reign. Perhaps strangely, given their connections and expertise, these activities petered out during his later years. But this was not due to any loss of favour or status.

The answer was far simpler, and far more brutal.

The urgency of total war in the Holy Land was reflected in changing practices in Britain. Up to this point the role of the master of the Templars in England had often been, de facto, a lifetime position. As the situation in the East collapsed, however, the masters were increasingly summoned out for more hands-on service in the Holy Land.[1]

This also applied to the other ranks of the order. An acute shortage of men in the East meant that the brothers were shipped out from the provinces to the front line more quickly – and the manpower crisis of the crusader states inevitably caused knock-on manpower problems in Britain.

The severity of the demographic crisis that engulfed the order becomes clear when looking at the trial transcripts of 1308–11. The fighting men had been shipped off to the East. Those left behind were increasingly defined by what they were not, rather than what they were – they were not Templar soldiers at the heart of the order. Instead, they were generally administrators or lawyers, farmers or fixers. They were often old, frail (both mentally and physically) or otherwise unsuited for military service.

Far from being heavily involved with the fighting, very few of the Templars on trial had even been to the East. One brother, Henry Danet, the commander of the order in Ireland, seems to have served in the crusader states for two years before sailing back from Cyprus in the winter of 1307–8, an unusual and dangerous time to be travelling. The unlucky Templar arrived in Ireland on 1 February 1308, just two days before the brothers there were arrested. William de la More and Robert Scot had both served in the crusader states. And Brother Totty (or Thoroldeby) testified, not very convincingly, that he had participated in a naval action while on active service in the eastern Mediterranean.[2]

But that was all. The fighting British Templars were gone long before the order was suppressed.

There were some who missed the trials. A number of British Templars, the younger, fitter ones, were still in Cyprus and presumably remained there until they returned to Britain – at which point, with the dust having settled, they could perform whatever kind of penance was required. The men collected their pensions or, if they were lucky, slipped off to quietly resume their lives as best they could.[3]

FIGHTING FOR A FUTURE

The Templars struggled to maintain their positions of influence in Britain – and they simultaneously took on even more of the responsibility for defending the dying European settlements in the East.

This was an increasingly thankless and desperate responsibility. The crusader states had lost any semblance of critical mass in terms of land and colonies. As the settler population fell, so the number of men available for military duty fell too. The Christian cities became increasingly marginalised on the regional political stage. Shockingly, even the small armies that could still be raised were increasingly turning on each other – bereft of any realistic future, the Franks found the illusion of purpose in fighting ever more futile civil wars about the minutiae of baronial rights, family landholdings or commercial privileges.

The local nobility had failed. The burden of sustaining the Holy Land fell ever more heavily on the shoulders of the military orders. The papacy, and their loyal agents in the form of the Templars and the Hospitallers, continued to hope that the situation could be turned around – and a series of crusades were called to try to change the long-term situation in the East.

Some of the enthusiasm for crusading faded as the century progressed. The prospect of a decisive and sustainable victory in the Middle East seemed increasingly unlikely.

But on expeditions where there was a significant British contribution, the old crusading pride, often carried down different generations of the same families, could resurface again. The chronicler Matthew Paris could be cynical and cranky, and he had no great love for the Templars, but he wrote movingly of the final moments of the English knight William Longsword and his brave death alongside the Templar knights at the battle of Mansourah in 1250. And he was fulsome in his praise for the Englishmen who died on Richard of Cornwall's crusade of 1240–1.[4]

This volatility of attitude was reflected in the way the British Templars were viewed. The image of the order shifted dramatically in line with their actions. They were brave, elite soldiers fighting what was an expensive and ultimately unwinnable war. The forlorn nature of the task was becoming clear, and not just with hindsight. When their bravery was to the fore, they were idolised. When they lost, as they inevitably would, the sacrifice of their defeats was met with increasing frustration.

FUNDRAISING AND LOBBYING

From a very early point, the preaching of the crusade in Britain was as much about raising money as it was about getting recruits for armies. Campaigning, or even the preliminary act of getting to the East, was an expensive business.

Pressure to generate help from Britain for the Holy Land was continually being applied by the Templars. On 4 March 1260, the grand master wrote to the order's treasurer in England, the gloriously named Brother Amadeus, to ask for more men and money from the British province. He wanted to ensure that the local brothers were lobbying Henry III as hard as they could to ramp up support.

The big prize, and the primary purpose of the letter, was to get Henry to give the order a loan. As the grand master wrote, 'We pray the lord king of England, and also the queen to beseech him, to have pity on us and help relieve our lack of funds by lending us ten thousand marks of silver. To this end we strongly exhort you to put as much pressure as you can on the king, insisting energetically, to obtain this favour, and to give us in writing your views on this.'

The financial situation of the order was dire. The letter, effectively an internal memo, could not have been blunter. The grand master made it clear that 'because of the important and countless expenses incurred in fortifying our . . . castles and the city of Acre to improve matters, our house is suffering and has suffered such huge runs on our money that it is recognised that we are in a dangerous financial situation'.

Without outside help, he wrote, 'we will be forced completely to default in respect of the defence of the Holy Land . . . for times are so bad in these regions at the moment that it is not possible to borrow money either against interest or against pledges . . . Yet we have had to quadruple our expenses on the fortifications since we cannot hire labourers unless we feed them and pay them danger money.'[5]

Communications from the crusader states were as frequent as the rudimentary systems of the time allowed. In 1243–4, for instance, the grand master wrote to the brothers in Britain and mentioned in passing 'that we are bound to inform your fraternity of the state of the Holy Land by letters or nuncios as often as the opportunity presents itself'.

As well as writing on their own behalf, the Templars also added their voice to other appeals for aid from Britain. These included increasingly desperate entreaties from the crusader states sent in 1244, 1254, 1260 and 1263. The Templars (and to a slightly lesser extent their Hospitaller comrades) were the most assiduous writers of diplomatic begging letters from the East. They exceeded the monarchs, princes and prelates of the East in their lobbying programme – and even the surviving correspondence represents, inevitably, just more or less random survivors from a far greater number of original letters.

With Templar help, the lobbying continued – there were no fewer than twenty-six embassies to England alone from the crusader states in the period 1216–1307.[6]

Crusading had become far more difficult, but no one gave up in a hurry.

THE STRUGGLE FOR EGYPT

Despite, or perhaps because of, the continuing turmoil following the civil war and John's death in 1216, men found time for crusading – there was significant support in England for the Fifth Crusade (1217–21) – and its extended campaigns in Egypt. But the expedition had collapsed by the summer of 1221. The crusaders managed to negotiate their way out and returned home.[7]

Unlike the Third Crusade, there was little coordination of the English contribution to the expedition, but large numbers of enthusiastic British noblemen and their small armies took part. Prominent English crusaders in the war included Philip d'Aubigny, King Henry's 'most faithful master and teacher' of the martial arts, Savaric of Mauléon, the earls of Chester, Winchester, Hereford and Arundel, and two of King John's many illegitimate children.[8]

Even the bishop of Winchester, Peter des Roches, took the cross a few days after the major Egyptian port of Damietta was captured by the disparate crusading army. Optimistically, but largely theoretical in nature, Peter was elected bishop of Damietta in his absence by the crusading army.[9]

English women also went on the crusade and sometimes seem to have had darker, or sadder, reasons for taking part. Mariotta, the daughter of William of Yorkshire, joined the Fifth Crusade after having made accusations of rape. A certain Lecia also went to Jerusalem on the same crusade after having been connected in some way (which is not entirely clear now) with the murder of her son. Similarly, Agnes of Middleton in Yorkshire went to Jerusalem amid speculation that she was doing so to avoid a pending court case.[10]

The English effort may not have been centrally controlled, but the men and women gathered together as a natural and distinct group on the crusade. Two English churches were even briefly established inside Damietta, dedicated to saints Thomas Becket and Edmund the Martyr respectively. The latter church was even decorated with some (extremely short-lived) wall paintings of his martyrdom, commissioned by an English knight named Richard of Argentan.[11]

Philip d'Aubigny provides an extreme example of the way in which English family crusading traditions reverberated down the generations. Philip's father had died on the Third Crusade, and Philip himself was an enthusiastic participant on the Fifth Crusade. Disappointingly (but perhaps luckily for him), he arrived on 5 September 1221 – too late to get involved in the fighting but just in time to join the evacuation of Damietta.

Undeterred, Philip took the cross again in 1228, and once more in 1234–5, alongside members of his family and other English knights. He died on crusade and, as he wished, was buried at the very epicentre of Christianity, in the Holy Sepulchre at Jerusalem.

Philip's death was sad, but also brought posthumous glory and dignity to his family. Matthew Paris wrote that he was 'a noble devoted to God, and brave in battle' who, 'after fighting for the Lord during several pilgrimages to the Holy Land, at length closed his life by a praiseworthy death there, and obtained a holy burial in the Holy Land, which he had long desired when living'.

His tomb slab still survives. The short message carved on it resonates strongly with Matthew's comment about the old crusader's desire to be laid to rest close to the site of Christ's suffering. It simply says: 'Here lies Philip d'Aubigny. May his soul rest in peace. Amen.'[12]

The Fifth Crusade attracted a lot of attention from the British Templars and their followers. The brother knights and the new British recruits to the order doubtless shipped out with their own contingents of troops in train, but the order's English patrons also stepped up to do their part.

One patron, John of Harcourt, showed where his devotions lay in the most powerful way possible. On his deathbed in Egypt (*in extremis agens in exercitu Damete*), John still found time to give the order lands in Leicestershire. This was a pious and very tangible expression of his support – it reflected his belief that helping the Templars was both the most chivalrous thing to do, and would also, like his participation in the crusade itself, benefit his immortal soul.

As the siege of Damietta ground on, other pious English supporters of the Templars gave up their lives, but not without first putting their affairs in order. Emery of Sacy, for instance, gave the brothers land and a mill in Southampton as he lay dying outside the city. Of even more immediate value to the order, the earl of Chester gave 50 marks to the Templars in their capacity as expert military architects to enable them to build a fort in the siege works.[13]

The list of British Templar patrons in the fighting was long. Ranulf III of Chester (who gave the order several donations of land, including property in Lincolnshire) stayed on campaign in the East for at least two years. Other patrons with their small contingents of English soldiers included Eustace of Grenvill, Hugh of Sandford, Geoffrey of Say II and Robert of Vaux. Few men could give up everything to devote themselves to the order and this was particularly difficult for those who were married. But association with the Templars, both spiritually and militarily, was a powerful statement made by many devout English knights and noblemen.[14]

RECOVERING JERUSALEM

The crusade of the Emperor Frederick II in 1228–9 (often called the Sixth Crusade) was, not surprisingly, dominated by the Germans. French and English crusaders also participated, however, with the latter being led by the church militant in the forms of the bishops of Exeter and Winchester. Roger of Wendover wrote that 'forty thousand tried [English] men were said to have marched, besides women and old men'. The number is completely implausible, but this exaggerated claim is at least evidence of the crusade's popularity. Significantly, much of the support it attracted in England came from those with Templar connections.[15]

The Templars found it difficult to coordinate their efforts with those of Frederick II – irritatingly for all concerned, the emperor's long-standing conflicts with the papacy had deteriorated still further. Ironically enough, the leader of Christendom on the crusade found himself inconveniently excommunicated.

In the event, it all went better than everyone expected – embarrassingly so, in fact, given the excommunicate state of the principal Christian negotiator. Frederick managed to recover both of the hugely significant religious sites of Jerusalem and Bethlehem, together with much of their old lands in western Galilee. He also concluded a truce for the Latin Kingdom of Jerusalem which would last for ten years.

The army that eventually assembled in the Holy Land included, according to one of the continuations of the chronicler William of Tyre, 'many English'. But for some of these enthusiastic volunteers, the trip to the Holy Land would, literally, be a bridge too far.

A group of heavily, probably far too heavily, armed English crusaders happened to be crossing a river at Ferrybridge in Yorkshire in 1228. The bridge collapsed and many were drowned. When the bodies were recovered, they were found to have the large sum of almost £20 on them. Unhelpfully for the crusading cause, but with a fair degree of pragmatism, the money was put towards the repair of the bridge, rather than the defence of the Latin East.[16]

For those who finally got there, the crusade itself was unglamorous but prosaically successful. Instead of high-risk battles, it focused on the more tangible issues of money, diplomacy and building works. William Brewer, the bishop of Exeter, for instance, went on the crusade in order to fulfil his uncle's vows to go to the Holy Land. While in the East, William was able to call on a bank account in Acre held in his uncle's name by the Templars. He drew down the substantial sum of 4,000 silver marks from the order, so he presumably had his own retinue of men with him too.

The bishop of Winchester, Peter des Roches, also provided much needed financial help. He probably carried with him the money raised by the English tax of 1222, which had been levied to provide help for the Latin Kingdom of Jerusalem.[17]

The English contingent played a significant role in refortifying the coastal cities and particularly the ports of Jaffa and Sidon. These cities were the bedrock of the much-diminished crusader states. The Templar bank account and the treasure chests of the two English bishops were put to good use.[18]

Even in between crusades, however, the Templars continued to haemorrhage men and materiel, necessitating a continual trickle of reinforcements from Britain and the other provinces.

In June 1237, the Templars made a characteristically aggressive but overly ambitious raid on Turkic-held Darbsak, north of Baghras. They were intercepted and in the resulting battle 'more than a hundred knights of the Temple fell, and three hundred crossbowmen, not including some other secular [troops] and a large number of foot-soldiers'.

We know that some of the English Templars were engaged in the battle. One of them was singled out for his outstanding heroism on the day. 'In this unlucky conflict,' wrote Matthew Paris, 'an illustrious English Templar knight, named Reginald of Argenton, who was [the Templar] standard-bearer on that day, was slain; but he, as well as others who fell, left a most bloody victory to their enemies, for he unweariedly defended the standard until his legs and arms were cut off.'

On hearing of the bloody defeat, the military orders in England rushed to provide help. Even the Hospitallers, despite their rivalry with the Templars, sent men and money from their London commandery to help their comrades and shore up the ranks in the East. The dramatic scene of their departure clearly made an impact on those who saw them leave.

'The Hospitallers,' Matthew wrote,

sent their prior, Theodoric . . . a fine knight, with a body of other knights and paid retainers, and a large sum of money, to the assistance of the Holy Land. They, having made all their arrangements, set out from their house at Clerkenwell, in London, and proceeded in good order, with about thirty shields uncovered, with spears raised, and preceded by their banner, through the midst of the city towards the bridge, that they might obtain the blessings of the spectators, and, bowing their heads, and with cowls lowered, commended themselves to the prayers of all.[19]

It looked, and probably felt, like the departure of men who were not coming back.

With the help of these warrior monks and others, the northern borders were eventually stabilised. Reinforcements were found and the pope intervened to help his own vanguard – he (and King Henry) provided ransom money for the Templars who had been captured. The survivors were freed.

But the frontiers could not hold indefinitely.

RICHARD OF CORNWALL ON CRUSADE

If Henry could not travel east in person, at least his brother Richard, earl of Cornwall, could go in his stead. Richard had already taken the cross in 1238, when he gave a large sum of money to Baldwin II, the Latin emperor of Constantinople, during his first visit to England.[20]

English recruits and 'volunteers' for this crusade could be found in the strangest of places. Richard Siward, for instance, was an inveterate rebel and long-term military enthusiast. In 1236, not for the first time, he found himself in custody. Luckily for him, preparations were in hand for a crusade. He was offered the possibility of commuting his prison sentence to that of fighting in the East. Perhaps not surprisingly, given his warlike temperament, Richard found the offer far more congenial than remaining incarcerated in Gloucester prison. He took the cross as a 'get out of jail free card' and went with Richard of Cornwall on his crusade (1240–1).[21]

On 11 October 1240, Richard arrived at Acre with his small English army. He was horrified by the dysfunctional nature of the Frankish state he found there. Despite the appalling threat posed by Muslim armies, the different local factions were engaging in almost open warfare with each other. This was hardly encouraging for those who had sacrificed much to come to their rescue.

Richard, like many others, found this self-indulgent posturing bitterly frustrating. He later wrote of 'the seriousness of the difficulty in bringing relief to the country on our arrival when we saw the nobles who were likely to help us leaving for home'.

The earl and his men eventually had enough of the infighting. They moved down to Ascalon to negotiate with the Egyptians. In a peace treaty of 1240, he persuaded them to return much of Galilee, including Belvoir, Mount Tabor and Tiberias, to the Christians. Under the terms of the new agreement, Frankish prisoners were released and only Nablus and the old province of Samaria, both of which had large Muslim populations, remained outside of Christian control.

The truce was a success but it was all very wearing. Richard had negotiated effectively but painfully between different Muslim enemies and, ironically, even more painfully between the many mutually antagonistic local Frankish factions. He was devout, and he and his army had done good work. But they were glad to be heading home again. As Richard wrote, with obvious relief after the treaty had been agreed, 'We propose to return home to English soil as quickly as we can.'[22]

Once again, English supporters of the Templars had been heavily represented on the crusade. Richard himself signed at least one confirmatory charter for the order. Simon de Montfort, one of the most eminent members of the crusade, gave the brothers lands and the place known as 'Rockley Woods'. Another prominent English crusader, William Peverel, confirmed a grant of land to the Templars by his family, perhaps conscious of the acute dangers posed by a long sea journey. He finished the paperwork, with a fearful eye on God's favour, just a few hours before setting off back home with the much-relieved earl of Cornwall.[23]

On 3 May 1241, Richard left the Latin East. His army was small and his stay in the Holy Land had been short. But his was a very successful and popular crusade – an exemplary intervention.

The national pride in an English-led crusade that had enjoyed at least some success was palpable. Richard was fêted when he arrived home. As Mathew Paris wrote, when 'the men returned that was great joy and celebration'. Henry rushed down to greet him and his men when they landed at Dover 'and the king and almost all the nobles loaded him with various presents'. When they got back to London, 'the city was decorated with banners and hangings as if for a festival'.[24]

Even after Richard's achievements, however, things were looking distinctly unpromising for the Templar brothers who were left manning the front line. Just three years later, most of the order's remaining knights in the Holy Land were killed or captured at the battle of La Forbie (17 October 1244). Only thirty-three brothers escaped. Casualties cascaded from the top of the order downwards. They included, according to the chronicle of Eracles, 'Armand of Périgord, master of the Temple, who [later] died in prison'.[25]

The order was once more on the verge of collapse, and desperately needed help from Britain.

The British Templars continued to do everything they could to encourage recruitment. In 1247, a Templar knight brought a crystalline phial containing drops of Christ's blood back to London. The relic, believed to have been filled while Jesus was still on the cross, had been authenticated by the senior clergy of the crusader states. However implausible it may seem to modern eyes, relics such as this generated a spark of spiritual immediacy for those who might consider taking the cross.[26]

Keen to keep crusading enthusiasm alive, the master of the Templars also gave Henry III's wife, Queen Eleanor of Provence, 'a great book' of stories from the siege of Antioch, which had taken place during the First Crusade. Victory in the East, it seemed to imply, was still possible, if only one had sufficient faith – and, of course, funding for a big enough army.

It all helped. But for the Templars, fighting the good fight was far more tangible. Their blood was more literal than anything found in a relic or a storybook.

The magnitude of the disaster at La Forbie helped galvanise support for the crusader states in the West, for a time at least. After the usual protracted bouts of political manoeuvring and painful fundraising, the Seventh Crusade (1248–54) eventually set off, led by King Louis IX of France – but it ended in disaster.[27]

After its failure, an already difficult situation became progressively worse. The crusader states were now fringe players, political entities who existed only at the whim of their vastly bigger Muslim neighbours. The heavily outnumbered Christian forces were increasingly unable to achieve anything other than the most temporary military success – and even that at great risk.

Frustrations at this helplessness began to emerge, even amongst the Templar brothers. In April 1261, for instance, they launched an attack on Turcoman tribesmen near Tiberias. Even if it had succeeded it would have been insignificant. Instead, things went badly wrong. The all-important charge failed. Sixteen Templar captives were later ransomed, but the rest were dead and 'no more could be found alive'.[28]

The pressures were unremitting. Later that year, the town of Sidon was destroyed by the Mongols. The walls were severely damaged. The Templars had to step in to 'buy' the lordship. In reality, they were the only people with enough cash to pay for the privilege of taking on the liability. They were forced to find the money for the necessary rebuilding work.[29]

And still the crisis showed no sign of abating. The Templar castle of Safad was besieged and captured in July 1266. The garrison had surrendered under terms of safe conduct, but the Mamluk sultan changed his mind once they left the castle and had them executed. The butchered prisoners were mourned throughout the Holy Land. The shock of the loss was soon compounded by other disasters. On 15 April 1268, the order's castle of Beaufort was captured after a short siege. The garrison, some 480 men, according to one source, traded their freedom for the lives of the women and children. The chivalrous Templars were taken into slavery.

A few weeks later, the ancient Christian city of Antioch was overrun, too. With its loss, the Templar castles in the Amanus mountains, including the fortresses of Gaston and Roche de Roussel, had become completely untenable – they had to be hurriedly evacuated.[30]

The order was firmly on the retreat. There was only one end in sight.

14

✧

EDWARD I – LAST THROW OF
THE DICE: 1270–1291

*I have the sign of the cross on my body. This affair [the defence of the
Christian East] is my chief concern. My heart swells at the thought of that.*
Edward I to Mongol envoys, 1287[1]

There were sometimes doubts about the depth of Henry III's commitment
to the crusading cause. But there were none about his son Edward.

Like his ancestor Richard the Lionheart, Edward was exactly what the
order needed. In him England had a leader who was a dedicated warrior
and personally brave – he had an enthusiasm for war which was combined
with a pious and deeply personal devotion to the crusading cause.

In Edward I the British Templars once more had a crusader king – a
true *Rex Crucesignatus*.

THE 'LORD EDWARD'S' CRUSADE

Crusading glory was not quickly forgotten.

The 'Lord Edward' (later Edward I) went on crusade in 1271–2. When
he arrived in the Holy Land, he was compared to another English crusader,
a man who had similarly strong support from the Templars. As one
contemporary poet wrote: 'Whilst Edward is in his vigour, behold, he
shines like a new Richard. Thus the Britons have a double claim to honour,
by the wars of Edward equally and by the valour of Richard.'[2]

The order was eager to help burnish this glory in any way it could – militarily, logistically and even spiritually.

It is easy, in our more secular age, to underestimate the power of relics. We do not understand the way in which physical contact with religious objects could help the pious create deep connections to long-distant events in the Holy Land. But spiritual victories went hand in hand with more temporal ones, forming a vital part of motivating the devout knights of Europe to continue the struggle. In 1272, Templar grand master Thomas Bérard helped legitimise the achievements of Lord Edward's crusade by sending pieces of the True Cross back to London, together with precious relics of saints Barbara, Euphemia, Helena, Philip, Laurence and Stephen. Heavenly victory could be made as tangible, and as glorious, as that won on the battlefield.[3]

Edward certainly saw himself as the heir to crusading glory. While Henry might be somewhat reticent towards the crusades, his son Edward was positively pushy. In 1267, he proposed himself to both his father and to papal legates as being the most suitable leader for a forthcoming crusade.[4]

People had always been suspicious of Henry's putative crusades – the more cynical had seen them primarily as political vehicles or as money-making schemes. But Edward's expedition tapped into a sense of national pride and an underlying popular enthusiasm for crusading. In June 1268, having succeeded in making his case for leadership, Edward took the cross at Northampton, alongside other members of the royal household, the earl of Gloucester, Gilbert of Clare and almost 200 other knights.[5]

The 'Lord Edward's crusade', as it became known, was inevitably expensive. Financing any expedition to the East was a huge stretch and could push entire kingdoms into debt. Edward's expedition was no exception. Henry organised special taxation in support of his son's efforts and a tax of one 'twentieth' was levied as a means of generating the funds required.

This 'twentieth' raised a very helpful £30,000 – but it was still nowhere near enough. On 27–8 August 1269, Edward, in his capacity as duke of

Gascony, borrowed 70,000 livres tournois from King Louis IX of France, partly to finance a Gascon contingent but mainly to provide transport, horses and supplies for his crusading army setting out from England. Edward committed himself to bringing his troops with him to embark at Aigues-Mortes with the rest of what later became known as the Eighth Crusade.[6]

On 26 July 1270, Edward gave a total of 22,500 marks to his leading followers and – indirectly, of course – to their military contingents. In return for this subsidy they were to provide him with their services on crusade for a year. Each man was to receive 100 marks.

Presumably this would have translated into some 225 knights, though these would have been accompanied by far larger numbers of 'other ranks' – crossbowmen, sergeants, mounted squires and other lower-status soldiers. The money provided by King Louis also implies that there was an additional Gascon contingent of some 125 knights. William of Tripoli, who was relatively well informed and in Acre in the early 1270s, estimated that Edward had approximately 300 knights with him – a figure that accords well with these estimates.[7]

Lord Edward was himself a Templar patron and several of the order's donors accompanied him on the campaign. The earl of Atholl, for instance, David of Strathbogie, died at Tunis in August 1270 shortly after giving the Templars an estate at Chingford in Essex. Luke of Tany, his comrade on the expedition, likewise gave them lands and meadows nearby.[8]

The Templars did everything they could to help. In addition to all the money raised in England, Edward had to borrow heavily from the order once he was in the Latin East, just to keep his crusade afloat. As well as the up-front costs of raising, transporting and supplying his army, he now also had heavy in-region costs to bear. Employing local mercenaries and carrying out extensive repairs to castles and other fortifications was not cheap.[9]

The resulting debts were crippling. In 1273, once the crusade was over, he was still paying off his loans to the Templars, giving them 2,000 marks in part repayment of the huge sum he owed – he had borrowed almost 30,000 livres from the order during the crusade, as well as a further £23,560 lent to him by the Temple in Paris.[10]

The order used its financial centre at the New Temple as a base from which to make these loans to Edward and other English kings. These were mostly short- or medium-term loans, ideally for no more than one year. The Templars were doubtless trying to make themselves useful to the crown in doing so but, given that they needed to provide funding for the Latin East, they also made sure that these were real loans – ones that required repayment.

Even for kings, collateral had to be provided and there were fixed penalties for non-payment. The order could not afford to be shy when asking for their money back either. In 1288 they had to write to Edward I to remind him that he needed to repay a loan of 4,000 marks. We do not know if this reminder was interpreted as impertinence, but relatively soon afterwards, in 1291, Edward I moved the wardrobe back into direct royal control at the Tower of London.[11]

The crushing costs of campaigning in the Middle East were also felt by Edward's noble followers. While they were in the Holy Land, various English crusaders found themselves financially embarrassed. They were able to call on help from Edward and the Templars. Roger of Clifford, John of Grailly, John of Vescy, Otto of Grandson, John II of Brittany, Hamo l'Estrange and even Edward's brother, Lord Edmund, were obliged to borrow money from local financiers in Acre. The master of the Templars repaid the loans on their behalf, providing security on the basis of his own standing, and the lands of the indebted lords.[12]

Two separate crusading forces eventually left England in 1270–1. Prince Edward departed in August 1270, followed by his brother, Edmund of Lancaster, the following spring. Edward arrived in North Africa at the tail end of the French campaign in Tunisia, shortly after the death of King Louis and that of his youngest son. The crusade disintegrated.

Edward refused to accept defeat – and he would not admit that the end of the crusade marked the fulfilment of his vows. He over-wintered in Sicily and the following year he and his small Anglo-Gascon army set off for the Latin Kingdom of Jerusalem. They arrived in Acre, the capital, on 9 May 1271, ready to continue the fight.[13] Edward was enthusiastic, but his forces were far too small to achieve much in a region that had to contend with huge Mamluk armies and vast neighbouring states.

There were a couple of military exploits. These were self-conscious attempts to evoke the glory of English crusading in the blunt manner of a warrior king. In the summer of 1271, soon after he had arrived:

> the Lord Edward mounted a raid and went to attack a rich village called St. George which is about three leagues from Acre. The Templars and Hospitallers went with him, as did the other men of Acre . . . But a number of our men died there, on account of honey from bees and other things which they ate, as footmen were accustomed to do, so that they died on the road, from heat and from exhaustion and from the hot food which they had eaten.[14]

Honey and 'hot' foreign food (whatever that meant) may or may not have been to blame. But the English troops were clearly very poorly acclimatised.

The attack was a statement of intent by the new arrivals. The limitations of the action were all too clear too, however. St George is barely 10 miles east of the Christian capital of Acre – this was hardly a long-range threat to Sultan Baybars. And the casualties that the troops took from the climate and the unfamiliar conditions showed just how ill-prepared they still were.

A couple of months later, when the weather was somewhat cooler and the men had become more used to local conditions, Edward tried once more. Again, the results were less than impressive. The English attacked but failed to capture the small castle of Cacho. It is also clear that, although the castle was close to Christian territory, they would have felt unable to hold it even if they had taken it. The Franks' military capabilities had been embarrassingly diminished. These were merely ineffectual raids, full of danger and with very little meaningful upside. But Edward lacked the forces to do anything of greater significance.[15]

Edward did the best he could under the circumstances. He helped bolster local defences before he left – he built another tower in the defences of Acre and left behind a small number of paid troops (*stipendiarii*) to carry on the good work.[16]

The local nobility negotiated a treaty with the Sultan Baybars in April 1272. It was designed to last for ten years and ten months. The terms of the agreement show just how limited the remaining Frankish possessions were. The Christians were to keep the narrow coastal strip from Acre to Sidon and their pilgrims were to have access to Nazareth by the pilgrim road. The remnants of the county of Tripoli were already protected by a truce of the previous year. But that was it. Apart from those slim toeholds, all of Palestine was back in Muslim hands.[17]

Even after the truce had been signed, however, the crusade held dangers for the heir to the English throne. Baybars was impressed by Edward. And he was famously ruthless. He did not want Edward coming back with a bigger army to finish what he had started. He arranged for an Assassin, who ostensibly wanted to convert to Christianity, to take up employment in Edward's household and, in June 1272, a night-time attack was launched to kill the prince while he was in his bedroom at Acre.[18]

The timing of the attack is telling. Planting an Assassin by these means requires an unhurried process of establishing trust. More specifically, it also takes a lengthy period of religious instruction to show the sincerity of conversion – inveigling your way into a household by these means was slow and methodical. We know that the Assassin had been in place for at least a year, as he had been instrumental in planning the attack on St George the previous summer. The pathologically untrustworthy Baybars had clearly been planning to have Edward killed during the entire process of the treaty negotiations, which had concluded just a few weeks earlier.[19]

We have an account of the attack, which, in a fashion-conscious aside, shows what a well-dressed thirteenth-century crusader lord wore in bed. When Edward opened his bedroom door he was said to have been 'dressed only in an undershirt and braie [loose-fitting breeches]'. Linen breeches, loose-fitting or otherwise, were fine for rest but less than ideal for a fight to the death.[20]

There was no small talk. The Assassin walked up 'and stabbed him on the hip with a dagger, making a deep, dangerous wound' – presumably Edward had made a reflex blocking action and moved the trajectory of the dagger thrust downwards. The prince may have been preparing for bed but, in a telling indication of the violent times in which he lived, he also had weapons close at hand. Edward 'caught up a dagger from the table which was in the chamber, and stabbed the Saracen in the head and killed him'.[21]

The Templars had done everything they could to support Edward on his crusade. Quite apart from the financing, the grand master, Thomas Bérard, had been with him throughout, offering advice, military expertise and local knowledge. Some said, probably with hindsight, that the Templars had advised against taking Turkic converts at face value. There were also claims that the order had provided an antidote for a poison supposedly administered during the attack, presumably smeared along the dagger edge. Whatever the truth of the matter, everyone knew that the Templars were at the heart of this English crusade.[22]

The attempted murder scarred Edward for life, in more ways than one. It had been a threat, not just to his own life, but to the lives of his family. Edward's wife, Eleanor of Castile, had been in the same room when the attack took place. She had gone to the Holy Land with him and gave birth to their daughter Joan of Acre while out there. In keeping with the family tradition, Joan would herself vow to go on crusade, back to her birthplace, in July 1290.

When Edward took the Cross once again in 1287, he referred directly to the way in which God had saved him from the Assassins fifteen years earlier. Having recovered from his wounds, Edward and his troops set sail from Acre in October 1272, preceded by his brother Edmund, who had returned to Europe in May. His was not a grand crusade but, unlike many, the prince left the Holy Land in better condition than he had found it.[23]

When Edward arrived in Sicily in December, on his way home, he heard the news of his father's death. The succession, particularly to an heir so far from home, went surprisingly smoothly. The 'Lord Edward' was now King Edward. His troops, and those of the British Templars in his expedition who were permitted to return, went back to England.

THE HOLLOWING OUT OF THE WEST

Edward never returned to the crusader states. He remained interested in helping the Latin East, however. The king used the English Templars and their network to send horses, cloth and cash to bolster their defences, even while he was heavily involved in campaigning in Scotland.[24]

While Edward's attention inevitably refocused on the British Isles, the order was increasingly forced to pay more attention to the demands of the Holy Land and the terminally grim trajectory of military affairs on the eastern front.

Most tangibly, this focus was reflected in the increased absences of the order's masters. Guy Forest, for instance, was the first British Templar master of Edward's reign, but he was in post for just one year and even in that short time he was twice absent from the kingdom. He then set off for military duties in the Holy Land, leaving the provincial post vacant for two years.

His successor, master Robert of Turville, held the office for a more extended period (from 1276–90) but he too was absent for most of this time. Ominously, there were also indications that the military pressures on the order were taking their toll on local loyalties.

Robert began to style himself, pointedly and clumsily, as 'master of the Templars to whom all the Templars in Ireland, Scotland and England are subject'. Perhaps with allegiances unravelling, and with the provincial master absent for such long periods of time, it was felt necessary to reiterate the correct order of the local Templar hierarchy. But it feels as though Robert was protesting too much – legislating against the problem only served to prove its existence.

As so many of their men were fighting in the East, so the Templars' relationship with the crown changed – their role in government had to be radically scaled back. By 1286, the New Temple was no longer employed in the service of the Crown, and, by the 1290s, the order's financial dealings with the government in England had come to an end.[25]

This shift was nothing more than a recognition of the order's changing priorities – there is no evidence of a loss of royal favour. The last British master, William de la More, held a position of great affection in the royal household. The brothers continued to have influence at court. And the order still helped the crown from time to time as ambassadors, fixers and diplomats.

Edward continued to act as a patron and had confirmed their privileges when he came to the throne. In 1280, he made sure that the annual payment of 50 marks to the order was resumed. He also confirmed other donations, such as lands at Stableswood and Cressing and Edmund of Cornwall's grant at Istelworth.[26]

But no amount of goodwill could disguise the shocking drain of Templar manpower in Britain. Exact figures are unavailable, but it is clear that, although many men were heading to the East, very few were coming back. The relatively small numbers of brothers arrested when the order was suppressed was a testament to the sacrifices they were making on the front line. In the whole of Scotland, for instance, only two brothers were available for interrogation.

And many of those left in Britain were elderly, broken men. The Templar care home at Denney in Cambridgeshire was, apart from the headquarters in London, the largest concentration of Templars in Britain, but it was full of men who could no longer serve. One was described as insane, perhaps suffering from severe PTSD, and most of the rest were too old and frail to fight. With all available combat troops being called to the crusader states, the order in Britain was fast becoming a shell.

There is little biographical information about individual brothers, but a few scraps exist for one of the knights – a certain Brother Robert the Scot. What we know of him is suggestive of the personnel and psychological pressures facing the Templars. Robert had first fought as a knight in the East in a secular capacity. He had eventually joined the order in the Holy Land, and had been 'received first in Castle Pilgrim [that is, 'Atlit, in the Latin Kingdom of Jerusalem]'.

For reasons that are now unclear, Robert resigned from the order. His departure was said, frustratingly vaguely, to have been 'from fickleness' – perhaps he was shocked by the severity of the fighting or the strictures of the tight discipline. But he grew to regret his decision. With impeccably poor timing, he rejoined in Cyprus in 1291, just as the last Templar forces in Palestine were facing their greatest challenge – and greatest casualties. By the time the inquisitors questioned him in 1307, Robert was back in England, but in the care facility at Denney. Perhaps frail in mind as well as body, his fighting days were over.[27]

This manpower drain was reflected across the rural commanderies. When the order was closed down, the asset-strippers who arrived to survey the Templar estates were expecting rich pickings. Instead, they were shocked by what they saw laid out in front of them. Balsall, for example, was in a dreadful condition. It had once been a shining example of best practice in British agriculture. Now it was decayed and run down – under-invested and under-managed. What had gone so dramatically wrong?

As we have seen, the estate of Balsall, actively developed under Templar management, had been a new and thriving settlement – an example of how to tame nature and exploit it to the full. A mill had been built and new settlers brought in. Now, a quarter of a century after the fall of Acre, things were very different. By the time the Hospitallers took over Balsall, in 1322, the entire estate was run down and near derelict. The home farm was almost unusable – all the cooking implements were gone, the fields lay unsown and the animals had been sold or slaughtered.[28]

Was this decline due to over-exploitation and greed? There had certainly been a few local conflicts in the declining years of the order. These incidents might be used as evidence of a debilitating unpopularity. But all were relatively minor – they were just the usual rural disputes about land rights and localised privileges. In 1275–6, for instance, the Templars at Studley (part of the wider preceptory of Balsall) were accused of demanding an annual payment of 8 shillings from the village of Cotton – a rent, it was claimed, to which they were not entitled.

There were some complaints too about the withdrawal of services from various small properties nearby – probably services withheld from royal land holdings in the area. And there were the usual vague disputes about the levying of 'oppressive' dues. But all of this was the normal vocabulary of rural litigation. Similar accusations were levelled at most landowners, including the Hospitallers and other religious institutions, on a regular basis.[29]

There was a deeper malaise, however. The poor state of their British agricultural assets was a reflection of the lack of brothers on the ground. By the time the Templars were suppressed, several of their estates were clearly extremely run down and under-staffed. The drain on manpower at the end of the thirteenth century had been fierce.

The estate at Rockley in Wiltshire is another striking example of decline. It was said to have been a commandery, but by the end of the thirteenth century one would have barely recognised it as such. The refectory and chapel were still standing, but empty – there were no Templar brothers left to eat their meals or say their prayers. The chattels and contents of the estate, the chests, ploughs and even the loose lumber, had all seen much better days. By 1308 it was as derelict and rudderless as the British order itself.

Rockley was not alone in this decline. Other houses too were empty and obviously decaying, even before the order was closed down. Similar examples can be found in Hampshire, Sussex, Oxfordshire and Buckinghamshire – houses that had previously had preceptors in residence were found to be empty of brothers by 1308. Estates that had once had bustling dormitories, such as Hirst in Yorkshire and Dokesworth in Cambridgeshire, were down to their last two brothers when the bailiffs arrived to make their final call.[30]

Anecdotal evidence of decay is reinforced by the numbers. There were approximately sixty Templar estates in Britain and we have evidence of over fifty preceptories. Managing these holdings effectively must have been hugely labour intensive. On top of all that, the order also required men for legal and financial activities, together with the recruitment drives and training required for the fighting brothers, and all the diplomatic, military and administrative tasks that accompanied their governmental duties.

But when the order was closed down, there were only about 150 British Templars to arrest, many of whom were too elderly or infirm for work. Regardless of all the hired hands, managers and tenants, there were an average of only two brothers for each estate. It is no wonder that the Templar properties were in decline. The vibrant, expanding estates of earlier years were a distant memory. It was a powerful metaphor for the decline of the order as a whole.[31]

Other economic indicators of agricultural activity were similarly depressing. Mills were a strangely specific but striking example of the order's rural deterioration. They were a central part of any astute lord's money-making efforts. If he controlled the local mills, he could charge his tenants handsomely for the privilege of using them. So, on any well-run estate, the mill, as one of the few highly profitable and hi-tech pieces of equipment available to a medieval landlord, would be operational and in first-rate condition.

But with the Templars' estates in 1308, this was definitely not the case. Their mill on the River Fleet, embarrassingly close to the order's

British headquarters in the New Temple, was in such a poor state that it had to be completely written off. All its timbers were sold off as lumber. The mill, which had previously been valued as a prized asset, generating significant revenues, ended up being sold for less than the cost of carting the timbers away.

There were other Templar mills in London, this time on the other side of the river at Southwark. They were similarly unimpressive. In theory there were six watermills but one of them was completely broken and all the others were in a state of disrepair. The buildings associated with the mills were so decrepit that they were found to be beyond repair. Like the mill on the Fleet, they were just pulled down and sold as lumber.

The London mills were no isolated case. The asset-strippers at the Templar estate in Rothley (in Leicestershire) were also disappointed. Instead of acquiring a going concern, they found themselves the proud possessors of a mill that was completely broken, generated no income and, on the contrary, required an investment of 64 shillings just to get it operational once more.[32]

We should perhaps not be surprised by this decline. The 'decay' of the Templar estates in the late thirteenth century was an unavoidable choice rather than wilful mismanagement. A series of Church Councils had, quite rightly, stressed the need for the order to deploy as much of its manpower as possible in the war zones of the Middle East. In complying with these requests, the Templars were making the correct strategic choice – they prioritised fighting over farming. But the net result was the same.[33]

The lack of manpower was compounded by reputational issues. The crusading movement was viewed with increasing scepticism. This scepticism was reflected in a gradual decline in donations to the order. Gifts of land started to tail off markedly from the 1260s onwards and by the end of the century the Templars were forced to purchase land if they wanted to make any significant acquisitions.[34]

As the order increasingly lost its lands and fortresses in the Latin East, so there was greater pressure to improve the cash flow from their estates in the West. It was the only way to fill the financing gap. Despite increasingly high land prices, the Templars purchased significant new properties in Lincolnshire and Yorkshire from the mid-1280s onwards, generally in locations where they could consolidate and improve their existing holdings.

This process had its own logic. Modern private equity houses would approve of such ruthless 'buy and build' strategies. But, with failure in the East accompanied by an increasing display of agricultural largesse in the West, it is perhaps not surprising that some rural neighbours of the order thought differently, beginning to question its purpose and privileges.[35]

This was not just a rural problem. In London, the order used its control of the land around the River Fleet, just north of the New Temple, to take water away from its neighbours and to engage in some spectacularly predatory property developments. The Templars diverted water supplies to their mills at nearby Baynard's Castle, and in doing so they lowered the level of the Fleet to such an extent that others found they were no longer able to use their boats on it. A few years earlier, the Templars had also deliberately planted willow trees along the banks to hinder river traffic on its way. And, with the commercial competition suitably disadvantaged, they then began to build a quay along its banks, too.

By 1306, the dispute about the order's abuse of the River Fleet was so bitter that it was even being debated in Parliament. A petition was started to try to stop the Templars' efforts to exploit their commercial position still further. The fact that their enclave was exempt from most local laws, including that of the authority of the City of London, served only to heighten the resentment and anger.[36]

The Templars' extensive privileges, which underpinned some of these aggressive commercial activities, did not help, either. Concessions and exemptions had been originally designed to help the flow of money to the East. But they did little to improve the image of the order amongst those in the West who were footing the bill or those who had to live with the by-products of the process. Unforeseen commercial consequences tainted the entire process.

In the 1270s, for instance, the so-called Hundred Rolls enquiries into those who had over-claimed their rights unearthed several poisonous and long-standing disputes between the Templars and their neighbours. Having tax exemptions allowed, and even encouraged, the order to undercut their local competitors.

Traders in Grimsby, amongst others, complained of the way the Templars pursued what they felt to be unjust and oppressive commercial policies. The men of Sussex similarly argued that the order was corruptly extending their exemptions to people who were not their tenants – this created a two-tier hierarchy of privilege in the area and disadvantaged all those not associated with the order.[37]

Other members of the Church were also sometimes at loggerheads with the order. They provided some of the most hostile witness statements during their later trials. The mixture of privilege, independence and tax exemptions was deeply corrosive for relationships with the local clergy. Even in the 1180s, when Archbishop William of Tyre composed his chronicle, there was much bad blood between the order and those who they were fighting to protect. William claimed that the Templars had quickly become 'very troublesome, for they drew away from [other clerics] their tithes and first fruits and unjustly disturbed their possessions'.[38]

These were not abstract issues, confined to predictable ecclesiastical jealousies in Palestine. Foremost on the list of ecclesiastical financial resentments were exemptions from market tolls and other taxes. Privileges like this inevitably created jealousy amongst their neighbours and helped generate all manner of lies and malicious gossip.

A monk named Hildebrand of Hitchin, for instance, wrote in 1297–1305 that the Templars at the nearby estate of Dinsley were continually making a nuisance of themselves with their unspecified acts of licentiousness and arrogance. The Templar brothers, he claimed, were so drunk and dissolute that in their evening feast it is 'credibly confirmed' that their carousing can be heard in the town.

The accusation was concocted out of spite and jealousy. The phrase 'credibly confirmed' was a nice touch. It was, of course, nothing of the sort, but it did serve to provide some spurious authenticity for those who knew little of the local geography. In fact, the entire episode was an obvious fabrication.

At the time that Hildebrand was writing, we know that there were almost no Templars at Dinsley. The few brothers there were elderly and infirm, hardly candidates for the hard carousing that the bitter monk envisaged. More to the point, however, Dinsley is several miles from town. However acute their hearing, the good burghers of Hitchin were not listening to Templar feasts and drinking games running late into the night.

The stories were false – but the envy and resentment were real.[39]

As the number of brothers in Britain declined, one would expect, as part of this shift, to see evidence of greater numbers of brother knights, sergeants and other Templar troops appearing in the eastern Mediterranean. And this was indeed the case.

Taking Nicosia as an example, one Templar claimed that no fewer than 400 brothers were present at a chapter meeting there in 1291. It is important to remember that this would have represented just a part of their overall fighting capacity – other soldiers would have included sergeants, squires, Turcopole horse archers and mercenaries.

Similarly, when an 'Inquest' was carried out into the order's possessions in Nicosia in June 1308, it was clear that this was a serious military base. It catered for very large numbers of armed men. There were almost 1,000 crossbows on site and a similar number of breastplates; there were 640 helmets in storage and huge quantities of swords and shields, arrows and leg armour.

The fighting men, and their arsenals, had been sent where they were most needed – to the eastern frontiers.[40]

DESTRUCTION IN THE EAST: 1273–1291

King Edward regularly talked of the needs of the Latin East, and British volunteers continued to serve, even when a full crusade was not possible. But the enthusiasm of individuals, whether kings or squires, could not have been inspired by any great prospect of success. On the contrary, the news from the remnants of the crusader states grew steadily worse.

In 1275, William of Beaujeu, the new Templar grand master, arrived in Acre. He was horrified by what he found. He immediately wrote from his command base in the city to King Edward. In the past such letters to royalty in the West had often played on the tantalising possibilities of success (if, of course, 'your majesty can come quickly with an army'). Now the only card the Templars had left to play was that of desperation and imminent catastrophe.

The outlook was uninspiring. William felt that there was little in prospect except failure and defeat, which 'will cause us to fail in our duty and abandon the Holy Land in desolation'.[41]

But crusades to the East were impossible without peace in the West. Edward was inevitably beset by pressing domestic matters. He took the Cross again in June–October 1287, but military and political events in Wales, Scotland and Gascony were compelling priorities that he could not ignore.[42]

The Templars held on, but the pace of military decline was irreversible. In 1289, even Tripoli, the last great Christian city in the region apart from Acre, fell. The Templars had sent in reinforcements to their troops, but the defenders were vastly outnumbered. Templar casualties in the fighting were horrendous.[43]

The order faced imminent extinction in the East. And it had been hollowed out in the West.

15

DECLINE: 1291–1307

It should have ended there.

This was the last charge of the Templars. Like the order itself, it began with bravery and ended in horror.

18 May 1291. The early morning calm in the besieged city of Acre was broken by visceral screams. Death and fear. Panic spread almost instantaneously – Muslim troops had broken through the outer walls.

The Templar grand master, William of Beaujeu, responded as quickly as he could. He gathered his men. They needed to seal the gap in the wall – fast. But their numbers were pitifully few. There was no army left, just a few brave soldiers. The Templar cavalry were no more than 'ten or twelve brethren and [William's] own household troops'.

There was no chance of success. They all knew it. But the Templars would not go down quietly. Their duty was clear. They had to buy time for the civilians to retreat to the citadel. The doomed band charged down the dry moat between Acre's two sets of walls and headed for the St Anthony Gate, where enemy troops were pouring in.

The Mamluk assault teams lined the walls and rained death down on the crusader cavalry below. Shockingly for those on the receiving end, they also threw clay hand grenades full of 'Greek fire', or naphtha. This was a particularly vicious form of medieval napalm. It stuck to its victims and burnt ferociously. Casualties amongst the brother knights were appalling.

There were British Templars in those last brave moments. The chronicler known as the 'Templar of Tyre', William of Beaujeu's secretary and a member of his household, was an eyewitness. He left a moving account of the horrors he saw that day – and there was one incident in particular that he found too hard to forget.

An English squire had his horse killed under him. As he struggled to get up, pots of Greek fire exploded all around him, spraying his head and his clothing. He was so badly hit 'that his surcoat burst into flames. There was no one to help him, and so his face was burned, and then his whole body, and he burned as if he had been a cauldron of pitch, and he died there.'

The last Templar defences were eventually mined and collapsed some ten days after the rest of the city had fallen. Appropriately enough for such a mutually destructive end, the final tower 'collapsed outwards towards the street, and crushed more than two thousand mounted Turks' when it did so. There were no survivors from this final, desperate garrison of Templar diehards. The brother knights had given their all – but it was not enough.[1]

1298: DEATH OF A MASTER

Edward was, as Baybars had sensed, a natural warrior with the potential to become the leader of multiple crusades. But by 1291, before he could return to the East, Acre and the other Frankish fortresses had fallen into enemy hands.

The Latin East was lost.

This was an unprepossessing backdrop against which to launch another crusade – an already difficult situation was beginning to look as though it had become completely impossible. Edward could not gather momentum to get a new English crusade underway after 1291 – but then neither could any other European ruler.

Instead, Edward turned to war against Scotland. He saw Scotland as a client state, more like one of his northern baronies than an independent kingdom. He claimed the right to act as judge and arbiter in all important Scottish matters. The Templars knew who to favour in this conflict. It is perhaps no coincidence that, at this point, Robert of Turville, the English master and the most senior Templar in the province, began in 1286 to use the title 'Master of England, Scotland and Ireland'.

The next two masters, Guy Forest (1291–4) and his successor Brian le Jay (1296–8), both used the provocative title of 'Master of the Templars in England, to whom the other houses in Scotland, Ireland or in Wales are subject'. William de la More, the last British Templar master, also adopted the title, and he too was at pains to emphasise the dependent relationship of the non-English parts of the Templar province.

This largely mirrored reality. The general chapter in England had over-sight over the other parts of the province, even down to the level of super-vising and confirming relatively small grants of land in Scotland. But it had never felt necessary to emphasise the subsidiary status of the other parts of Britain quite so brutally.

In part this was just a reflection of the power politics of the time. The English king had far more resources than other parts of the British Isles. And Edward was the only monarch in the region capable of launching, funding or leading a crusade. In this context it was not irrational for the Templars to prioritise their relationship with the English crown. Previously, however, they had felt able to do so while maintaining equally good rela-tionships with the Scottish kings – the order had, after all, wide-ranging property assets, extensive privileges and almost 200 years of goodwill to protect in the Scottish realm.

By 1291, as the last Christian fortresses in the East collapsed, matters reached a logical but perplexing conclusion. Brian le Jay (at that point master of the Templars in Scotland), took an oath of fealty to King Edward. In itself this was not unusual. This oath obliged him to raise a certain number of soldiers on the king's behalf – but again this was entirely normal. It represented Brian's obligations as a landowner, rather than a more substantial commitment by the Templars as an institution.[2]

It certainly did not commit Brian or the Templar brethren to fight personally on the king's behalf. On the contrary, there were strict instructions forbidding any of the military orders from taking up arms against fellow Christians. But the master pushed things further than any of his predecessors. The Templar preceptories in the north were offered as staging posts and logistics depots for Edward's soldiers heading off on their Scottish campaigns. Finally, in a demonstration of brutal partisanship, Brian (by this time master of the entire British province) followed the king on campaign in Scotland.

Shockingly, the Templar master died fighting alongside Edward at the English victory in the battle of Falkirk on 22 July 1298.[3]

The matter was not entirely clear cut. When Brian le Jay took his oath of fealty to Edward I he was not alone – he did so alongside the Hospitaller commander in Scotland and many other senior religious figures. Similarly, although he took two companions with him (Peter of Suthchirche and Thomas of Caune) on the Falkirk campaign, which culminated in his death, neither of his two military comrades were Templars – they are not referred to as 'brothers' (or *fratres*).[4]

Both the Templars and the Hospitallers had previously been involved in Edward I's wars – and this was perhaps a reflection of Edward's senior status within the crusading movement as a whole. Richard Poitevin, for instance, a Templar brother and the lieutenant-commander of the Temple in England, seems to have been involved in military action on the king's behalf in Wales in 1282. So too were the Hospitallers in 1294–5.[5]

Brian le Jay probably just got carried away. He performed personal service for the crown in his capacity as an enthusiastic warrior and a loyal subject. But the fact that the master of the British Templars felt able to do so, even to the extent of fighting in person, was ominous. This was a sign that the ties that bound the order together, and the singular objective that sustained it, were unravelling.

As individuals, the British Templars were predominantly Anglo-Normans and, as the order began to lose its strategic focus after the loss of the Latin East, they increasingly acted like it. They had become biased, particularly with regard to the government of England. While resources were needed to shore up the crusader states on an almost daily basis, such behaviour made sense. Influence at the English court could be converted into tangible benefits for the crusading movement.

With the loss of that central objective, however, the partisan nature of the order's engagement in the province became more visibly just that – provincial and partisan, with far fewer redeeming features. The British Templars were turning inward and becoming more nationalistically focused.[6]

They were losing their way.

EAST AND WEST: A RECKONING LOOMS

Though events prevented him from leading another crusade to the East, the Holy Land was always on Edward's mind. In the months shortly before his death, he swore that after his Scottish campaign of 1306 he would put down his sword for ever. But even then there was, he emphasised, one exception – the Holy Land would always have an overriding call on his services.[7]

As late as 1302, Edward wrote to James of Molay, the master of the Templars, that he still dreamed of 'going to Jerusalem as he had vowed . . . upon which journey he has fixed his whole heart'. This was not just a dramatic turn of phrase. Edward meant this quite literally. When he died, he did indeed leave his heart to the Holy Land – a nice gesture, perhaps, but not very useful. More helpfully, he also left a financial bequest to fund a force of 100 knights to serve in the East for a year.[8]

Edward's energies and resources were continually diverted towards more local military problems. Even in the midst of these campaigns, however, he maintained his interest in the East. James of Molay, the newly appointed grand master of the Templar order, made a point of contacting Edward before any other western ruler and visited England in November 1293.

The grand master stayed over for Christmas, meeting with Edward and lobbying the king on the order's behalf. James was back on the Continent by the early summer of 1294 but in the meantime he made a point of visiting Eagle and Bruer, where he held a chapter meeting. Even after he had left, the retired and current English masters, Guy Forest and Brian le Jay, were given permission to go to France to visit the grand master.[9]

In a vivid illustration of the way in which the able-bodied brothers were increasingly based in the military frontline of the eastern Mediterranean, when Guy Forest was made master for the second time in 1291, he was already elderly and in poor health. He remained ill for the whole of his term as master, but no fit fighting men could be spared to replace him.

William de la More eventually took over from Brian le Jay and remained in office for almost a decade. He was a popular man at court. Edward valued William's counsel and company so highly that when he asked permission to visit James of Molay in Cyprus in 1304, Edward wrote a note of recommendation for his friend. The letter was so fulsome in its praise that Edward stressed, in some embarrassment, that Brother William should not be shown the contents of the letter.

Despite their reduced capacity to help within government, the British Templars remained on excellent terms with the English crown.[10]

A REPUTATION AT RISK: PRIDE BEFORE THE FALL?

But the loss of the Holy Land meant a loss of focus – and this was all the more dangerous for an organisation that was powerful and, on occasion, undeniably over-proud. Neither were calculated to improve their popularity.

Like many monastic orders, the Templars were sometimes criticised for their ostensibly lax behaviour. Charges of widespread satanism, homosexuality and (ironically under the circumstances) womanising later emerged. These accusations were almost unheard of before their cataclysmic fall from favour in France in 1307. But the order's vulnerability to accusations of venality and drift only became more pointed as the military situation in the Holy Land collapsed into despair.

Even by the middle of the thirteenth century, one Anglo-French poet could confidently play to the crowd by writing that:

The Templars are the bravest men,
And they certainly know how to provide for themselves,
but they love pennies too much.
When prices are high
They sell their wheat
Instead of giving it to their households.

This was not an isolated viewpoint. Shortly before the dissolution of the order, a Provençal poet reflected what he knew many of his audience already believed when he wrote that the Templars in the West: 'rest in the shade, contemplating their golden hair; since they often give a bad example to the world; since their pride is so great . . . tell me . . . why the pope puts up with them, when he sees them wasting the riches that they are given for God's sake'.[11]

These accusations were untrue or, at the very least, grossly unfair. For most of the twelfth and thirteenth centuries, the Templar estates were, as we have seen, efficient and productive. That productivity was put to good use in sustaining the huge military efforts to defend the Holy Land. Most of the 'golden-haired' British Templars were fighting bravely in the forlorn attempt to save the Latin East, rather than enjoying a bucolic life of luxury at home. Many, perhaps the majority, died while on active service.

But the underlying problem was now their lack of purpose. And this was less an accusation than an instinctive recognition of reality. Addressing this issue became progressively more difficult in the last decades of the thirteenth century. The crusading movement in general, and the Templars in particular, were perceived to be expensive and increasingly pointless expressions of a lost cause.[12] Almost imperceptibly, their image was shifting towards a toxic blend of pride and arrogance, venality and redundancy.

It seemed to some that the Templars had become more interested in making money than in making friends. Focused as ever, they succeeded in both regards. They made a lot of money. They did not make a lot of friends. Given the situation in the Latin East, this was a high-risk strategy.

There were also broader issues about the credibility of the crusading movement as a whole. People always resent paying taxes. But a war of survival, or one with a strong moral case behind it, is different. Most people just hunker down and sustain the burden. For a war that is being waged far away, with little obvious benefit for those at home, the case for sacrifice (financial or otherwise) is far less compelling. After 1291, the defence of the East was a fight that had become increasingly abstract – and very probably unwinnable.

To make matters even worse, there were some embarrassing and undeniable instances of wrongdoing. Like any organisation employing large numbers of people, many of whom were dealing with huge sums of money, individual brothers occasionally succumbed to temptation.

The Templars, despite (or perhaps because of) their role in investment banking, could be untrustworthy. Gilbert of Hogestan's pillaging of the Saladin Tithe in 1188 was the most prominent example. But there were other examples, too. We know, for instance, that Brother Hugh of Stockton and some of his Templar comrades accepted bribes (specifically, a silver goblet) to release criminals from their care at the preceptory at Bisham.[13]

Above all else, however, there was the reality of the military catastrophes that had been unfolding in the Holy Land.

Ironically, the Templars' greatest strength was also their greatest weakness. They received more criticism than the other military orders, partly because they were the ones most unequivocally focused on warfare. They were the men most tainted by defeat when battles were lost, and they were the most obviously underemployed when the war to sustain the crusader states had ended.

Every 'brand' is a promise. And the Templar brand had promised much – military success, an enduring Christian community in the East, a chance to turn back the tide of Turkic invasions. But none of this had proved possible. The Templars were the highest-profile military order and the exemplars of the crusading movement. The depth of their fall was in direct proportion to the heights they had aspired to.[14]

The order had sacrificed the most to defend Acre, the last great city of the Christian East. But it had still failed.

And with that failure came consequences.

REARRANGING DECKCHAIRS

By April 1292, a new grand master had been elected for the leadership of the Templars: James of Molay.

At the time, Molay must have seemed like the ideal candidate. He was of a mature age (in his mid-forties by the time of his appointment) and had already been in the order for twenty-seven years. He was steeped in the history, politics and rituals of the Templars. Above all, he had a long-standing military background and had probably served as a soldier in the crusader states since the 1270s.

Given the military situation facing the order in 1292, choosing a bluff warrior to become master made a lot of sense. Taking refuge in activity is often an attractive option. But his strengths were also his weaknesses. The length of his military experience had made him rigid and unimaginative. His age had made him knowledgeable about tactics and processes but had not given him insight into strategy. His long years of service had taught him much, probably far too much, about the way the order did things. He was not inclined to innovate or change.

Most importantly, his focus on military affairs made him a less than flexible leader when it came to negotiating new roles and launching effective diplomatic initiatives – this was a man used to obedience, rather than someone practised in the arts of persuasion.[15]

Molay's vision for a putative 'counteroffensive' against the Mamluk armies which had conquered the Holy Land was firmly set in the past. He helped organise a last foray to set up a base on the island of Ruad, just a few hundred yards off the coast of Syria. Not surprisingly, it was an embarrassing fiasco. Afterwards, James of Molay was vehemently opposed to anything other than large-scale crusades.[16]

But, in an era when such large-scale crusades were extremely unlikely, this stance began to beg the question: what was the point of a military order which could not operate by sea and which did not have the resources, or stomach, to attack the enemy by land?

NEW IDEAS AND NEW PURPOSE?

Despite the difficulties, there were those who still wanted to carry on the fight. There was talk in the papacy about the possibility of a new crusade. And, for the Templars, in Britain and beyond, this meant hope.

In 1306 this talk became more real. The papacy, under the leadership of the enthusiastic Pope Clement, started to gather advice about the kind of expedition that would be most likely to succeed. If another crusade could be launched, the Templars would have a clear purpose once more.

With the distorting benefit of hindsight, we tend to see the fall of the last major Christian strongholds in 1291 as the end of the realistic prospects for crusading in the East. After all, if Palestine and Syria could not be held with the help of huge castles and fortified cities, what chance would a fragile seaborne invasion have, however well resourced or well motivated?

This inescapable truth was not readily apparent to everyone at the time, however. The emotional desire to liberate the East could trump the most compelling military logic. There were still pockets of optimism amongst those who chose to believe and the pope was amongst those believers. Pope Clement was wholeheartedly committed to the crusading cause and made every effort to bring the French monarchy along with him.[17]

The pope tried to progress detailed planning for the crusade. We know of at least thirty treatises written in the decades following the fall of Acre. Each discussed different ways to recapture the Holy Land and keep the war in the East alive. There were varying degrees of realism. Some were mere wishful thinking, composed by cranks or hobbyists. Others were more thoughtful and detailed. Almost all of them, however, regardless of their differences in other areas, were united in assigning an important role to the military orders. There was a clear opportunity for them to regain their sense of purpose.[18]

Extensive planning sessions focused on two main topics. Firstly, what kind of expedition should be launched to save the Holy Land? And, secondly, given the need to coordinate increasingly scarce resources to best effect, would it make sense to amalgamate the two main military orders?

At the time, these discussions appeared to be the normal cut and thrust of military and political debate. What James of Molay did not appreciate, however, was that this was the Templars' last chance – his decision would decide the fate of the entire order.

As if to prove the wisdom of the idea of amalgamating the two orders, discussions about the nature of a crusading intervention broke down almost immediately. The Hospitallers wanted to capture Rhodes with a relatively small naval expedition and they had no intention of allowing Templar involvement in their project. Given the limited nature of their objectives, the Hospitallers' project was eventually successful. Between 1306 and 1310, relatively small Hospitaller naval forces, with limited assistance from other interested parties, captured the island from its Christian Byzantine rulers. They made it their headquarters and a forward base for aggressive naval action in the eastern Mediterranean.

The Templars, for their part, were even more inflexible and less realistic. James of Molay, far from being content with a small force, suggested that it would be essential to have no fewer than 12,000–15,000 armed caval-rymen on a crusade. These men would be supplemented by up to 50,000 foot sergeants who would act as archers and crossbowmen. He also proposed that this vast force should be transported by a huge armada across the Mediterranean, using Cyprus as a jumping-off point and logistical base.

He knew exactly what he was asking for – and how unlikely it was to ever happen. Just by way of comparison, the army of the Latin Kingdom of Jerusalem, which was destroyed at the battle of Hattin in 1187 and which was, incidentally, the largest force ever fielded by the crusader states, included only some 5,000 cavalrymen – and of these just some 1,200 men were knights. And, quite apart from the unprecedented numbers of cavalry that Molay was asking for, his suggestion also implied that, in addition to carrying the huge baggage train and other supplies required, the expedition would be able to source and transport tens of thousands of horses to the Middle East in one trip.[19]

By pitching his demands at such an unrealistic level, many would have thought Molay unwise. The more cynical, perhaps, may even have suspected a hint of delaying tactics – that he was trying to defer the moment when he and his men would return to the traumatic and blood-drenched battlefields of the Middle East. He was demanding levels of manpower and materiel that he knew could never be delivered by the politically fractured monarchs of western Europe.[20]

STRONGER TOGETHER?

There was one last lifeline. James of Molay could have amalgamated his order with that of the Hospitallers. This was what his masters in the papacy and many outsiders wanted. And, despite the rivalries between the two orders, the logic behind such proposals was compelling.

Each order had its own unique heritage and areas of expertise. But it was hard to argue with the underlying rationale of consolidation, particularly in the light of the increasingly unhelpful rivalries between the Templars and the Hospitallers. Mutual antagonisms had been regularly played out in the cramped and inward-looking cities of the Latin East. Occasionally, they had even led to violence between the different factions of the vastly outnumbered Christian forces.[21]

The fall of Acre in 1291 had inevitably focused minds considerably on the role of the military orders. In 1291 and 1292, a series of Provincial Councils were set up by the papacy to generate discussion about the best way forward for the crusading movement. In almost every case, the idea of amalgamating the military orders was broached. It was also proposed, entirely rationally, that the master of this new, consolidated military order should be crowned as king of Jerusalem. This new style of leadership would, it was hoped, make succession issues far less divisive than had previously been the case.[22]

But Molay made the wrong decision yet again. He was so dedicated to the order that he was blinded to the bigger picture. Molay fought hard, far too hard in fact, to preserve the order's independence and assets. He could foresee no change, no adaptation to new circumstances. Under his command, an ostensibly strong but strategically vulnerable institution was becoming increasingly fragile – and if they would not bend, the Templars were in danger of breaking.[23]

Molay chose to focus on the differences between the Templars and the Hospitallers, rather than their profound similarities. Even he was forced to recognise the huge cost savings and efficiencies that a union would bring, but he rejected such base advantages as being beneath the dignity of himself and his men. He argued that the Templars were the better soldiers as they were part of an order 'founded expressly for military service'. The Hospitallers, he wrote, spent much of their time on (presumably less manly) activities such as tending to the sick.

His biggest mistake, of course, was to hammer home a very dangerous point. He inadvertently confirmed that the Templars were only good at doing the one thing that most people thought no longer feasible or sustainable: fighting it out on the ground in the Middle East against huge Mamluk or Mongol armies. There were no new ideas. No sense of new purpose.

He did not know it, but Molay had just signed the order's death warrant.

SAFE AT THE HEART OF THE ESTABLISHMENT

The storm was gathering.

But the extent of the danger was still barely visible in Britain. The Templars were influential and powerful. Talk of union with the Hospitallers had been raised on several occasions since the fall of Acre. It had been rejected each time. The order had its detractors, of course, but, lacking the imagination of vulnerability, it felt safe.

The Templars were firmly embedded at the highest levels of society. They were trusted advisers and respected professionals. They worked and socialised with the king and his administration. And this sense of belonging amongst the social elite was encouraged by a new idea. A new way of looking at war, society and the role of the upmarket warrior had emerged – chivalry.

As this new cult developed in Britain, it gradually encompassed a unique and heady blend of military prowess, ethical aspirations and a semi-religious idealism. The Templars, as the iconic warriors of Christ, were the natural caretakers of such an ideology.

The process and ceremony of 'knighting', one of the central signifiers of this mystical–military ideology, was increasingly carried out in churches, with religious blessing and priestly participation. Not surprisingly, chivalry and knighting were quickly and intimately associated with the order. Ironically, the most prestigious and large-scale knighting ceremony of the age involved the British Templars and it took place just a few months before the order was suppressed.

In 1306, Edward I of England, the warrior king and long-time supporter of the Templars, sent his own son Edward of Caernarvon, soon-to-be King Edward II, along with almost 300 other candidates, to be knighted at Westminster Abbey and the nearby St Stephen's chapel. Preparation for this profound and highly spiritual event was vital. Each of the candidates was expected to spend the night before the ceremony in quiet reflection. Significantly, on this most important of chivalric occasions, prospective knights were sent to spend their vigil in the place deemed most appropriate for holy warriors: the Templars' British headquarters, in the church of the New Temple.

The squires' night of vigil deliberately mirrored that time of lonely introspection experienced by all warriors on the eve of battle. But theirs was a symbolic battle. Alongside the Templar brothers, in the emotionally charged confines of the New Temple church, they reflected on the spiritual and physical battle of preparing to be a knight and of living up to the ideals of a pious but muscular warrior elite.

The following morning, the young men rode slowly towards Westminster for the final ceremonies. The solemn and profound nature of the services was only slightly undercut when King Edward I, ever the pragmatist, took the opportunity to make a public but far more prosaic vow: he swore that he would soon give the Scots a good kicking and subdue them to his will. He wanted everyone to know it. But, despite his rather boorish interruption, the religious mystique was pervasive and the association with the Templars was strong.

The day ended with drinking and feasting. The British Templars were held in the highest favour – they were amongst friends and helping to lead one of the foremost social and intellectual movements of the day. All was well.[24]

The order's loss of purpose was presumably temporary. The Templars were at the heart of the English establishment. They were basking in the warrior king's friendship.

Everyone was safe.

16

◇

FALL: 1307–1312

October 1307. Friday the thirteenth. Of course.

Shocking dawn raids took place in Paris and across the rest of France. The French Templars were arrested en masse, in what almost amounted to an internal coup d'état. There was no warning of the suppression. The axe fell as suddenly as a guillotine blade. Philip IV's troops moved in force against the order. The king's motives, and those of his closest advisers, in carrying out this extraordinary putsch are still not entirely clear. It seems that Philip was genuinely credulous about the prevalence of heresy. But he was even more genuinely in need of large amounts of cash.

For the Templars, this was a dangerous combination.

The death of Edward I in the summer of 1307 allowed King Philip of France to take command of the crusading movement. Perhaps bizarrely to our eyes, he started this process by destroying the Templars.

The order in France were close allies of the monarchy and, as in England, often acted in its service. But the relationship was a complex one. The Templars were also answerable to a higher, supranational authority, in the form of the papacy. They were largely redundant in their role as the crusader states had, for all practical purposes, ceased to exist. And, most importantly for Philip, they were rich.[1]

They were accused of a series of crimes that were said to have long taken hold and corrupted the order. They had, it was said, held private meetings.

It was claimed that certain of the brothers had indulged in homosexual acts or defrauded their pious patrons. And that they had failed to give as much to charity as might have been hoped. This was disappointing, but hardly unexpected in any large organisation.

But the accusations grew increasingly grave and suspiciously shrill. The Templars had denounced Christ and regularly spat upon the cross. They had started to worship devils and idols, creating their own 'anti-Christs' for a new 'anti-Christian' religion. The Templars were revealed as a secret sect at war with the very heart of Christendom.[2]

It was true that the Templars had never been universally popular. Any organisation as successful, privileged and prosperous as they were inevitably made enemies – that had been the case since the earliest years of their formation. They also had monastic and militaristic goals which were hard to reconcile and almost impossible to achieve, even under the most benign conditions. They were expected to simultaneously embody the military virtues of the perfect Christian knight, together with the fierce spiritual discipline of a religious order.

More importantly, they were also expected to protect the Holy Land, fighting at the very extremities of Europe against what were, for all practical purposes, unending waves of Mamluk, Turkic and Mongol enemies. With the benefit of hindsight, it is clear that the Templars had unachievable goals and, with the loss of the Holy Land, their entire *raison d'être* was in question.

Nonetheless, the shocking sins of the Templars were a huge surprise to everyone. There was no backdrop to such significant complaints. The order's high profile had exposed them to close scrutiny for almost 200 years. But if anyone had seen them worshipping devils or developing a new anti-Christian religion, they had forgotten to mention it until now.

WEAKNESS AND DRIFT

Some of the same monks who were tried, tortured and later executed were on royal service, helping the king of France's officials, when the order for the suppression was issued. In a strange twist of fate, some Templars had to be escorted back to Paris, under arrest, by the very people they were helping.

The order was entirely unprepared. The combination of shock, dislocation and torture – particularly the latter – was overwhelming. Almost everyone, from the master down to the newest novice, confessed to everything that was put to them. It quickly emerged that the depths of their heresy were profound – perhaps suspiciously so.[3]

The timing of the attack on the order was largely driven by King Philip's wishes and the internal timetable of the French court. Events in England in the weeks running up to the suppression were certainly helpful for him, however.

Edward I, a staunch supporter of the order, had died on 7 July, just a few months before the French authorities launched their brutal crackdown. If he had still been alive, the bellicose and self-confident king would almost certainly have launched a fierce defence of the Templars. At the very least, he would have been massively unimpressed by the ludicrous charges levelled at the order by his French rivals.

The British Templars suffered from the lack of protection that he would undoubtedly have offered them. Edward II, the new young king, remained, like his father, positively disposed towards the order and made no secret of his lack of enthusiasm for shutting them down in his territories. He was, however, in a far weaker position to help.[4]

Edward was young and still uncertain on his throne – he had been king of England for just four months and was still uncrowned at the time of the raids on the Templars. He also had financial problems to face. His father had been a successful warrior king but, in the traditional way of warrior kings, he had left an empty Exchequer behind him.

Edward had few immediate allies with which to face down the French coup. And he was engaged to be married to Isabelle of France, Philip IV's daughter. One would expect that, like King Philip himself in France, he had every motivation to suppress the order and to confiscate its lands – this was a chance to fill his coffers while at the same time pleasing his new father-in-law. And yet he did nothing of the sort. Instead, after a couple of weeks spent in anxious reflection, Edward wrote to the French king to express his dismay and query the truth of the charges levelled at the order.[5]

In England, the Templars were popular within government. They were an intimate part of life at court. Edward had grown up in a household of which the Templars were valued members. His father had treated them as brothers in arms when he was in the Holy Land and as trusted advisers when he was at home. Even after Edward I had returned from the wars in the East, he had continued to maintain close contact with his old comrades. He was still writing to the master of the order, James of Molay, as late as 1304.

King Philip quickly sent one of his confidants, master Bernard Pelet, to the English court to explain what had happened and to get Edward's support for his actions. Bernard set out the charges and the evidence as powerfully as he could. He fully expected the English government to follow suit in shutting down the order and ransacking their possessions.[6]

But Edward remained unimpressed. The actions of the French king lacked all credibility in England. Far from arresting the brothers, on 4 December Edward wrote identical letters to the kings of Castile, Portugal, Aragon and Naples in which he fiercely defended the reputation of the Templars. The guilt of the order, he suggested, was 'hardly to be entertained'. He wrote instead that the brothers were part of an organisation that 'shines bright in religion'.

A week later, Edward wrote to Pope Clement in even stronger terms. He made it clear that he did not believe the accusations against the order. He advised His Holiness to delay any form of judgement until he had seen all the evidence. He suggested that the pope should discount the 'rumour of infamy', a rumour indeed full of bitterness, terrible to think of, horrible to hear, and detestable in wickedness'.[7]

The Templars had been integral allies of the English crown for many generations. Whenever the monarchy was threatened, whenever the country seemed about to descend into chaos, the Templar brothers rushed to support the king, however imperfect he might be. They were not just trusted by the English establishment, they were a vital part of it. To be told to end this long-standing and close relationship by outsiders, and particularly by the king of France, was appalling.

As practical proof of his belief in their innocence, Edward continued to use the services of the Templars. He borrowed carts off them to transport household items down to Dover. He approved requests for Templar brothers to be appointed for legal cases. It was, in a glorious show of defiance, business as usual.[8]

Even so, the order's position was not as strong as they would have wanted. Their voluntary merger with the Hospitallers, which would have been a rational response to their mutual lack of corporate objectives, had been discussed and rejected. Others were now looking to make sure that the 'merger' took place involuntarily.

HONOUR AND DEFIANCE

Trust and honour were deeply important aspects of medieval government, and cannot be underestimated. There was also something deeper, however. Edward's innate loyalty to his advisers was understandable but entirely insufficient to explain his actions. If they were guilty, he would quickly have cast them aside. Instead, it is clear from his actions that Edward and his advisers did not believe the charges laid against the order. Far from following his own interests in disowning the Templars and making a land-grab for their estates, Edward defended them for as long as he could.

But at the end of the year, on 14 December 1307, Edward received a papal bull ordering their arrest. The issue could no longer be avoided. His response to the pope was polite but terse – just two sentences acknowledging his unwilling compliance.

On 20 December, instructions were sent out to detain all Templars, albeit in comfortable conditions, and to make an inventory of their assets.

The arrests took place on 9–11 January 1308. About 144 members of the order, of whom only 15 were knights, were rounded up and taken into custody. When the arrests were set in train in Wales, it became apparent that there were no Templars to arrest. This was incontrovertible evidence of how painfully thinly spread the order had become.[9]

The Templars were a military order par excellence and one might assume that they would have put up a sharp defence against anyone seeking their destruction. Given their well-deserved reputation as the vanguard of Europe's warriors, the suppression should (in the popular imagination at least) have consisted of a series of desperate charges and heroic last stands. But nothing could be further from the truth.

In fact, the military assets of the order in the West were, quite rightly, negligible. The soldiers and the fortifications were in the East. Little or no resistance was put up when royal officials in different countries moved in to suppress the order.

The Templars in Britain were no exception. Even if castles had existed, there were no garrisons with which to defend them. Their rural properties were usually simple manor houses, often with a series of buildings clustered around a courtyard – perhaps with workshops and sleeping quarters, sometimes a small chapel. These were administrative centres, with enclosures designed to keep chickens in rather than armed men out.

Similarly, the order's urban properties tended to be domestic and residential buildings rather than towers or keeps. As in the countryside, they were sometimes built around a courtyard with a hall or chapel, but these were primarily designed to deter burglars rather than determined soldiers.

Much the same was true of the Templar personnel. Entirely correctly, Templar knights and their soldiers were mainly deployed in the East, fulfilling the order's prime objective of defending the Holy Land. The brothers who lived in the West tended to be small in number. Many were elderly or infirm, wounded and recovering or professional administrators. Even if the order in Britain had wanted to defend itself, there was very little they could have done. Without warriors or castles, the defence of the order would have had to be undertaken in the courts rather than on the battlefield.[10]

But there was no violence on either side. Unlike the brutality of the French attack on the order, the English arrests were far more informal, almost shame-faced. The sheriffs were told to give the men a relatively generous financial allowance to make their stay in captivity more comfortable, and they were explicitly ordered not to put them in a 'hard and vile prison'. Where secure accommodation was not considered comfortable enough, as in the case of York, the prisoners were released to live in private houses or allowed to go back to Templar estates, riding their own horses. This was not the kind of high-security intimidation that had been seen in France.

Meanwhile, in a show of outward acquiescence, on 9 January 1308, the king's officials entered the New Temple and William de la More, the English master, was arrested. But this again was more about the appearance of compliance than anything more severe.

William was confined in Canterbury, but in comfortable quarters. He lodged with some of his brothers as companions and was even paid financial expenses by the English crown to ensure that his stay was not too onerous. Within a few months, William was quietly released. By July 1308, he was given access to six of the Templars' manors in order to provide an appropriately comfortable living for him and his men.[11]

Edward never turned against the Templars. All the evidence suggests that he believed, entirely correctly, that they were innocent. When the participation of England in the process of winding up the order became unavoidable, he did everything he could to make it as humane as possible. Their 'imprisonment', at least until outsiders arrived, involved bail or an 'open prison', rather than being thrown into a dungeon.

Edward's every action demonstrated continuing loyalty. His attitude suggested a hope, perhaps even an expectation, that the whole ghastly episode was just a dreadful mistake which might still be rectified.[12]

But it was already too late.

SO IT BEGINS . . .

By the end of 1308, over a year after the putsch against the Templars in France, even Edward was forced by papal pressure to take things more seriously. Master William de la More was arrested once more (on 28 November) and orders were issued that the Templar prisoners should be guarded in a more visibly rigorous manner.[13]

Almost a year later, in the autumn of 1309, papal inquisitors finally arrived in England. Hurried (and presumably somewhat embarrassing) orders had to be issued to round the 'prisoners' up again. The sheriff of Kent, for instance, was told to arrest 'all Templars wandering about in your bailiwick and send them to London as the king understands that diverse Templars are wandering about in secular habits'.

One suspects that even this letter was perhaps accompanied by a verbal message placing it in a more realistic context. It was probably sent just for show, for the benefit of the papal inquisitors, rather than for its ostensible recipient. The sheriff who received the letter was a confidant of the king and was doubtless all too aware of his lord's real feelings about the persecution of the Templars.[14]

Accompanied by senior English clergy, papal inquisitors began to interrogate the Templar prisoners. The brothers in England were corralled together in three locations – London, York and Lincoln. Similar instructions to round up the prisoners and provide assistance to the papal inquisitors were sent to Ireland and to the English governor in Scotland.[15]

The 'interviews' in Britain were based on eighty-four charges which had been brought against the order. These ranged from relatively minor offences (such as not fully understanding the difference between 'sin' and a 'fault') through to more imaginative charges of idolatry and participation in satanic rituals.[16]

The interrogations were a farce. Not surprisingly, in the absence of evidence and without the use of torture there were no confessions. The prisoners testified that the order was run as a conventional religious organisation. They denied the existence of any 'secret' meetings other than the usual services. The men vehemently contradicted any suggestion of satanic rites, devil worship, heresy or sodomy.

This was all in stark contrast to the testimonies of the French brothers, who had been tortured or threatened with torture. There, men had been forced to confess to everything, no matter how ludicrous.[17]

One fortunate French Templar, a brother named Himbert Blanc, had been in England on a business trip on the morning of 13 October 1307, when Philip's men had launched their surprise attack on the order. Because he was arrested in England, he was interrogated under English law rather than with the brutality of the French system. It is fascinating to see the very different results of the process.

The brothers in France were all quickly suborned into admitting the most spurious and incredible accusations. Himbert, however, was adamant that all the charges were trumped up. He was a senior Templar and an experienced military man. A letter from Pope Clement V, written just months before Philip decided the order were heretics, referred to him as 'admiral of the galleys dispatched to aid the Holy Land'.[18]

He had been in the order for almost forty years and had fought in the Holy Land under William of Beaujeu. As a stark indication of Himbert's age and the appalling casualty rates suffered by the brothers, he testified that there had been thirty Templars to witness his entry into the order, but that he was the only one still alive.

Such a man was not to be cowed – he had no intention of being bullied into saying anything other than the truth. Like the blunt old soldier he was, Himbert was outraged and angry rather than compliant. Throwing down the gauntlet at his accusers, he said that if anyone 'had confessed the aforesaid errors, they had lied'.[19]

English law was different to that of France. There was no tradition of royal control of the judiciary. English courts did not have an inquisition at their disposal, as many of the major heresies on the Continent, such as Catharism, had never become problematic. Third-party witnesses were required and, as there were precious few available for the so-called 'secret' rites of the Templars, there was almost no evidence. Most importantly, English law relied on a locally selected jury, rather than torture, to deliver results.

As normal legal procedures had failed to deliver the desired outcome, the papal inquisitors began to demand that torture be used to generate appropriately dramatic confessions. At the Council of Canterbury (confusingly held in London on 24 November 1309), they began their lobbying in earnest and, just over two weeks later, over two years after the raids on the order in France, they asked the king to approve the widespread use of torture against the Templar brothers.

Edward could not bring himself to fully condone such barbarities against his faithful servants, but neither did he feel he could stop the process altogether. The king feared that he, and perhaps England as a whole, might be excommunicated if he made an outright refusal. He replied ambiguously and the possibility of interrogation with torture was unleashed.[20]

Even now, there was little enthusiasm, however. Increased pressure was applied during interrogations. But the almost total lack of results from the questioning that took place in the spring of 1310 shows that full-scale torture was still being avoided – the inquisitors complained that they could find no one in England to carry out the torture to their satisfaction. They tried (and failed) to get the English Templar prisoners sent to France, so that they could be questioned more 'thoroughly'. But no one in England wanted to make such a fateful decision. A Council held in York, in May 1310, decided to postpone everything until the following year.[21]

Everyone, it seems, was stalling for time, hoping that the whole embarrassing problem would just go away.

THE LONDON CASE STUDY

The interrogations were carried out in different places across the British Isles and in each case the process was different. But there was also an underlying similarity: incredulity. In most cases it is clear that even the prosecuting authorities were unconvinced about the charges they were supposed to be pursuing. Only the papal inquisitors acted with any vigour and even they were often blocked. The secular authorities in England did everything they could to be unhelpful without being overtly obstructive.

There was widespread interest in the trials and interrogations in London. Judging by what we know of events in Canterbury, large crowds would have gathered at critical moments in the process. Although they were arch rivals, not a single Hospitaller came forward to perjure themselves against the Templars despite the fact that, as the ultimate recipients of the orders' lands, they had most to gain. The Templars in London also had a large number of tenants, employees and business associates, many of whom were disgruntled and who could have testified against them, but almost none did so.[22]

Even senior members of the clergy were at times blatantly unwilling to take part in action against the Templars.

William Greenfield, the archbishop of York, was very much of the 'dog ate my homework' school of thought when it came to excuses. He gave a series of spectacularly unconvincing reasons why he could not attend proceedings in London. He said that he could not leave York as his cross could not be carried in front of him when he left his province. At one point he claimed that he was too unwell to travel. Later, he suggested that he was too busy to leave York. And, getting into his stride at this point, he finally complained that he did not receive notice of meetings until it was too late for him to set off.[23]

But the process itself could no longer be stopped. The London examinations took place in stages, as the inquisitors sought to build their case – identifying weakness, focusing on irregularities and exploiting the occasional confusion of men under stress.

From 23 to 25 October 1309, three Templar brothers were interrogated, but not under oath. This was what modern market researchers would call 'dynamic piloting' – a chance to make sure that the charge-sheet 'questionnaire' was working correctly and to allow the interrogators to hone their interview techniques before the real work began.

On 25 October, interrogations under oath started in London. They continued until 17 November. A total of forty-three Templars were questioned. Eager to exploit weakness, the inquisitors concentrated their persuasive efforts on those men who had only recently joined the order, assuming that they would be the easiest to break – but almost nothing incriminating emerged during these sessions.[24]

The second round of Templar interviews in London started on 29 January 1310. This time there was a new charge sheet – less ambitious in scope, but far more specific. There were twenty-five questions, focusing on the order's structure and procedures. As they had hoped, this more arcane line of questioning threw up a few issues with which the inquisitors could work. There was particular fun to be had around the Templar brothers' understanding of doctrinal matters. Some of the men were unclear about the procedures for absolution, for instance, or the technical difference between a sin and a crime.[25]

There were also some supposed irregularities in how the brothers had been received into the order. These centred on the issue of secrecy and how the Templars were able to use the privacy of these 'secret' meetings to suborn new recruits into the alleged satanic cults that substituted for the order's ostensible Catholic faith.

Annoyingly, however, as with the hundreds of conspiracy theories that have swirled around the internet ever since, there was no evidence to support any of this. Brother William Raven, for instance, testified that he had been accepted into the order by the master, William de la More, at Templecombe. But he also estimated that there had been 'around a hundred secular persons . . . in the chapel'. So much for secrecy.

And the description he gave of his induction was likewise entirely orthodox – there was a pledge of loyalty to the Rule of the Templars, promises to serve God and the Virgin Mary, vows to obey his superiors (particularly important in an order with a military focus) and a recognition that he should never behave violently towards fellow Christians. There were no blasphemous rituals involved in this deeply orthodox church service.[26]

Some of the Templar brothers were less bright than others. It is clear that few were bookish. Their ability to produce the correct answers was not helped, of course, by the fact that many of them could not read or write. This should not be a surprise – the order was focused on war rather than theology and that was reflected in the interests of the men it recruited. And some unfortunates had joined the order only shortly before the arrests took place.[27]

Inevitably, occasional instances of ignorance about the more arcane aspects of their religious life became apparent. A couple of the brothers were found to be unsure about the nature of absolution and whether it was a sacrament when administered by a preceptor (correct answer: it was not). But these were entirely understandable mistakes. There was nothing that would constitute genuine heresy.

But that was the best the inquisitors could come up with. The process ground on. On 3–4 March 1310, there were more interviews, but few new insights. As the process produced frustratingly little incriminating information, the papal inquisitors felt obliged to lobby to have the brothers' prison conditions made harsher. As a result, the prisoners in London were now chained and placed in solitary confinement.

Even this led to no major breakthroughs, however. On 8–9 June 1310, the final London interviews took place. Once again, nothing of real value emerged. Almost three years after the arrests in France, and after huge efforts on behalf of the inquisition, there was still almost no evidence against the British Templars.[28]

THE IRISH CASE STUDY

If the process in England was conducted with little conviction, the examinations in Ireland were, if anything, carried out in an even more desultory fashion – and with just as little result.

The Templar brothers in Ireland were arrested on 3 February 1308. But their conditions were not harsh – they were paid pensions until 14 April 1309, after which King Edward's Justiciar gave them three estates with which to support themselves.[29]

The process lacked energy from the beginning. On 29 September 1309, King Edward had to write again to order that Templars who were not yet detained should be rounded up. There was likewise no rush towards interrogation and the trial did not get underway until February 1310. Some Templars died during the interrogation process, but only of old age or infirmity. Fourteen brothers were imprisoned in Dublin Castle. The interrogations produced almost no information of substance. Each was questioned three times, but, apart from their master, none said anything that would incriminate either themselves or the order.[30]

Henry Danet, the master of Ireland, gave his testimony on 18–25 February. He was an English outsider. Unfortunately for him, he had arrived in Ireland only a few days before the suppression. He inevitably knew little about his new sub-province. Feeling vulnerable and disorientated, he was perhaps eager to show at least a minimal level of cooperation with his inquisitors.

Henry had joined the order in February 1304 at the commandery of Bruer in Lincolnshire. He made a few incriminating remarks about how the order operated in the East. He also attributed some heretical practices to Templar brothers from the Iberian peninsula, but he later changed his mind and testified that there were no 'errors' or heresies of any kind in the order. And what he had originally suggested was seemingly mistaken. The trials in Spain and Portugal produced no evidence of heresy. Otherwise, Henry said nothing negative about his own behaviour or that of the order in Ireland.[31]

He contradicted himself so often that it must have been obvious, even at the time, that much of his evidence was false. Presumably he was just saying whatever he believed the inquisitors wanted to hear. Significantly, none of the other Irish brothers corroborated his evidence.[32]

There were a couple of minor grudges and prejudices to be aired. One Templar priest complained, in the traditional manner of disgruntled employees, about the lack of prospects for promotion in his job. But it was all relatively trivial.[33]

No one seemed interested in pursuing matters too far or uncovering things that might require further action. Even the authorities' choice of witnesses to be interrogated was highly suspicious. Henry Danet's predecessor as master of Ireland, a man who would have known far more about the order's operations, was not questioned. There were also several English Templar fugitives in Ireland at the time, men whose status as fugitives made them extremely vulnerable: taking flight could, of course, be construed as an admission of guilt. These men were accordingly the most obvious candidates for severe questioning. Instead of being interrogated, however, they were paid an allowance by the Irish authorities (thus proving definitively that government officials were aware of their presence) and excluded from the trial process.[34]

The only witnesses produced against the order in Ireland were outsiders. They were deeply underwhelming. Most were friars who repeated second-hand gossip and tittle-tattle of the most inane kind. There was some recycling of urban (or rural) myths. And there was the vague and insubstantial accusation that the Templars had been subject to 'scandal'. But there was nothing to suggest more than small-town grudges.[35]

Of the forty-four witnesses who gave evidence against the Templars in Ireland, very few even pretended to have had first-hand dealings with the order. One of the jealous clergy of Dublin, for instance, accused them of being inattentive in church. Another claimed that they did not look with sufficient interest at the host during Mass. Yet another said that they were guilty, but when pressed as to the specifics of that 'guilt', he seems to have forgotten what it might be and was forced to say that he did not know.[36]

There was just one matter of potential substance. Walter the Bachelor (the Templar master of Ireland *c.* 1295–1301) had been found guilty of fraud and of theft from the order. He was taken to London for sentencing by the general chapter. Walter was excommunicated for his sins and sentenced to a spell of eight weeks' imprisonment in the order's cells. The ex-Irish master was a broken man by this point, however, disgraced and shunned by his brother knights. He 'was placed in prison and in fetters'.

Conditions in the cells were harsh. More ominously, it was said that 'some duress was done to him'. There were suggestions that he had been deliberately starved as part of his punishment or perhaps tortured in other ways. His short stay became even shorter. Walter died after only a very brief period of incarceration. He was buried outside the order's cemetery.[37]

The inquisitors tried to prove, on the basis of no evidence whatsoever, that Walter had been murdered because he had threatened to reveal the Templars' secret heresies. There was repeated questioning about why he was not buried in the normal manner. The Templar witnesses merely riposted, entirely plausibly, that this was because he had been excommunicated for theft, not as punishment for being a whistle-blower.

The Templar order was suppressed soon afterwards. Their inquisitors, struggling to find any real evidence of systemic wrongdoing in the order, were eager to pursue the Bachelor affair in more detail. Walter's crimes were an obvious area of investigation, but this line of questioning quickly ran into the ground. The order had discovered his crimes and he had been punished – harshly perhaps, but correctly.

Either way, there was little of substance with which to accuse the order. The fact that the inquisitors were reduced to clutching at such flimsy straws only demonstrates how little genuine wrongdoing there had been within the Irish Templar houses.[38]

Taken as a whole the evidence against the order in Ireland was laughable. Once the interrogations were over, it appears that the brothers were not even required to perform penance or go through the motions of abjuring any supposed heresies before their release. And there was no verdict of 'guilty as charged' – the authorities seemingly just wanted the affair to be brought to a painless conclusion as quickly as possible.[39]

The order in Ireland, as in the rest of Britain, went out with a whimper rather than a bang. The Templar leader, Henry Danet, was released on bail in the autumn of 1312 and so, presumably, were all the others. The king continued to pay pensions to the Irish Templar brothers but, from April 1314 onwards, the Hospitallers, who had received the order's properties, took over responsibility for their care. The last remaining Templars in Ireland were seemingly allowed to go back to their homes. They faded into a quiet life, hopefully enjoying their pensions while they did so.[40]

THE END IN BRITAIN

The process elsewhere was similarly anticlimactic.

By 1299, the post of Scottish commander seems to have become vacant – it may even have been scrapped altogether. The lack of an elaborate organisational structure is not altogether surprising – there appears to have been only two Templar brothers (William of Clifton and William Middleton).

Both were of English origin. And neither seems to have served in the East. Disappointingly for the inquisitors, they were not prepared to make false confessions. Instead, external witnesses had to be produced in order to gather the usual litany of trivial gossip. Most seem to have been driven by petty jealousy and bitter local disputes. However much they disliked the Templars, there was little of substance to be dredged up.[41]

After several years and several hundred interrogations, the evidence against the British Templars was derisory, consisting of little more than a series of denials from the brothers, supplemented by hearsay and gossip from a relatively small number of outsiders. By May 1311, the frustrated inquisitors left England to report back to their masters.[42]

Ironically, the breakthrough in terms of evidence took place, presumably much to the inquisitors' chagrin, soon after their departure. In June 1311, three Templars were at last coerced into making a form of confession.

One confession came from Brother Stephen of Stapelbrugge. He had gone on the run and was vulnerable as a result – escape could be interpreted as an admission of guilt. More to the point, he was also tortured.

Another confession came from Brother Thomas Totty. Thomas had been absent for over a year, and could likewise be pressurised. He was certainly imaginative. Totty at first suggested that he had been a spy for the order and argued, in a statement uncorroborated by any other witness, that this was why he had gone on the run. After a gap of a few days, during which time Stephen of Stapelbrugge was tortured, Thomas Totty changed his story and also 'confessed'. He too had presumably been tortured in the interim. He made allegations against other British Templars, but even under torture he was careful to implicate men who were beyond reach of the inquisitors. He mentioned only those who were insane (John of Hauvile) or dead (Brian le Jay and Guy Forest).

John of Stoke, the treasurer of the New Temple, was the third man to break. He confessed on 1 July 1311. Like the other two brothers, John was vulnerable. He had been slow in coming forward to answer questions. Perhaps, as treasurer, there were also some allegations of financial misconduct hanging over him. John confessed to a series of offences, all of which followed the French confessions so closely that it was obvious that he had been heavily coached or prompted – and perhaps tortured for good measure.[43]

Despite the testimony of these three outliers, the other British Templars steadfastly refused to confess to any major defects. But, by this stage, many of them had had enough. They realised that matters were moving to an inevitable outcome and they just wanted to bring things to a quick and bloodless conclusion. Almost sixty English Templars confessed to minor infringements to get the process completed.

In return for this nominal compliance, they were given penances, to be completed in the monasteries of other orders. At the end of July 1311, in York, another twenty-four Templars were similarly reconciled with the church. In a form of words designed to get matters concluded, they personally confessed almost nothing but admitted the shame of the charges themselves.

There were two diehards in England who refused to make even such minor compromises with the truth – men who would not be bullied, however much they might be intimidated. The master, William de la More, was one. He was interrogated by some of the most senior clerics in the land, including the archbishop of Canterbury, but he steadfastly refused to make a false confession. He was sent to the Tower of London because of his obstinacy.

The other was Himbert Blanc, the preceptor of the Auvergne who had been captured while visiting England. He made a similarly robust stand and denied everything. As a result, he was sent to 'the most vile prison in double chains' until he could remember something more substantial to confess to. His fate is unknown, but he was still alive, and in custody, in February 1314.[44]

THE END

The differences in the process between France and England were shocking. This was particularly striking given that relations between the brothers in the two countries were extremely close. Both were almost certainly just as guilty – or just as innocent – as each other. The key driver of this difference was obvious: torture.

In France, where torture was routinely applied to suspects, there were almost universal confessions, and of the most explicit kind. The cliché is true – men will say anything to get the pain to stop. But in England, in the first two years of the process, there were no admissions of guilt. It was only as torture, or the threat of torture, was introduced into the process that even a few 'confessions' began to emerge from a handful of the more vulnerable brothers.

But with torture or without, there needed to be an ending. By March 1314, the papacy, under continuing pressure from the French crown, tried to bring the debilitating process to a final conclusion. Four of the most senior French Templars, including Geoffrey of Charney, the master of Normandy, and James of Molay, the grand master, all of whom had previously made confessions under torture, were brought before a special

Council in Paris. They were condemned to life imprisonment for their supposed crimes.

This was not what they had been expecting. Faced with this final humiliation and left with no further hope that sanity would prevail, James of Molay and Geoffrey of Charney retracted their spurious confessions. After seven years of imprisonment and torture, the two men decided to make a stand.

James of Molay had his faults as a leader. He had not always shown good judgement. But in his final hours he tried to make up for his mistakes. His defiance was duly punished. The two men were burned alive by the French king on the Île-des-Javiaux, still refusing to admit the trumped-up charges. As the last embers of the fires died away, 'their ashes and bones were collected as sacred relics . . . and carried away to holy places'. All 'who saw them [had] much admiration and surprise for the constancy of their death and final denial'. Personal bravery was their last substitute for hope.[45]

The end in Britain was far less dramatic. The English Templars were pensioned off but do not usually seem to have gone back to secular life. They generally served their penances out at different monasteries. Some may, in effect, have become informal Hospitallers. The houses of their old rival military order were allowed to take in two Templars to fulfil their penances, while other institutions could only take one. By 1338, it seems that just thirteen brothers were still alive and receiving a Hospitaller pension – an indictment perhaps, not just of life expectancy in the fourteenth century but also of the advanced age of many British Templars when the order was closed down.[46]

Pope Clement was eventually persuaded that the Templars were innocent, but by then it was too late. They had little real role left and were crippled by a terminally tarnished reputation. The order was wound up. Its assets were transferred to its more adaptable rival – the Hospitallers.[47]

Many of the British brothers had died in the course of their questioning. Five died in the Tower of London alone, but this was due to age and infirmity rather than torture. The shock of arrest and the discomfort of confinement doubtless did not help. But men such as Thomas Tholouse, for example, the preceptor of Upleadon, were already very old by the standards of the day. When he died in the Tower, Thomas had already served the order for forty-three years.[48]

None of the British Templars was executed. William de la More, the last master of the British Templars, passed away in captivity in London on 20 December 1312. But he died of old age rather than torture. He was still firm in his beliefs and bravely protesting the innocence of the order.

Unlike many of his comrades in the British Templar administration, William de la More was a man of action. He was a Yorkshireman and a soldier and had seen action in the East at a time when conditions there were dangerous in the extreme.

William served in the crusader city of Tripoli (now in modern Lebanon) in the period running up to its final capture by the Mamluks in April 1289. If he was still part of the garrison at the end, he somehow managed to escape the massacre that ensued. By 1294 we find him taking over the far less arduous job of Templar commander at Ewell in Kent. And with the death of Brian le Jay in 1298, William took over as British master.[49]

When he was arrested in 1308, he had already served the order for almost a quarter of a century. His service to Edward I was remembered and respected by his captors. In happier days, Edward had commended William to grand master James of Molay. He wrote fondly of the 'grateful and laudable services that William has rendered to the king and his realm . . . and for the great affection that the brethren under him are said to bear towards him, as his friendly bearing and honest conversation merit'.[50]

Death in prison was a quiet but inglorious ending for such a man. Like the order itself, he deserved far better.

17

◇

MEDIEVAL CONSPIRACIES – GUILTY AS CHARGED?

The order was gone – found guilty of the most outrageous charges.

The Templars are the subject of many modern conspiracy theories. But, even at the time, they were accused of astonishing vices and plots. Given the number of such accusations, is it possible that they were guilty of some of them? Surely there is no smoke without at least some fire?

The calf provides the answer.

At the beginning of this book we encountered calf worship by the Templars. We saw that the normally specialist pleasure of kissing a calf's anus was supposedly widespread, but only within the county of Yorkshire. In a world of crazy accusations, of licking cats and worshipping black-faced fiery demons, this seems, at first glance, to be just more of the same.

But the bovine bottoms of northern England were far more significant than that.

A WELL-TURNED CALF . . .

The interrogation of the Templars in France was not a search for truth. It was a search for incriminating evidence – and it did not matter overmuch whether that evidence was true or false.

In terms of methodology and process, the key to understanding the Templar confessions across all the provinces of Europe is to recognise that

250

they were neither spontaneous nor unprompted. Interrogation was based on responses to a series of extremely detailed (and extremely leading) questions. Significantly, these leading questions were often accompanied by torture or its credible threat.

In France, victims were told what to say and then tortured until they said it. The brothers were taken through a highly structured interrogation process that involved confessing to a wide range of outrageously implausible activities.

The charges, and the confessions, included participating in blatantly heretical and satanic initiation ceremonies; denying Christ; spitting or trampling on the crucifix (sometimes, when the inquisitor was becoming bored or excitable, this list was also extended to include urinating on the cross); worshipping idols, particularly of a pagan head; engaging in sodomy and a range of other sexual activities with women or, more commonly, with other members of the order; obscenely kissing their fellow brothers in profane masses, on the naval, on the penis, on the lips or at the base of the spine. 'Base of the spine' was usually just a more delicate way of saying 'anus'.

The list was detailed. As an informal 'questionnaire', it was repeated so often that it becomes boring to read the transcripts. More importantly, it obviously says more about the fantasy lives of their accusers than anything that had happened in reality.

The allegations were, of course, manufactured. This was hysterical nonsense, exaggerated by superstition, gullibility and greed. The notion that generations of pious volunteers, some of whom were taken from the most influential families in Europe, had failed to mention all this was stretching credulity too far.

Over a period of almost 200 years, we are expected to believe that thousands of the most entitled and devout men in Christendom had turned up for their induction programme into the Templars, only to be told on page one of the Welcome Pack that the order was in fact a satanic cult. Seen from a distance, the accusations are a joke.

There were doubtless individual transgressions. In any organisation involving the activities of thousands of different human beings, that is always going to be the case. There were occasional problems with sexual behaviour and instances of theft or fighting. All of these were mentioned, and specifically forbidden, in the Rule of the Temple, the order's operating handbook. There was an implicit recognition that transgressions were bound to happen from time to time and would be punished accordingly.

But beyond the normal vagaries and weaknesses of human behaviour, the charges were obviously trumped up. They were based on almost no evidence other than irredeemably compromised confessions wrenched from frightened men under torture.

The foundations of the charges were riddled with inconsistencies and illogicalities from top to bottom. The supposed location of many of the perverse and satanic initiation ceremonies, for instance, was in rooms of the Templars' tower complex in Paris. These rooms were shared, on a daily basis, with many of the king's lawyers and officials – the same men who were now making the case for the persecution. The idea that generations of devout royal bureaucrats, working closely with the Templars throughout their careers, had failed to notice anything untoward happening in adjacent rooms beggars belief.

But confronting the obvious absurdity of the charges brought against the Templars only serves to raise far bigger questions. *How* was it possible to make such charges stick? And, even if it were possible to do so, *why* would anyone want to?

CREATING GUILT: THE BACKSTORY OF HERESY

The inquisitors had a pretty clear idea of what they were going to find, even before the questioning had begun. They knew this because they had gone back through their records to find out what heretics got up to.

The claims of satanism and sorcery levelled against the Templars seem absurd from our perspective, but they had precedents at the time. Such accusations were a proven means of putting an opponent off-balance and, more to the point, they were tactics that worked. King Philip the Fair and his advisers were fighting dirty and they knew what kinds of fictitious details they needed to find. These were charges that had been established over time and which had achieved the spurious patina and credibility of age.

In 1233, for example, a papal list of heretical activities in Germany contained an uncannily similar set of practices. The 'heretics' were said to kiss animals and other sect members on the mouth and on the anus. A black cat then appeared, whose anus the lucky initiates also kissed. Idols were worshipped. And finally, just to round off a perfect evening, everyone took part in an orgy. Tiny practical details were added to give extra credibility. Once these 'German heretics' started going back to Mass, for instance, they were allegedly allowed to take Holy Communion – but they were, of course, expected to spit the wafer out into a toilet.

The parallels with the charges brought against the Templars are striking. It is shocking to see the cold-blooded planning that went into the process. These were not just fabricated charges – they were entirely prefabricated.

Someone was told to go back through the filing cabinet, see what was already there and make the charges up. Like lazy policemen, they just reiterated whatever it was that people expected devil worshippers to do. They may not have been the 'usual suspects', but they were certainly the 'usual charges'.[1]

And those tales were certainly there in the files if only one wanted to look for them. Suspiciously similar stories of idols, orgies and demonic animals could be found in the ecclesiastical records of previous centuries. Walter Map, archdeacon of Oxford, writing around 1182, told of heretics kissing a huge cat on the genitals and on the anus. 'When they have found him they kiss him. The hotter their feelings,' Walter wrote, clearly getting into his stride at this point, 'the lower their aim: some go for his feet, but most for his tail and privy parts.'[2]

Similarly, the bishop of Paris, William of Auvergne, wrote almost a hundred years before the trial of the Templars that the followers of Satan worshipped a cat and that they kissed the cat on its anus. Just for a change, they were also said to occasionally kiss a toad on the mouth. Even the Cathars were believed to worship a cat. Again, unimaginatively, they also had a special predilection for its anus. The suspects might be varied, but one could not accuse the inquisitors of being inconsistent.

So, when King Philip's Parisian lawyers wanted to add a bit of local colour to the charges, they needed to look no further than the traditional fantasies. They could then cut-and-paste these stories into the inquisitorial topic guide for use with tortured prisoners. Once the line of questioning was established, it could then be confirmed by forced confessions and everything else would fall into line.

This narrative also sought to associate the Templars with supposedly Islamic practices. The suggestion was that they had, in some unspecified way, been corrupted by their long-standing dealings with the Muslim states of the Middle East. Thus, the Templars could be accused of worshipping idols and dragging the crucifix along the ground – and the fictitious links with heretical and idolatrous practices could be made even stronger.

The Templars were evil. Their wealth was gained by a pact with the devil. So, the logic went, why not take that ill-gotten wealth and give it to the king of France, where it could be put to good use? A converging spiral of narrative and motivation, superstition and greed, led inexorably to the fall of the Templars.

The strategy was crude but effective. If you make the stories salacious enough, they will become high profile. If you throw enough mud, some of it will stick. And if you tell a lie, make it a big one.[3]

Torture was the other main element of the strategy. Torture is a powerful but deeply flawed way of gathering evidence. It is fine for volume. Torture someone enough and they will keep talking almost indefinitely. But if one is looking for the truth, the quality suffers profoundly.

There were legal rules about what degrees of torture were permissible. But in the case of the French Templars, torture was not only used legally, it was also systematically misused. One Templar priest in Albi testified that his feet had been burnt over a fire. 'Burnt' in this context did not just mean an uncomfortable toasting. The process was so vicious that two bones dropped out of the dead flesh in his gruesomely barbecued foot a couple of days later.

The Templars were brave. In Paris, where torture was used from the outset, thirty-six Templar brothers died rather than make false confessions. But they were not super-human. Torture of this ferocity was effective – men would eventually say whatever they thought the inquisitors wanted to hear.[4]

One French Templar, Brother Ponsard of Gizy, summed up the pros and cons of the methodology. He was very clear and disarmingly honest about the power of torture. When he appeared in front of a papal commission in November 1309, he was adamant that the charges were trumped up. They were, he said, entirely false. But he also added helpfully that, if they wanted to torture him, he would readily agree with whatever they suggested. He wanted it on the record that he would happily confess to anything.[5]

Where witnesses were able to speak freely, the results of questioning were far different. In England, Ireland, Scotland and Cyprus, for instance, where the brothers were not generally tortured or put in fear of their lives, there were almost no false confessions.

Away from the threats of the inquisitors and torturers, a very different (and far more prosaic) story emerged about the Templars. But, as a story that lends itself much less readily to lurid tales and conspiracies, it has tended to be overlooked.

THE STATE OF THE EVIDENCE

Under English law, pressurising the Templars was difficult. This meant that the net for gathering evidence had to be cast far wider. Witnesses from outside the order were persuaded to come forward, whether because of jealousy or because of petty disputes they had with the Templars or even perhaps, on occasion, because they had been paid to do so. But, however well motivated they might have been, they still produced almost no first-hand evidence against the order.[6]

This is where the Yorkshire calves (literally) rear their lovely heads and in doing so reveal not just the absurdity of the charges but also the process by which it was manufactured.

The idea of routinely kissing cats' anuses is absurd enough. But why would anyone extend this charge to the even more unlikely practice of kissing calves' bottoms? And why was it only happening in Yorkshire?

The answers to these questions show, in the absence of widespread confessions, how evidence against the order in Britain was fabricated.

All across Europe, or rather all across those parts of Europe in which torture could be used, the Templars confessed to kissing a cat's anus. As we have seen, this was a fabricated charge, based on the unimaginative prompt-ings of inquisitors who had been searching through the files to find the 'usual activities' of heretics.

But there was never any mention of calves. Cats were commonplace around medieval chapels. They were also small enough, if that was your unlikely inclination, to be conveniently introduced into satanic services. In Yorkshire, however, we do not hear of cats. Instead, they were replaced by highly incongruous and inconveniently large calves. This bizarre circumstance is mundane but profound in its implications.

It appears that an inexperienced clerk or inquisitor in Yorkshire misread the list of things that witnesses were 'supposed' to have seen. The Latin word for 'cat' (*catum*), which was introduced into interrogations in France and beyond, was probably mistranscribed as 'cattle' (*catellum*). This mistake was, coincidentally, made more plausible by the fact that many Christians in the Middle Ages believed, falsely of course, that Muslims worshipped a calf.[7]

Armed with this prompt sheet about what they were expected to have seen, the witnesses duly obliged, but they struggled to make their testi-mony fit this strange, and strangely specific, narrative.

Very creatively, one Master John of Nassington, an official based in York, said that he had been told that 'certain other knights of the county [of Yorkshire]' had been invited by the Templars to a great banquet at their commandery in Hirst. Extremely ill-advisedly for a supposedly conspiratorial order focused on devil worship, the brothers then started telling anecdotes about their evil activities.

They casually dropped into conversation with their guests that they 'had assembled there for a certain solemn feast that they used to hold, at which they adored a certain calf'. As always, master John did not claim to have been present at the dinner. This was just hearsay of the most improbable kind. But at least he had done his best. He had constructed the kind of imaginative story that the inquisitors were expecting to hear – one involving the Templars and the satanic worship of a calf.[8]

William of la Forde, the rector of the church of Crofton, about 10 miles south of the commandery at Newsham, had a similar story to tell. William said that he had been told by a fellow priest (conveniently now dead) that a Templar (also conveniently now dead) had confessed to a wide variety of sexual and heretical offences. There was a spectacular highlight to this third-hand tale. When this Templar had joined the order, William told the inquisitors, 'it was said to him that he should let down his breeches, turn his back to the crucifix, which weeping he did. Afterwards, a certain image was shown to him like a certain calf placed on a sort of altar, and he was told that he should kiss the image and venerate it, which he did.' The same Templar also told his confessor, who then told a colleague, who then told master John, that 'the brothers of the Order of the Temple had sexual relations with each other'.[9]

The misreading of *catum* for *catellum* shows that the witnesses had been carefully primed before they gave their evidence. More specifically, it demonstrates that they had even been told what to say. When 'witnesses' were told to say that they had seen a cat being worshipped, that is what they said. When a clumsy interrogator told them that they had probably seen a calf being worshipped, that was given in evidence instead.

But the need to find evidence of a 'calf' caused other problems and unforeseen consequences. What did this calf look like? Quite apart from the obviously dubious nature of the testimonies, this clearly caused deep confusion amongst the witnesses. They did not know how to describe the animal.

William of la Forde, not unnaturally, imaginatively chose to interpret it as a small statue, or perhaps a model set in a tableau – and his model calf was part of much more wide-ranging sexual misbehaviours. John of Nassington, however, was a more literally minded man. His calf was a real creature, with an equally real and well-attended anus. Given the limited and flawed brief with which they had been presented, both of these were legitimate interpretations, and both men told their own highly creative versions of the supposed events.

The stories obviously have no real value as evidence, but they show us the extent to which this entire process was a charade. It is clear that, in the absence of confessions, disgruntled neighbours were just lined up to perjure themselves and read out semi-scripted accusations.

The hearsay nature of the evidence produced in this way was still embarrassingly underwhelming, however. We know, by comparing manuscripts, that the evidence was later changed in an attempt to make it appear more incriminating. The testimony of one of the Yorkshire witnesses was altered to attribute it to the Templars themselves, rather than to third-hand gossip, thus turning it into a 'confession'.

In this later, doctored, version of the testimony, the story of the Yorkshire calves was recorded as having been given 'by two brothers of the Temple in England. The first says that they adored a certain calf, the second that a certain commander and brothers received by him adored an idol, also, a certain other cleric testifies about the adoration of the calf.' Every attempt was being made to distort the evidence and smear the order.[10]

Interestingly, the 'Case of the Yorkshire Calf-Kissing' was not the only instance in which a mundane mistranscription was to have significant consequences during interviews. The charge sheet in France was originally drawn up to investigate the 'suspicious' secrecy of the order. Specifically, it focused on the supposed way in which meetings were held at night (*de nocte*). In England, however, the text was mistakenly transcribed as being *de vocte* – that is, 'devotedly'. This inevitably led to some tortuous (and entirely irrelevant) discussions.[11]

The importance of the Yorkshire calves lies not in the facts presented in the stories (there were none) but in what they tell us about the process of gathering evidence and, more generally, what they tell us about the suppression of the Templars as a whole. The process only became transparent because of a laughable mistranslation and the equally laughable attempts on behalf of witnesses to live up to the expectations of the inquisitors.

The incompetence was so ridiculous that it would be amusing under different circumstances. But it was also evidence of a far darker side: it shows the lengths to which the inquisitors were prepared to go to convict the British Templars.

THE ENEMY WITHIN

Calf molestation was not the only accusation made against the order in Britain. Other charges were more vague but, on the surface at least, more plausible.

One such charge was that of aiding and abetting the enemy.

The underlying idea was that the Templars had become so immersed in the politics of the Middle East that they conspired with the local Muslim authorities to further their own interests – that the order had lost its way and somehow become 'traitors to Christendom'.

The origins of this claim dated back to the middle of the twelfth century, not long after the full militarisation of the order. There were always tensions between those who visited the Holy Land as crusaders and those westerners who lived there. The latter, frequently of mixed race, were often dismissively referred to by crusaders as '*pulani*'.

Crusaders came looking for action and glory. Western settlers, on the other hand, had a far better understanding of the local situation. They were generally more measured and cautious in approach – they knew what was realistic and what might lead to disaster. As a result they were often seen as cowardly and 'effeminate' by their comrades from the West. Similarly, crusaders were essentially military tourists and, like all tourists, they occasionally behaved extremely badly. When they left, the local Franks had to pick up the pieces and face the prospect of retaliation.

Under these circumstances, relations between the two groups were often difficult. This was particularly true when things went wrong and a scapegoat needed to be found. The Templars, as the military elite of the crusader states, were often caught in the middle of such tensions. Although they had a provincial network back in Europe, they were fully embedded within the military and political life of the Middle East. They even had their own extensive networks of spies and diplomatic contacts.

Under normal circumstances this was a great advantage for the crusader states. When campaigns began to unravel, however, as was frequently the case with the outnumbered crusader armies, they often took the blame – it was easy to throw accusations at the all-too-fully acclimatised Templars and their suspiciously sophisticated relationships with the local Muslim states.

As the siege of Damascus ground to a potentially disastrous conclusion in 1148, for instance, the Templars and the local nobility worked hard to extricate the crusader army from a situation in which they faced almost certain annihilation. Gratitude for their actions, however, came only in the form of outlandish accusations of treachery. The face-saving device of choice for a failed expedition to the Holy Land was to come home and blame the Templars and the local '*pulani*' for their perfidy.[12]

Having a sophisticated approach to dealing with the enemy did not always endear the Templars to bluff military visitors – men profoundly unencumbered by any insight into the nuances of eastern politics or warfare. But the claims of grand 'treachery' made against the order are relatively easily countered.

Muslim sources inevitably revelled in any act that revealed signs of Christian disunity. They were quick to boast of instances of treachery or apostasy. With the Templars, however, there were no such stories. Far from being seen as collaborators by their enemies, thirteenth-century Muslim historians used the word 'Templar' as a touchstone for loyalty and fanatical military excellence. When the Mamluks defeated the crusader armies of King Louis IX, the victors were described as being so fierce that they could be called the 'Templars of Islam' (*Dawiyat al-Islam*).[13]

The reputation of the military orders in Muslim chronicles was that of being strong and consistent in their fighting capabilities. In their eyes, the Templars were the foremost enemies of Islam, soldiers in charge of the most threatening castles and men to be butchered when captured. Visiting crusaders may have sought solace for their failures. But the Muslim enemy knew exactly who their most dangerous and incorruptible foes were.[14]

There were other, more insidious claims associated with the accusation of 'treachery', however. One of the criticisms levelled against the Templars in England was that their leaders had deliberately sent awkward men over-seas to die – men who did not want to become part of a satanic cult, for instance, but who were presumably too shy to mention it to their friends and relatives. The accusations were made by four witnesses, but it is telling that these extraordinary charges were only made by non-Templars – and it is clear that these accusers suffered from a fundamental (and possibly wilful) misunderstanding of the nature of the order.[15]

One of the witnesses, a Carmelite friar named Robert of Maidenesford, said that he had been told by a servant, who remained conveniently anonymous, that because a brother 'did not agree to their cursed profession he was sent secretly to overseas regions and there was killed by those to whom he was sent'. But Robert was no ordinary cleric – he was clearly a disreputable character and was later outlawed in Towcester for his role in a murder conspiracy. The imaginative Carmelite was allegedly party to a plot to burn a man to death in an oven.[16]

Two jealous Dominican friars testified that troublesome British Templars were given sealed letters to take out to the East. Highly dramatically, the contents of these letters were later found to include instructions that the recipient should kill the bearer. But this hearsay was just a variation on an old trope, common in medieval romantic literature. It eventually found a suitably dramatic and equally factual home in Shakespeare's *Hamlet*.

Finally, a Franciscan friar from London, John of Bercia, made a similar accusation. He claimed that he 'knew a certain knight called Walter le Sauvage of the household of the late Earl Warenne [John de Warenne who died in 1304] . . . who having entered the Order of the Templars was banished and carried away so far within two years that neither the Earl, although he inquired, nor his other friends could find what had been done with him'.[17]

Evidentially, this was extremely slim pickings. But there were two germs of truth, which may have led to such tales being circulated.

Some British criminals had indeed been sent out to the East as part of their punishment or penance – but this was not specific to the Templars and does not seem to be what the order was accused of at the trials. And it is certainly true that the fate of some of the brothers who had gone to the Holy Land on active service remained unknown.

Across such distances and in an era of only rudimentary communication, this was inevitable. Men who were taken prisoner might be executed, be sold into slavery or languish in captivity for decades. In the absence of any equivalent of the Red Cross they might, from a practical perspective, just 'disappear'. This must have been extremely painful for the men's families. Their grief and resentment are entirely understandable.[18]

But the nature of these witnesses is telling. As far as we know, none of them had ever set foot in the East and their accounts were based on rumour and hearsay. Significantly, those warriors who had fought alongside them in the Holy Land and who would have been able to provide credible testimony against the order were absent. Veteran crusaders or men such as their arch-rivals, the Hospitallers, refused to bear false witness.

Of course British Templars were sent abroad, very possibly to die in defence of Christendom – that is, after all, what they had signed up to do. Far from being a 'crime', maintaining the flow of reinforcements out to the Holy Land was a major part of the function of the western provinces of the order. The need for such reinforcements was unremitting.[19]

The levels of overseas service are hard to determine but it is certainly not surprising that many men did not come back. Most brothers were not questioned about it during their interrogation and did not spontaneously raise it as a subject. Of the twenty-seven Templars across western Europe who did mention it, however, almost all had served abroad, perhaps indicating, not surprisingly for a military order, that being transferred to the East was commonplace.[20]

Many British Templars died in the East. Each death was a tragedy for them and their families, but they were volunteers and that was their job. The British houses were entirely correct to send their men to the crusader states to help fill the ranks. The fact that eccentric accusations such as this were made at all, and ostensibly taken seriously, shows the depths to which their inquisitors were reduced.[21]

In the absence of real evidence, or real crimes, they were just scraping the barrel.

GREEDY AND AVARICIOUS?

Then, as now, when people mentioned the Templars their minds often turned to the prospect of treasure. And it was only a short step from the idea of treasure to the sins of greed and avarice.

After their fall, the legend of 'Templar greed' and the riches that it generated became commonplace. Historians ever since have bought into this trope. As one fifteenth-century Dominican theologian commented, 'They had fallen into many vices because of their great wealth.'[22]

Ironically, for an order founded on the principle of poverty, the idea that the Templars were fabulously rich goes back to its origins. This was not entirely irrational. They were given substantial privileges, tax breaks and properties with which to fund the defence of the Holy Land.

The money for crusading had to come from somewhere. Other members of the clergy were inevitably disadvantaged by Templar privileges and particularly by the tithes this diverted away from their own coffers. The properties and tax breaks were similarly unpopular to varying degrees. Everyone wanted to recover the Holy Land. But not everyone wanted to pay for it.

It is not difficult to see how the legends grew. There were times when the two enticing but distinctly different ideas of 'treasure-hoards' and 'crusading' impinged on each other. English crusades were glamourised and part of that glamour was attached to stories of the treasure the men took with them to the East. This was certainly the case, for instance, with the expeditions of 1227, 1240 and 1290. Beyond the expenses involved, however, which were naturally considerable, almost all these tales of 'Templar treasure' were pure fantasy.

Part of the criticism focused on what the order did (or rather did not do) with their supposed riches. Why, it was asked, did the order not do more in terms of charitable giving or offering hospitality to those in need?

The alleged lack of charitable giving or hospitality was routinely denied by the Templar brothers, however. Most pointed out that 10 per cent of the bread baked in a Templar house was allocated for charity and that further gifts of meat, clothing and money were also made to the poor. Hospitality was not a core obligation of the order, unlike their rival order, the Hospitallers, but it was often said during the Templar trials that it was freely given, nonetheless.[23]

And, far from covertly hoarded 'secret treasure', the property owned by the British Templars was very carefully documented – partly by the order itself in records such as the 'Inquest' of 1185, but also, as the Templars were closed down, by third parties. The royal keepers of the confiscated lands produced detailed annual accounts and any expenses they incurred were recorded in the royal Pipe Rolls. An initial inventory of the British Templars' assets was also made by royal officials in January 1308, when the brothers were first arrested, and yet another inventory was ordered to be made a year later, on 4 March 1309. Any satanic idols or secret treasures were not going to remain secret for long.[24]

But the accounts show that the personal possessions of the Templars were, despite the lurid accusations, surprisingly simple. At the British order's headquarters in London, we find that the king's men seized only a few sets of clothes and wall coverings; two crossbows and a few swords; two books and some sundry iron forks and firestands. Of precious metals there were none, with the poignant exception of the property of one Brother Richard of Herdwick, who, rather churlishly under the circumstances, had his two silver cups and twelve silver spoons confiscated.

Much the same situation was repeated across Britain, doubtless to the disappointment of the bailiffs. At the Templar house of Kilcloggan in County Wexford, for instance, there were a few items of furniture and some stored food. The church was found to be well equipped, as one might expect, with vestments and some silver plate. But there were no great riches – merely a normal religious establishment. Any hidden treasure remained just that – firmly hidden.[25]

There were, indeed, some valuables to be found within their preceptories. But these were 'valuables' of a kind that generally have far less obvious appeal to modern audiences. On the contrary, they were largely pious items, in direct contradiction of the other charges of heresy.

At the chapel of the preceptory of Bisham in Berkshire, for instance, there were many books, some valuable. Doubtless the brothers were very proud of these. But there was nothing whatsoever to suggest any idolatry. The less than exciting contents of their small library included a large, two-volume book of saints' legends and stories; a martyrology; a psalter; four copies of the Gospels; and a book with the office of the Blessed Mary. This deeply conservative book collection was supplemented by the appropriate religious objects – crosses, relics, candlestick holders and so on.

These were the possessions of a prosperous and decidedly orthodox religious community, with no evidence of the garish totems of a devil-worshipping cult. There was no sign of anything more racy or controversial, either in terms of value or of doctrine. The inquisitors and money men (like modern conspiracists) were disappointed at the lack of rich pickings.

Even the New Temple headquarters were a major disappointment for the bailiffs. True, the quality of the relics to be found there was impressive, but it was difficult to put a monetary value on such items. Some of the relics strained credulity, even amongst those who were motivated to find value in them. As befitted a military order, the chapel had, in pride of place, the sword with which, allegedly, Henry II's knights had killed Thomas Becket. Not all were entirely convinced, however, and the provenance of the relic was not being oversold – the sword was merely described as being Becket's murder weapon, 'as it is said'. Similarly, and perhaps suspiciously to the more cynical, there were no less than two crucifixes which were said to contain the wood on which Jesus Christ was crucified.

There were certainly a number of valuables held in the vestry but nothing out of the ordinary for the provincial headquarters of a major religious order – rich furnishings, of course, and beautiful fabrics, some reliquaries, ivory and high-quality silverwork. But again, little beyond that which might be described as 'rich-pious'.[26]

Was there any hidden treasure? The inventories of the British Templars' goods show no hoards of money or jewels, no idols, nothing really out of the ordinary. A total of fifty-three silver spoons were mentioned in the inventories, six of which were at the convalescent home in Denney. This amounted to one spoon for every two Templars arrested – hardly a treasure trove.[27]

Despite a complete lack of any evidence, some have tried to argue that this merely indicates the brothers had time to hide their treasures and other secret goods before the king's men arrested them. Interestingly however, in France, where the order was taken completely by surprise, similarly no treasures were found. The reason was simple – there were none.

A SECRET CULT?

At the risk of appearing overly literal, it is perhaps worth stating the obvious. A secret satanic cult requires, above all else . . . secrecy.

But the Templars were never an enclosed order, shut off from the rest of society. On the contrary, even as third-party witnesses condemned the Templars for being secretive, the context of their testimony often made it clear that the order was well integrated within most echelons of society. Witness statements confirmed that outsiders were regularly invited into Templar houses and chapels. The brothers were happy to chat, gossip or to engage in business just like other men of their class.

The Templars were not devoted to charitable works – their focus was on warfare in the defence of Christendom. But they often offered hospitality to travellers, nonetheless. The evidence of such hospitality suggests that, far from being secretive, the order was actually more engaged with the outside world than most other religious communities.

Many commanderies, such as those at Garway, Eagle and Bruer, offered hospitality to outsiders. One friar, for instance, mentioned that when he and a comrade stayed at the preceptory in Flaxfleet they were lodged adjacent to the Templars' dormitory and not in a separate guest house, as would have been more normal. This was far more welcoming, and inclusive, than one would have expected.

The Templars, like most religious orders, certainly held some 'secret' meetings, but this was, they said, because during those sessions the brothers confessed their sins or talked about transgressions against the Rule of the order – these discussions were naturally undertaken in private.

Testimonies at the trials demonstrate that, far from being withdrawn, the Templars were in close contact with other parts of society and led a much more sociable existence than one might expect from monks. Many non-Templars worked, and sometimes even lived, in the order's houses, whether as servants or as secular priests. They would surely have spotted if the order had decided to focus on devil worship and idolatry rather than mainstream Christianity.[28]

This level of public access is corroborated by other evidence given in the trials. One witness statement given with regard to the Templar commandery at Sandford, for example, makes clear that non-Templars were allowed into the order's chapel there – they were only prohibited on special occasions. Perhaps even more surprisingly, there is also evidence that outsiders were occasionally even allowed to attend full chapter meetings, including sessions at the New Temple in London and in Paris.[29]

If the brothers were trying to run a secret society, they were doing a spectacularly bad job of it.

THE 'SECRETS' OF THE NEW TEMPLE

The headquarters of the British Templars provides a compelling case study for assessing the levels of secrecy that were actually enforced by the Templars.

Soon after they were established in Britain, the brothers had built a church and chapter house just outside the western walls of London at Holborn – it later became known, unimaginatively, as the Old Temple. The Holborn church was sold in 1161 and the order moved to far more prestigious accommodation – a large precinct just to the south of their old chapter house, called the New Temple, well placed on the road out of London to Westminster and with its own frontage on the Thames. The changing real estate was a tangible manifestation of their changing status, both as an increasingly important military power in the Latin East and as a more influential player in the government of Britain.

The New Temple had the walls, the money and the treasure boxes that have helped to create 'the Templar legend'. And yet, as with so much of the mythology, almost nothing was what it seemed. Despite the over-elaborate

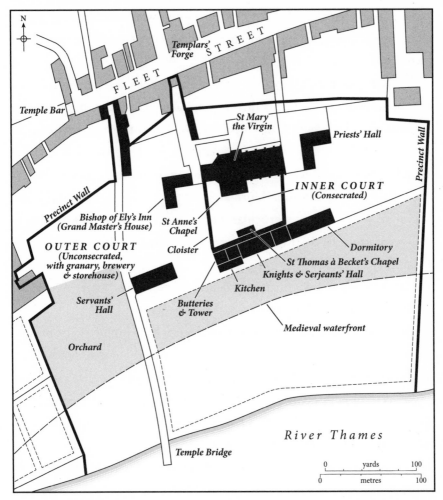

5. The New Temple, London *c.* 1250, possible reconstruction (After Nicholson 2010 (II) and Gatti 2005)

conspiracies with which the order and the New Temple have been associated, their headquarters were a remarkably public place.

The precinct was indeed one of the most important financial centres in Britain, but it was not just used for Templar money. It was used by the kings and bishops of England, and even by the more affluent citizens of London, as a place to store their treasure. It was the medieval equivalent of a safety deposit warehouse. Numerous legal documents were witnessed, signed and stored there – lawyers habitually used it as a storage facility.

Loan agreements often specified that the money would be liable for repayment at the New Temple and so too did bills of exchange issued by merchants.

The Templar buildings in the new precinct housed so many valuable and incriminating documents that in times of civil disorder they became a target in their own right. On 13 June 1381, for instance, participants in what later became known as the 'Peasants' Revolt' burned down the Templar buildings which, after the dissolution of the order several decades earlier, had morphed into an informal version of the Public Records Office. The offices attracted the particular attention of the angry rebels because they were eager to destroy evidence of the restrictive land tenancies to which they objected.

But it was not just financial clients, lawyers and rioters who were attracted to the New Temple.

Even today, Templar sites in Britain tend to have public rights of way, often very ancient routes, running through them – these were not isolated or secretive places. As if to ensure that any vestiges of conspiracy were made even more difficult, there even seems to have been a thoroughfare going through the middle of the Temple precinct – the citizens of London had a right of way down to the river.

This right of way, which was said to have existed for 'time out of mind', was not just used by pedestrians: it was also a lane for transporting goods down to a wharf. It is evident that the supposedly most secure and private site owned by the order, their headquarters in Britain, had what was, in effect, a public road running through the middle of it.

The public were walking in and out of the precinct almost all the time. A London notary named Nicholas of Hynton casually mentioned that he had been invited into the New Temple for a drink by one of the Templar brothers. This was just an aside. Nicholas was not trying to make a point. Invitations such as this seem to have been entirely normal and unremarkable – hardly what one would expect at the headquarters of an ultra-secretive band of heretical sorcerers.[30]

The church of the New Temple was also generally open to the public for prayer. We know from the trial testimonies and later legal documents that outsiders such as members of the local community could attend mass there. Pilgrims and other visitors were allowed in to see the relics.

The New Temple was a vibrant and very public centre for finance and worship, law and government – the very antithesis of a malevolent nest of conspiracies, devil worship or secret societies.[31]

ENTRY INTO THE 'TEMPLAR CULT'

Another supposedly covert aspect of the order was the accusation that admission to the Templars was a secretive affair. Admission ceremonies were of particular interest to the inquisitors – this was imagined to be the moment when devout and enthusiastic volunteers would be introduced to the idea that the order was (obviously) just a front for satanic worship.[32]

The accusation is absurd on so many levels that it is hard to know where to start. Far from being secretive, the evidence suggests quite the opposite: admissions ceremonies seem to have been joyful family celebrations rather than sinister occult services.

Across western Europe, young recruits usually joined the Templar house closest to their homes. Their devout and often influential families would have been close at hand if there had been anything even remotely untoward to report, eager to support their sons in revealing any trace of heresy.

It is true that many men had indeed joined the order and later left. Sometimes this was because of misdemeanours, or sometimes because they did not take to the rigours of Templar life. But these men, often disgruntled and with every reason to hold a grudge, told no tales of satanism or heresy.[33]

In Britain, admission to the Templars seems to have taken the form of an initial service in a public area, in which the volunteer's friends and family could participate. It then concluded with vows being taken in a more private ceremony in the adjacent chapel. This was presumably followed by celebrations and farewells with well-wishers – at which point we are expected to believe that none of the new brothers bothered to mention that they had just become devil worshippers.

Significantly, the responsibility for closing the doors to the chapel for the second ('secretive') part of the ceremony, was given to an individual who held the office of *claviger* (literally, a key holder). But we know that even the claviger might be an outsider. One holder of the office, Hugh of Tadcaster, explicitly mentioned that he had held the position *before* he became a brother knight. And at the Templar commandery in Flaxfleet, a local Friar explained that he and other people (probably the proud members of the initiates' families) were waiting out in the hall next to the chapel during admission, before all going in together to celebrate mass.[34]

Most compellingly, and most obviously, however, was the lack of complaint from the new entrants to the order. New knights joined because they were 'inspired by zeal for the orthodox faith, [and] have made their profession in the order of the Temple, remaining in it until the end of their lives. If such men had known, seen or heard', one Templar said to the papal commissioners in Paris, 'of anything dishonest in the order of the Temple, especially the so detestable insults and blasphemies to the name of Jesus Christ, they would have cried out against them and revealed everything to the whole world.'[35]

His logic was unarguable.

A CATALOGUE OF IDOLATRY?

The most headline-grabbing charges laid against the Templars (and one of the reasons why they continue to feature strongly in the highly competitive world of modern conspiracy theories) were those of satanism – the accusation that, instead of being brave and orthodox monks, they were devil worshippers and heretics.

But perhaps the most stunning proof of Templar innocence is the biggest single piece of evidence that was *not* produced at the trial: the inventory of goods owned by the order. The most spectacular evidence in the suppression of the Templars was never produced in court, precisely because it was so compelling.

On the day that the order was dissolved in France, an inventory was ordered to be made of all their possessions. The brothers had, of course, no warning of their impending suppression and no idea that the inventory was going to take place. All their idols would still have been in their treasuries and chapels. All the other items used for their devil worship would similarly be in situ. And, of course, there would be a marked lack of standard Christian symbolism and treasured items.

The motive for creating an inventory was largely financial in nature – it was going to be a register of the windfall that Philip the Fair hoped to make. But it was also going to provide incontrovertible evidence at the trial. The satanic practices of the order would be on display. Their idols would be there for all to see. The Templars' heresy would be proved beyond doubt.

Except it never worked out that way. The inventories were thorough – fastidiously so. But they were not brought forward at the trial. Why, given the compelling and very tangible nature of the evidence they provided, was this not so?

The inventory began in the king of France's lands on 13 October 1307, immediately after the order had been suppressed. The Templars had no time to destroy any of their secret statues or hide their idols – surprise was total. The inventories were ordered to be completed on the same day as the arrests. This was not always possible, as they often took longer than a single day to complete, but the element of surprise was generally achieved. All the buildings and rooms were listed, together with – importantly – all of the movable goods within them.

Many of the inquests and searches started, not surprisingly, in the chapels of each of the local Templar commanderies. This was where valuables were normally kept. It was here, at the sites of their supposed religious crimes, that the most incriminating evidence would be found.

But the results were hugely disappointing for the inquisitors. There were many liturgical books, but all of them were orthodox. Surprisingly, if the charges were true, there was no hint in writing of any satanic worship. There were crosses – large and small, precious and valueless – but, again, all were normal items of Christian devotion. Interestingly, all the crosses were in suspiciously good condition. This was a particularly embarrassing finding, given that new entrants to the order were supposedly forced to trample on the crucifix and then urinate on it.

There were relics and precious reliquaries to put them in. There were many images of the Virgin Mary. But what was missing from the inventories – and this was why they were never produced as evidence in the French courts – were idols. Nothing resembling the pagan idols of 'Maguineth' or 'Baphomet' could be found, because they did not exist.[36]

Physical evidence of devil worship in Britain likewise was non-existent. The meticulous catalogues of possessions reveal nothing more than the pious reliquaries and other devotional aids that one would expect to find in one of the less academically gifted holy orders.

It is true that there were a few discrepancies in the answers given by the brothers in Britain, and these were sometimes pounced upon as indications of heresy. But the reason for those discrepancies was prosaic rather than conspiratorial – and it arose because of the unique characteristics of a career in the Templar order.

The example of a high-flying brother such as Robert of Sablé, grand master of the entire order and admiral to King Richard I, is clearly unusual. But it does provide clues to the career progression of the British Templars as they rose through the order. As we have seen, in the run-up to the Third Crusade, Robert went from being a secular knight and soldier, to admiral, to royal diplomat, all in quick succession. He then became a Templar brother knight and took on the leadership of the entire order within a matter of months. In a time of crisis, military decisions needed to be taken extremely quickly.

The Templars were, of course, unusual in aspiring to the qualities of both monk and soldier. This was reflected in many aspects of their life in the order and is deeply suggestive of the special nature of their calling. Most monastic orders, for instance, were conscious that a life of celibacy and prayer was not always easy – they knew that some new recruits would not adapt easily to the rigours of their new life. An extended probationary period was therefore quite normal amongst most monastic orders. Not so with the Templars, however.

Even on a good day, the fighting arm of the order was short of men. When things went badly, as they had in the Latin East in the late 1180s, the fighting Templars could almost be wiped out in a matter of weeks. Reinforcements were often needed extremely quickly. British recruits could find themselves immersed in the order and thrown into combat all within a few short weeks.

And even though Robert of Sablé's introduction into the ranks of the warrior monks was exceptionally meteoric, it was not uniquely so. We know, for instance, that the chamberlains of the Templar houses of Newsham and Eagle were both relatively new recruits when they were arrested in 1308 – one had been in the order for just a few weeks. The commander of Garway, a vital preceptory on the Welsh marches, had similarly been in the order for only three years when the suppression took place, and even the commander of the headquarters at New Temple in London had been a Templar for just five years.[37]

The brothers' high mortality rates and the relatively short lengths of time in post go a long way towards providing a more rational explanation for something that has often excited the imagination of modern-day conspiracists. Why did so many Templar brothers give only vague responses when they were being questioned during the suppression of the order? What were they trying to hide? Why could the British brothers not bring themselves to talk more definitively about the minutiae of Templar regulations or religious practices?

The answer, disappointingly for today's internet warriors, is mundane in the extreme. Far from being deliberately evasive or trying to cover up heretical practices, many brothers were soldiers who were still relatively new recruits. However helpful they were trying to be, many of the men simply did not know the right answers.[38]

Ignorance, rather than heresy, was the root of the problem.

SEXUAL PREDATORS?

In the thirteenth century, there was a popular association between heresy and homosexuality. This seems strange to our eyes, but it did have its own twisted logic – both were interpreted as examples of extreme (and extremely anti-social) lifestyles. Under these circumstances, it is not surprising to find that the accusations of Templar heresy were accompanied by suggestions of sodomy.

Charges of homosexuality were among the accusations thrown at the order from the very beginning. King Philip's 'order of arrest', dated 14 September 1307 (before the Templars had even been taken into custody), was at pains to point out that the brothers were 'comparable to the beasts of the field, deprived of a sense of reason, even more, going further in their lack of a sense of reason through its astounding bestiality'. Admission to the order involved, according to the king, 'a horrific and frightening coupling'. Homophobia and talk of '*bougrerie*', or buggery, was at the heart of the Templar trials.

All Templars were questioned about homosexual acts but none admitted any personal guilt. Under torture, many of the French brothers claimed that they knew of homosexual acts that had taken place within the order, but – suspiciously, and almost without exception – they claimed not to have seen anything or to have participated themselves.

Sodomy is explicitly mentioned in the Rule of the Templars as being completely unacceptable; the offence was punishable by expulsion or life imprisonment. The grand master, James of Molay, said that he was not aware of any such activity, but added (entirely accurately) that if it had taken place, known culprits would have been thrown out of the order.[39]

These accusations were deeply ironic. As we have seen, although the order was supposed to be a hotbed of homosexuality, secrecy and conspiracy, the Templar houses were far more in touch with their local communities than most other religious institutions. Their employees and tenants far outnumbered the Templar brothers themselves. Indeed, many of these employees were women and, although the British Templars took vows of celibacy, many women lived in and around the British Templar houses.[40]

There were limits, of course, in theory at least. The brothers were not allowed to have women perform more personal duties, such as washing their hair – these might presumably lead both parties into areas of temptation. But, on an everyday basis, interactions with women were frequent and, as far as we know, generally amicable. At their Flaxfleet house in Yorkshire, for instance, there were many female employees, including no less than twelve women who milked the ewes in the spring and early summer.

It seems that most, if not all, the British houses employed women – as cooks, as maids or as help around the farms. Interestingly, and very presciently, the Templars were equal-opportunity employers. They seem to have avoided the gender pay differentials that remain an issue in many instances even today – female cooks were paid the same as their male equivalents doing the same job.[41]

The issue of celibacy was never entirely clear-cut. Given the urgent need for new recruits and the inevitable lack of enthusiasm for sexual abstinence amongst the younger members of the British warrior classes, this was not surprising – the pressure was always going to be in the direction of exceptions.

Some brothers (those known as *milites ad terminum*, which might perhaps be translated as 'temporary knights') could join for limited periods of time rather than having to take vows in perpetuity. And the Templar

Rule, or statute book, of 1129, for instance, explicitly stated that married knights were able to enter the order for limited periods. Just for good measure, there were even equal-opportunity ways in which a married man and his wife could both join the Templars together – the couple merely had to apply as 'associates' to get joint status.

Embarrassingly for all concerned, several married women turned up at the Church Council of London during the suppression of the order. They asked, not unreasonably, if their husbands could be returned to them, given that the order was now being wound up. Rather peevishly, the Council refused. Many must have noted the irony – the presence of female partners was hardly indicative of a widespread, institutionalised culture of homosexuality.[42]

One can never pretend to fully know the sexual inclinations of others. It would be strange if same-sex acts did not occasionally take place within such a group of young military men. But is clear that homosexuality within the Templars, as with other religious orders, was seen as an offence and was actively discouraged.[43]

A BITTER 'RETIREMENT'

Refuting the accusations and contemporary conspiracy theories still leaves one last question, however. If the Templar order was innocent, then why was it suppressed?

Closing down the order was a multi-layered affair. Money and land made the process desirable. Arrogance made it easier. But it was redundancy that made it possible.

Guilt, or even the appearance of guilt, was just a legal nicety. Until June 1311, when torture was finally deployed in some of the British interrogations, there were no confessions. The obvious implication is that the charges were false – and, if they were false in Britain, they were probably equally spurious in other parts of the order.

Greed and credulity certainly had a large part to play. The Templars' riches (real in the case of their property portfolios and largely imaginary in the case of treasure or money) were undoubtedly attractive to those who thought they were well positioned to inherit it. But the final key to understanding the suppression of the Templars lies in their role – or, rather, lack of role.

It is no coincidence that, while the Templars had a useful role to play in defending the Latin East, no one accused them of anything substantive – certainly nothing remotely like the charges that were eventually brought against them.

The other military orders had been subjected to a few wild accusations, but these were widely – and correctly – assumed to be politically motivated. The Teutonic Knights had been accused of witchcraft by some of their opponents. The Hospitallers, who still exist today, had had false accusations of heresy hurled at them. Ironically, it was only the Templars, famously devout and disciplined in their approach, who had been left relatively unsullied.

But the order had not responded flexibly to the challenges of the time.

The Hospitallers had made major efforts after the loss of the Latin East in 1291 to renew their strategy and develop a more appropriate set of corporate objectives. They quickly started building a substantial military base in Rhodes and established naval patrols around the eastern Mediterranean. At the same time they also fell back on their original duties of looking after the sick. The other major military order, the Teutonic Knights, slipped easily into a crusading role on Europe's other eastern front – fighting pagan Prussia.

Only the Templars were left – underemployed and unfocused. Arrogance and a lack of imagination meant that they had been slow to adapt to the new world order. They continued to advocate boots-on-the-ground action in the Middle East to try to liberate the Holy Land once more. But this was their only idea, and it was far too ambitious and unrealistic – no one was buying what they had to sell. No European ruler believed that the Middle East could be reconquered, let alone held indefinitely, given the huge demographic and logistical problems involved.

The Templars were doubtless guilty of occasional arrogance and many minor misdemeanours. But their real 'crime' was that of redundancy. Critically, unlike the other military orders, they had not moved quickly enough to find an alternative role. They had failed to justify their continued existence. And now it was too late.

18

❖

MODERN CONSPIRACIES – DREAMS NEVER END

The solemn temples, the great globe itself,
Yea, all which it inherit, shall dissolve,
And like this insubstantial pageant faded,
Leave not a rack behind. We are such stuff
As dreams are made on.
Prospero, *The Tempest*

The Temple dissolves.

Dreams are cast on its ethereal remains.

But the British Templars are now a dream to be retold as any number of nightmares and paranoid imaginings. The absurd accusations and conspiracy theories of the fourteenth century have multiplied rather than dying out.

The once proud and dedicated order has become a blank page torn from a lurid novel. Blank because a lack of context, and a lack of hard evidence, allows us to write anything we want upon it. And lurid because of the vast number of baseless, almost laughable charges that have been thrown at them.

One of the best definitions of a pub bore, and I write this from bitter experience, is the amount of time it takes before the conversation – or, rather, monologue – turns to the Templars. They love them. If the order had not already existed, pub bores would have had to invent them – and, in some ways, given the absurd image the Templars currently have, that is exactly what they have done.[1]

The Templars have found their own seedy home in some of the darker corners of popular culture. They have also become a mainstay of cheap TV and take their place alongside the other stalwarts of the genre – sharks, Nazis and zombies.

Popular culture caricatures them in a variety of bizarre ways. Each would be unrecognisable to the brother knights – as hoarders and treasure hunters; as irrational fanatics; as evil Assassins; as members of arcane cults and secret societies; or even (and this is the ultimate absurdity, given that they were all devout Catholics) as devil worshippers.

The legends that arose after their dissolution – the conspiracy theories, the imagined links to other organisations such as the freemasons or the Illuminati – grotesquely overshadow and tarnish their true achievement.

ALL OUR SECRET DREAMS

The conspiracy theories associated with the Templars are highly tenuous at the best of times. But there is one elephant-sized point that is often over-looked. If the Templars were innocent (and, as we have seen, they almost certainly were), most of the foundations for conspiracies disappear entirely. They were not satanists, so there are no real links to the occult. They did not have huge riches, so there are no real links to treasure hoards. And so on.

None of this stops the conspiracy industry, however. Evidence is not the true arbiter of debate. The Templar mythology has much in common with the recently manufactured discussions about the authorship of Shakespeare's plays. The interesting issue is not 'who wrote Shakespeare?' (correct answer: he did) but, rather, why would anybody ask the question in the first place.[2]

The occult has been a perennial ingredient in this mythology. Charges of occultism were a central part of the French crown's attempts to discredit the order, if only because magic and sorcery were becoming closely associated with heresy in the early thirteenth century. The stories that emerged dated back to earlier centuries – some of the more esoteric, such as those that can be traced back to the tale of Perseus and the Gorgon, stretched back into early antiquity. The Templars have long provided a historically tangible link (albeit a largely spurious one) to more fanciful and ephemeral lines of thought. The accusations of orgies and sodomy play well to the magical role expected of the order, as does, far more obviously, the worship of idols and satanic familiars.[3]

Conspiracy, secrets and the supposed ability to control events serves, in our imaginations at least, to push the order into the realms of magic and beyond. It makes for an easy convergence with other groups with similar characteristics (real or imagined), such as Cathars, Illuminati or Assassins. The Templars provide both a blank canvas and a 'code', a secret solution, to the confusion of our everyday lives.

The internet is the obvious driver of such conspiracies in our own time. But the tradition of Templar false histories vastly predates it. The eighteenth century was a turning point. Freemasonry had begun to take off. There was a need to explain the origins of the new movement in suitably impressive and mysterious ways. This called for a grand, albeit spurious, backstory – something that linked them, for reasons of snobbishness, with the knightly classes of the Middle Ages. But it also needed to be a story with a whiff of magic, a dash of arcane knowledge and a huge helping of secrecy. The Templars were a perfect match.

In the 1760s, the German Freemasons began to retrofit, for the first time, their supposed links with the Templars. The order, it was claimed, had long been a centre for secret wisdom and profound magical insights. Luckily, just before he was arrested, James of Molay was able to package up all this information and pass it on to his successor. This new 'master' and hence the Templar order itself were thus (in the story at least) the ancestors of modern freemasonry.

We can only guess what James of Molay, one of the least imaginative of men, would have made of all this. He would undoubtedly be shocked to hear of a continuing association of the order with blasphemous activity – and the story is, of course, completely unencumbered by evidence.[4]

The new media of the early nineteenth century was the next breakthrough point. The social structure of western Europe was falling apart in the wake of the French Revolution. The idea that such cataclysmic change was unguided or accidental was far too frightening. Instead, it was more emotionally satisfying to blame the upheavals on conspiracies, secret societies and cults. The Templars, as a supposedly secret society closely associated with magic and sorcery, were natural candidates for the role of satanic *deus ex machina*.

The emergence of the Templars as a 'cult' was given a significant boost by the sudden popularity of the novel from the 1790s onwards. It is no coincidence that two of the best-selling novels of the period, Sir Walter Scott's *Ivanhoe* (1819) and *The Talisman* (1825), both feature the Templars very heavily, and very negatively. The world of popular culture, emotional need and Templar conspiracies had begun to converge.[5]

The search for an overarching explanation of an often inexplicable world lay at the heart of many of the new conspiracy theories – an unspoken desire for *completeness*, with the Templars acting as the lightning conductors of our need.

Sometimes there was an unimaginative literalism about it all – these secret intellectual riches became entangled with the idea of real buried treasure. Links with Cathar castles have been an obvious way of pulling several different strands together into one fun-packed conspiracy. Templar greed, Templar heresy and Templar sorcery converge easily and find thrillingly tangible form, for instance, in the 'secret treasure' buried in Montségur.

Evidence is not usually needed, but when people are so inclined, fraud can be resorted to. The nineteenth century saw a minor industry of its own in the form of Templar forgeries – mainly documents, but also objects such as coins and treasure caskets.[6]

And the same phenomenon has been seen, in an even more exponential fashion, with the more recent onset of social media, on-line gaming and the internet.

Many of these media changes have been exacerbated by the recent tendency to blur fiction and non-fiction. We are increasingly comfortable blending historical study with the wishful thinking of fantasy. This has taken Templar mythology into yet another direction and has created an entirely new industry of entertainment and speculation.

These two main literary influences, fact and fiction, started in different directions but have ended up converging. The book *The Holy Blood and the Holy Grail* began as a by-product of a serious documentary. It explored, amongst other things, purported links between the Holy Grail and real historical events. *The Da Vinci Code*, on the other hand, explores similar themes from a fictional perspective, but to many readers it has begun to assume the characteristics of truth and fact. A novel has turned into a treasure hunt with the characteristics of reality. It has created still more ways in which the Templars can be linked (with a finely stretched patina of historic truth) to many other associated conspiracies.[7]

The different genres feed off each other. And they feed off our desire for answers and certainty. The answers they provide are fantasies, but that barely slows the juggernaut down.

REVENGE OF THE RENEGADES

To address each of the Templar conspiracy theories in turn would be a lifetime's work – it would involve diving down endless rabbit holes in a never-ending pursuit of the unattainable 'Templar myth'. It would also give them oxygen, which they do not need. But, just to allow us to look at Templar myths within a broader context, it is perhaps worth looking at a couple of examples in more detail. The 'Mystery of the Missing Templars', the tale of the renegades who evaded capture, is a good starting point, if only because it acts as an enabler for many other downstream conspiracies.

As we have seen, the evidence strongly suggests that there were very few brothers left in Britain by the beginning of the fourteenth century. This evidence has been hotly contested, however. There have been recurring 'rumours' (that is, conspiracy theories and unsubstantiated tales) of huge numbers of Templars escaping arrest. According to this version of events, there were far more British Templars but many of them, presumably using their special forces skills, managed to avoid the inquisitors.

Most importantly, of course, the presence of fugitive Templars is an essential prerequisite for many other aspects of the Templar mythology – conspiracies are impossible without a critical mass of conspirators. Renegades were needed, and in large numbers, in order to turn the tide at the battle of Bannockburn, for instance. They had to be present to carry away their heavy treasure chests and precious items such as the Holy Grail. And the fugitive brothers were required to man the fleets that would take the Templars to America and other places in the (yet to be created) Spanish and British empires of the West.

Sadly for conspiracists, however, the evidence for the presence, or otherwise, of British Templar renegades is plentiful and clear.

We have a detailed inventory of the brothers' possessions, which was made immediately after their arrests. We also have a good sense of the normal range of personal effects that each Templar was allowed to keep with him. Combining these two arcane data sets, we can create a good correlation in most locations between chattels, prisoners and, by extrapolation, fugitives.

The evidence suggests that there were indeed some absconders. At Sutton, in Essex, for instance, there were items in situ which typically would have been the personal effects of two Templar brothers – there were two lances, two 'barhuds' (the brothers' distinctive travelling chests) and so on. But no brothers were there to be arrested when the king's men arrived. In the vast majority of cases, however, the items listed corresponded closely to the number of brothers arrested, even down to their individual barhuds.

Similarly, we have the extensive evidence of the lengthy interviews conducted with the captive brothers. These interviews included explicit questioning about those members of the order who had escaped arrest. The interrogations produced evidence of sixteen runaway brothers, a figure we know to be approximately correct, because their names tended to crop up in multiple interrogations. And, even of this sixteen, there is little that is mysterious – we know that the majority either gave themselves up in the coming months or were soon recaptured.[8]

Two brothers, John of Stoke and the splendidly named Michael of Baskerville, were away on business when the arrests were made and were at first assumed to have absconded. But in due course they came back and became part of the trial process. Two other brothers, William of Hereford (or Hertford) and Walter of Rockley, initially failed to present themselves for questioning in November 1309, but they were back by the following year.

There were others who, not surprisingly, were less than enthusiastic about being interrogated. A certain Roger of Stowe was a Templar priest who tried to avoid participation. He claimed, possibly correctly, that he had left the order before the arrest warrants were issued. He did eventually return to give evidence, but then seems to have disappeared.

Similarly, a handful of others, including Stephen of Stapelbrugge and Thomas Lindsey, tried to evade questioning. Very anti-climactically, it later transpired that they were living in Ireland and, like their Templar comrades there, were even receiving a government pension while they were doing so.[9]

Several of those who failed to participate were absent because of ill health or their advancing years. John of Hauvile (or Hamil), for instance, was at Denney but could not be interrogated because he was clearly insane (*demens*). Similarly, Brother William of Barnwell, serving at the commandery of Eagle, could not be interviewed properly because he was too frail and sick. But that was not the only reason. Questioning him would have been doubly frustrating – William was completely deaf.[10]

Only five British Templars disappeared without trace. Unlike in France, there was no element of surprise about the arrests. If anything, in an age without ID papers, photographs or biometric testing, it is perhaps surprising that more did not disappear. Presumably they just went back to the secure obscurity of their family networks. Or perhaps they adopted new names and re-established themselves elsewhere. What they could not have done is become an elite army and launch a decisive attack at Bannockburn.[11]

It is not difficult to see why most men decided to stay rather than run. Evading capture indefinitely was fraught with difficulties. Escape to the Continent, and particularly the most obvious destination of France, was unattractive in the extreme – Templar brothers there were being routinely tortured and executed by the French authorities. Common sense argued for staying in Britain and cooperating with the authorities. Being in a jurisdiction with no torture and the prospect of a pension at the end of an increasingly inevitable process must have seemed a far lesser hardship.

Escape to the East, even if it could be arranged, was only marginally more attractive. As we have seen in the case of Robert the Scot, some of the British brothers arrested in 1307 had certainly served abroad. But by the time he was questioned, Robert was middle aged, or possibly significantly older, and living in the Templar care home at Denney. At the very least, he was looking for a less energetic retirement than service in the East would ever have allowed – he had already served the order for some twenty-six years.

Other British Templar Knights, presumably now retired from active service, had also joined the order in the East, but came back home once they had done their duty. We know of British men, for instance, who had joined the order in Tripoli (in modern-day Lebanon), Cyprus, Sicily and even Armenia, where the order's troops had garrisoned many mountain fortresses over the previous two centuries. But by the time of the arrests the Templars in Britain had already been largely hollowed out and those available for interrogation were not the order's young soldiers.[12]

THE SCOTTISH CASE STUDY

One of the downstream stories that emerged from the 'Templar renegade' myth is that of their continuing role in Scotland. This gives us a chance to create a regional case study, if only as an example of the kinds of stories that have evolved and the unspoken agendas that lie behind them.

Evidence in Scotland is much sparser than in England or Ireland. There are, for instance, no surviving Scottish government records for the trial of the Templars. This accidental lack of hard data helps contribute to a spurious air of 'mystery'.[13]

Scotland has often been singled out (on the basis of no real evidence) as a possible location where renegade Templars, laden with treasure of course, fled after the suppression of the order. For some afficionados, these Templar renegades still exist today, running the world behind the scenes, presumably rubbing shoulders and occasionally sharing office space with the Illuminati, the Elders of Zion and the College of Cardinals.

These fugitive Templars proceeded to do wonderful things, seemingly propelled by a variety of different (and often irritatingly contradictory) motives. These motives change depending on the perspective of the author. They might be after revenge, driven by greed, supporting a proto-nationalistic agenda or acting as part of any number of other conspiracies – the Templars remain the blank canvas of our need.

There are three groups of Scottish stories that have achieved particular prominence. They range from the grand sweep of history-changing battles down to parochial point scoring and local property disputes. As always with Templar mythologies, there is something for everyone.

The battle of Bannockburn and the way the Templars tipped the tide of the conflict in favour of Robert the Bruce is one of the most enduring of these stories. It is composed of many interlocking and highly imaginative subplots, many of which play to a nationalistic agenda.

The first component is the tale of Templars escaping in large numbers from France, England and other parts of western Europe. Conveniently, these brothers gathered in the west of Scotland, particularly around Kintyre and Argyle, and carried on their weapons training. Then, as a dramatic climax to the 'revenge of the renegades' saga, this Templar army appeared at the battle of Bannockburn on 23/24 June 1314. These fearsome and hardened warriors formed up behind Robert the Bruce's army to support the Scots in their struggle for freedom. They instilled such fear in their

English opponents that they fled as soon as they saw the order's banners advancing menacingly towards them.

This is a great story, but it is entirely untroubled by facts or evidence. Firstly, there is no record of Templar fleets escaping France or any of the other provinces, regardless of the treasure hoards or Holy Grails that they might have been taking with them. Similarly, there is no record of any Templar properties in the areas of western Scotland that are claimed as the destination for these renegades. A few medieval grave slabs have been found in the vicinity. There are claims that these carvings have Templar connections. In fact, however, they are just evidence of fourteenth-century burials. There is nothing uniquely Templar about them, and there is no real evidence of any brother knights in Scotland in 1314.

But the presence of an 'invincible' Templar army at Bannockburn is the biggest myth. As we have seen, there were only two Templar brothers in Scotland when the order was suppressed, both of whom were embarrassingly English. Even more disappointingly, given the high-profile nature of the putative Templar intervention, every contemporary chronicle, whether English or Scottish, somehow forgot to mention them.

Perhaps more to the point, if any Templars had been on the battlefield, they would almost certainly have been fighting as part of the English army rather than on the Scottish side. The order had close connections with Edward I and had actively helped him live up to his reputation as the 'Hammer of the Scots' – they were indeed disturbingly partisan, but only in an anti-Scottish way.

His son, Edward II, had a similarly close relationship with the order and had protected them as best he could while they were being persecuted in other parts of Europe. If a Templar wanted revenge against a monarch, it would have been against the king of France and his Scottish allies rather than the king of England.

There were no large numbers of British Templar renegades upon which to build conspiracies, let alone create an elite army. Any force of Templar absconders at Bannockburn, for example, quite apart from the annoying detail that we know of no definitively 'Scottish' Templars at all, would have consisted of a maximum of half a dozen, probably very elderly (and very English) brothers.

To suggest that the Templars made the battle-winning charge at Bannockburn is a fantasy that flies in the face of all the evidence. It is also deeply insulting to the reputation of Robert the Bruce (himself, ironically, of Anglo-Norman heritage) and undermines his true achievements as a general.[14]

Rosslyn chapel is another Scottish Templar myth that has been given a recent media boost by its inclusion in the fictional *Da Vinci Code* book and its associated film. The chapel supposedly has close connections to the Templars and has 'associations' (whatever that means) with the Holy Grail.

Again, none of this is true. The chapel has no obvious links with the Templars at all. It is located 'just' 9 miles away from a Templar preceptory, but so are many other places. As I write this, I am sitting at a desk that is walking distance from one Templar preceptory and a short drive from another. When I go to the library, I am a ten-minute stroll away from a third Templar preceptory. Britain is not big and there were a lot of preceptories.

And the age of the chapel is so obviously unhelpful for conspiracists that one wonders how the myths ever gained any credence at all. We know that work on the chapel did not begin until 1446 and continued until 1484. Rosslyn was indisputably built some 140 to 180 years after the order ceased to exist. The building was commissioned by William St Clair, whose family, like the chapel itself, was said to have 'links' with the Templars. There are stories that a Catherine St Clair married Hugh of Payns when he visited Scotland in 1128, but this is almost certainly spurious. There is no contemporary evidence that Catherine even existed and the story overlooks the inconvenient fact that Hugh was a monk at the time – a religious man on a mission, bound by vows of chastity and on a whirlwind tour of western Europe. However tempting Catherine's charms may have been, Hugh was not looking to settle down with a Scottish wife.

In fact, the only evidence linking the St Clair family to the Templars suggests that, far from being close associates, the family had a grudge against the order. Henry St Clair and an earlier William St Clair were two of the few people who were prepared to give evidence (and probably perjure themselves) against the Templars at their trial.

Perhaps even less surprisingly, there is likewise no evidence providing any link, other than wishful thinking, between Rosslyn and the Holy Grail.[15]

For a final example of the Templar myth in Scotland, it is worth looking at the case of the (allegedly) evicted widow Christiane of Esperston. As we have seen, Brian le Jay, who was master of the Templars in Scotland in the 1290s, behaved in a very partisan fashion. He not only fought for King Edward I, but, so the story goes, famously tried to alienate as many of the locals as possible. In what was claimed to be a high-profile lawsuit, he was accused of stealing the lands of one Christiane of Esperston, a widow. As a wicked and vindictive landlord, he evicted Christiane from her house twice – once in 1292 and then again, just for good measure, in 1296.

The 'widow's eviction' incident should be treated with a great deal of caution. As usual, there is no contemporary evidence to back up the story. The first reference to it is in a self-seeking legal document dated to 1354, in which a plaintiff sought to take lands at Esperston away from the Hospitallers, who had inherited much of the Templars' property.

But it is telling that the tale of Christiane of Esperston's unjust treatment was never raised during the trial of the Templars. The inquisitors eagerly pursued all negative lines of investigation, no matter how trivial. Despite active encouragement, no one at the time came forward to mention the alleged incident.

It seems that the story, which came to assume epic folk-tale proportions, was part of a later property dispute – specifically, an attempt to claim ownership of the 'widow's property'. It cleverly managed to integrate a populist piece of anti-English propaganda into the narrative, designed to smear the Templars in general and Brian le Jay in particular for the support they gave to Edward I. But it was ultimately just a venal land-grab.[16]

Under close examination, each of the Templar myths slips away.

ARCANE TO MUNDANE: REVENGE OF THE LIBRARIANS

There is one final irony, one last prosaic counterpoint to the Templar fantasy.

Contrary to the glamour and secrecy surrounding the order, much of the explanation for their enduring reputation and the thousand conspiracy theories they have inspired lies in acts that are astonishingly trivial and mundane.

The Templar records were lost after the order was suppressed. Their rival and extremely similar military order the Hospitallers found a new role. They made an effort to adapt, and they were – slightly – less arrogant than the Templars. They survived. But the other thing that survived was their records. And, importantly, they make monumentally dull reading.

They are full of arcane disputes, petty wrangling over long-forgotten privileges that were barely worth squabbling about even at the time. Complaints about tenants getting drunk. Lists of livestock and fields they owned – or at least claimed to own – and long obscure disputes. Even arguments about water usage, which included painstakingly drawn circumferences drawn on parchment to show what was supposedly their right, the size and number of water pipes that might be used. Were they too small? Was someone trying to take some of their water away from them? And so on. The pettiness is mind numbing.

Some of the disputes are trivial, some less so. But they all share one quality – they are colossally boring. They are the dregs of old arguments, the dull everyday records of landownership and privilege, compiled by monastic orders with nothing better to do. The one thing they do not give scope for, however, is conspiracy. With records as prosaic and dull as this, the scope for glamorous and paranoid fantasies is almost non-existent.

With the Templars, however, it was very different. There is almost nothing left. We have only two surviving documents from their records relating to the Latin East – and even these are both copies rather than originals. The order's most critical archives, those that would have shown links with all manner of conspiracies – links with devil worship, receipts for the Holy Grail or the Shroud of Turin, for instance – have vanished.

The archives were initially held in their complex in Jerusalem, in the Temple of Solomon. The city fell to Saladin's armies in 1187, but their records survived this catastrophe and it seems likely that, like the Hospitallers, they had moved them out before the city fell. Parts of the archive may have been relocated to Acre after it had been liberated by the Third Crusade. We know, for instance, that they kept a treasury there, in a tower by the sea, until that city, too, fell into Mamluk hands in 1291.

Other copies were perhaps kept in the formidable Templar fortress at 'Atlit, newly built for the order in 1217–18. As 'Atlit was evacuated in a planned manner in 1291, rather than falling to a siege, their records would have been shipped out in safety.

So where did the records go? The most likely answer is that they survived the initial loss of the Latin East and, like most of the Templars' property, were given to the Hospitallers when their assets were transferred in 1312. After the retreat from the mainland, their records would have been shipped out to Christian Cyprus and, like the local Hospitaller archives with which they were presumably stored, they were probably destroyed when the Turks overran the island in 1571.

Their destruction was a nuisance for academics but it was more than just a sad historical footnote. The lack of real records created a vacuum. All that were left were a few stray scraps, the Templar confessions and their trial papers – the frightened, self-serving testaments of broken men, desperate to please their torturers. These were men eager to confirm any mad occult theory their inquisitors wanted to hear about, no matter how crazy or far-fetched.

The real, and incredibly mundane, records of the order were supplanted by the vivid imaginations of King Philip's inquisitors. The frenzied confessions that were forced from the brothers in their final, painful months replaced the reams of documentation about dull property disputes. And the void created by the loss of the Templar records established the perfect environment in which conspiratorial madness could flourish. These fantastical theories have multiplied exponentially in recent years – a phenomenon that is, of course, broadly in line with the growth of the internet.[17]

The trial of the Templars was so absurd that it would be funny if it were not sad – a Kafkaesque historical anecdote with a thousand unforeseen consequences and spinoffs. For most of the brothers, it was a personal tragedy.

But, even more depressingly, it was an inglorious and shoddy end to an order that had been an inspiration to generations of Europe's bravest knights.

ENDNOTES

ABBREVIATIONS

BD
: Baha al-Din Ibn Shaddad, *The Rare and Excellent History of Saladin*, tr. D. S. Richards, Crusade Texts in Translation, 7, Aldershot, 2001

Crusader Syria
: *Crusader Syria in the Thirteenth Century: The Rothelin Continuation of the History of William of Tyre with part of the Eracles or Acre text*, tr. J Shirley, Crusade Texts in Translation, 5, Aldershot, 1999

D'Albon
: *Cartulaire général de l'ordre du Temple, 1119?–1150, Recueil des chartres et des bulles relatives a l'ordre du Temple*, ed. G. d'Albon, 2 vols, Paris, 1913

Gervase of Canterbury
: Gervase of Canterbury, *The Gesta Regum with its continuation*, ed. W. Stubbs, 2 vols, London, 1880

IA
: Ibn al-Athir, *The Chronicle of Ibn al-Athir for the Crusading Period from al-Kamil fi'l Ta'rikh*, parts 1 and 2, tr. D. S. Richards, Crusade Texts in Translation, 13, 15, Aldershot, 2006, 2007

Inquest
: Lees, B. A., ed., *Records of the Templars in England in the Twelfth Century: The Inquest of 1185 with Illustrative Charters and Documents*, London, 1935

Itinerarium
: *Chronicle of the Third Crusade: A Translation of the Itinerarium Peregrinorum et Gesta Regis Ricardi*, tr. H. Nicholson, Crusade Texts in Translation 3, Aldershot, 1997

Letters
: Barber, M., and K. Bate, tr., *Letters from the East: Crusaders, Pilgrims and Settlers in the 12th–13th Centuries*, Crusade Texts in Translation, 18, Farnham, 2010

Libellus
: *The Conquest of the Holy Land by Salah al-Din: A critical edition and translation of the anonymous Libellus de expugnatione Terrae Sanctae per Saladinum*, ed. K. Brewer and J. H. Kane, Abingdon, 2019

Matthew Paris – Chronica
: Matthew Paris: *Chronica Majora*, ed. H. Richards Luard, RS 57, 7 vols, London, 1872–83

Matthew Paris – English History
: *Matthew Paris's English History*, vol. 1, tr. J. A. Giles, London, 1852

Matthew Paris – Hist. Ang.
: Matthew Paris: *Historia Anglorum sive historia minor*, ed. F. Madden, 3 vols, London, 1866–9

Odo of Deuil
: Odo of Deuil: *De profectione Ludovici VII in Orientem*, ed. and tr. V. G. Berry, New York, 1948

Proceedings	*The Proceedings Against the Templars in the British Isles*, ed. H. Nicholson, 2 vols, Farnham, 2011
Ralph of Coggeshall	Ralph of Coggeshall: *Chronicon Anglicanum*, ed. J. Stevenson, London, 1875
Ralph of Diceto	*The Historical Works of Master Ralph de Diceto*, ed. W. Stubbs, 2 vols, Rolls Series 68, London, 1876
Roger of Howden – Chronica	Roger of Howden: *Chronica*, ed. W. Stubbs, 4 vols, London, 1868–71
Roger of Howden – Gesta	*Gesta Regis Henrici Secundi Benedicti Abbatis: The Chronicles of the Reigns of Henry II and Richard I, ad 1169–1192, known commonly under the name of Benedict of Peterborough*, ed. W. Stubbs, 2 vols, London, 1867
The Templars	Barber, M., and K. Bate, tr., *The Templars*, Manchester Medieval Sources, Manchester, 2002
TTT	*The 'Templar of Tyre': Part III of the 'Deeds of the Cypriots'*, ed. P. Crawford, Abingdon, 2016
Usama	Usama Ibn-Munqidh, *The Book of Contemplation*, tr. P. M. Cobb, London, 2008
Walter of Coventry	Walter of Coventry: *Historical Collections*, ed. W. Stubbs, 2 vols, London, 1872–3
Walter Map	Walter Map: *De Nugis Curialium*, ed. M. R. James, rev. C. N. Brooke and R. A. B. Mynors, Oxford, 1983
WT	William of Tyre: *A History of Deeds done beyond the Sea*, tr. E. A. Babcock and A. C. Krey, 2 vols, Records of Civilization, Sources and Studies 35, New York, 1943
WT Cont	William of Tyre: *The Conquest of Jerusalem and the Third Crusade*, Sources in Translation, tr. P. W. Edbury, Aldershot, 1996

FOREWORD

1. Proceedings.

1. THE BRITISH TEMPLARS

1. France 2015 pp. 97–104; Tibble 2018 pp. 334–7.
2. Libellus p. 151; WT Cont p. 161.
3. 'Imâd ad-Din al-Isfahânî tr. Massé 1972, p. 27; IA II pp. 322–3.
4. IA II p. 324.
5. Proceedings II pp. 189–91; Nicholson 2009 pp. 230–1.
6. Nicholson 2021 pp. 33–4.
7. Proceedings I p. 379 and II p. 433.
8. Inquest; D'Albon. Note that the *Cartulaire général* is not a medieval cartulary but rather an assemblage of documents collected by d'Albon; Phillips, Simon 2010 pp. 237–46.
9. Barber 1994 pp. 310–13.

2. CRUSADE AND CONQUEST: 1099–1119

1. Riley-Smith 1980 pp. 177–92.
2. The Templar brothers were technically monks rather than priests, but the thought of monks shedding blood was inevitably still controversial.
3. Tibble 2020 pp. 18–26.
4. Barber 2012 pp. 37–49.
5. Phillips, J. 2009 p. 15; Cobb 2014 pp. 9–123.
6. Riley-Smith 2014 pp. 71–4.

3. BIRTH OF THE ORDER: 1099–1128

1. Raymond d'Aguilers p. 121.
2. Barber 2012 pp. 18–19; Phillips, J. 2009 pp. 22–7.
3. WT I pp. 524–6. See Nicholson 2021 pp. 14–16 for the 'Ernoul' account of the order's origins.
4. Boas 2006 pp. 2–4.
5. Barber 2012 pp. 133–4.
6. Forey 1986 pp. 143–7 and 165; Nicholson 2016a p. 2; Nicholson 2017 pp. 105–6.
7. Phillips, J. 1994 pp. 141–7; Phillips, J. 1996 pp. 19–43; Tibble 2020 pp. 81–3.
8. Orderic Vitalis VI pp. 308–11; Murray 2000 p. 236.
9. WT II p. 40.
10. Barber 2012 pp. 145–7; Phillips, J. 1996 pp. 19–43.
11. Barber 2012 pp. 146–7; Nicholson 2016a p. 3.
12. *The Rule of the Templars*; Barber 2006 pp. 9–10.
13. Barber 1994 pp. 11–19; Phillips, J. 1994 pp. 141–7.
14. *The Anglo-Saxon Chronicle* p. 259.

4. THE FOUNDATION YEARS: 1128–1135

1. Tyerman 1988 pp. 24–7; Tibble 2018 pp. 242–3.
2. Tyerman 1988 pp. 30–1.
3. *The Anglo-Saxon Chronicle* p. 259; Macquarrie 1985 p. 15.
4. Hollister 2001 p. 412.
5. WT I pp. 408–9; Schenk 2010 pp. 41–4; Tibble 2020 pp. 156–75.
6. Pringle 1997 pp. 106–7; Pringle 1998 pp. 89–109; Tibble 2018 pp. 155–7.
7. *Gesta Normannorum* II pp. 256–7; Hollister 2001 p. 412.
8. See John Walker's excellent 1990 thesis on the patrons of the British Templars: Walker 1990 p. 9; Inquest pp. xxxviii–xxxix; Nicholson 2010b pp. 1–2; Lewer and Dark 1997 pp. 18–19.
9. Johannis de Fordun p. 234; Macquarrie 1985 pp. 15–16. David's age is approximate – he was born *c.* 1084.
10. *Regesta Regum Scottorum* I pp. 289–90; Johannis de Fordun p. 234; Macquarrie 1985 pp. 16–17; Nicholson 2009 p. 219.
11. Matthew Paris – Chronica vi p. 521; Macquarrie 1985 pp. 49 and 125.
12. Macquarrie 1985 pp. 53, 53 n. 45 and 131; Nicholson 2009 pp. 234–5.
13. Lord 2002 p. 185; Barrow 1980.
14. Proceedings II pp. 21, 80–2, 101, 129–30, 164–5, 182–3, 420 and 420 n. 96; Barber 2006 pp. 227–8.
15. Proceedings II pp. 20, 34–6, 64, 101, 128–9, 164, 238, 274, 290, 304, 420 and 420 n. 96.

5. A NEW ARMY IN THE HOLY LAND: 1135–1154

1. Odo of Deuil pp. 124–7; Phillips, J. 2007 pp. 199–202.
2. Barber 1984 pp. 27–46.
3. Barber 1994 pp. 66–70; Tibble 2018 pp. 133–49.
4. WT II p. 196.
5. Tibble 2020 pp. 110–17.
6. Tyerman 1988 pp. 25–6.
7. WT II pp. 388 and 394; Tyerman 1988 p. 29.
8. Inquest pp. 213–15; Tyerman 1988 p. 32.
9. Tyerman 1988 pp. 25–6, 31 and 33; *The Conquest of Lisbon* pp. 55–7 and 57 n. 3; Inquest pp. 24, 80 and 99; Walker 1990 pp. 43–4; Nicholson 2009 p. 227.

10. Inquest pp. 33–5, 78, 79 n. 8, 111, 125, 132, 254–8 and 269–70; Walker 1990 pp. 43–4; Gooder 1995 pp. 5–7; Tyerman 1988 pp. 31–2; Phillips, J. 1996 pp. 231–9 and 266.
11. Barber 2012 pp. 188–92.
12. Barber 2012 p. 201; Tibble 2020 pp. 123–32.
13. Nicholson 1998a pp. 112–14.
14. WT II pp. 225–8; Barber 2012 p. 202.

6. STEPHEN AND MATHILDA – A GROWING INFLUENCE: 1135–1154

1. Orderic Vitalis VI pp. 310–11; Nicholson 2016a p. 3.
2. King 2012; King 1994; Crouch 2000. For an in-depth examination of the relationship between the Templars and the English monarchy, see the marvellous work by Irina Gatti 2005.
3. Crouch 2000 pp. 17–29.
4. Crouch 2000 pp. 30–49.
5. Crouch 2000 pp. 270–80.
6. Inquest xlvi–xlviii; Barber 1994 pp. 250–1; Gatti 2005 pp. 21–2 and 25–6; Nicholson 2009 pp. 220 and 225–6.
7. Gatti 2005 p. 26.
8. Tyerman 1988 p. 35.
9. Edbury 2020 pp. 5–6; Walker 1990 p. 94.
10. Inquest p. 49; Walker 1990 pp. 45, 158 and 282.
11. Inquest pp. 1 and 270; *Regesta Regum Anglo-Normannorum* III pp. 22–3; Walker 1990 pp. 267 and 285–6.
12. Inquest pp. xliii–xlv, 148 and 212–13; Gatti 2005 pp. 24, 26–7 and 221.
13. Lord 2002 p. 204; Walker 1990 pp. 278–87.
14. Albert of Aachen pp. 640–9; Fulcher of Chartres pp. 167–9; Guibert de Nogent p. 316; Tibble 2018 pp. 242–3; Crouch 2000 pp. 317–18.
15. Doherty 2017 pp. 878–9 and 884–8. If, of course, Hugh was not on the First Crusade.
16. Hurlock 2012 p. 147.
17. John of Worcester III pp. 292–7; Crouch 2000 pp. 11, 142 and 186–7.
18. Gatti 2005 pp. 24, 26–7 and 221.
19. Inquest pp. 146–7 and 203; Walker 1990 pp. 157–8; Nicholson 2009 pp. 226–7; Gervers 1996.
20. Lord 2002 p. 134.
21. *Regesta Regum Anglo-Normannorum* III pp. 310–19; Crouch 2000 pp. 317–18; Walker 1990 pp. 156–9; Gatti 2005 pp. 24–7.
22. Inquest pp. 24 and 78; Walker 1990 pp. 161–2.
23. Inquest pp. 15, 75, 137–40, 149–51 and 228 n. 9, and see: Cressing pp. 145–6; Cowley pp. 176–8; Dinsley p. 212; Uphall pp. 148–9 and 154–5; Shotover pp. 178–80; Witham pp. 149–53; Walker 1990 pp. 47, 156–7, 160, 163–4 and 170–1; Nicholson 2009 p. 240.
24. Walker 1990 pp. 280 and 284.
25. Walker 1990 p. 281.
26. Barber 1992.
27. Nicholson 2009 p. 21.
28. Tibble 2020 pp. 141–2.
29. Inquest pp. 65–6, 68–9 and 141; Levett 1938 pp. 232, 330 and 333; Lord 2002 pp. 78–81; Walker 1990 pp. 97, 165, 191, 262 and 285–6.
30. Inquest pp. 79, 112–17 and 260; Britnell 1968 pp. 13–21; Rodwell 1993; Walker 1990 pp. 30, 97, 156–9, 238, 254, 265–6, 286 and 294; Lord 2002 pp. 69–71.
31. Lord 2002 pp. 66–9.
32. Inquest pp. 1, 5, 9, 145–7 and 153–5; Britnell 1983; Ryan 1993; Hunter 1993; Lord 2002 pp. 62–9; Walker 1990 pp. 30, 98, 156–9, 254 and 286.

7. HENRY II – AGENTS OF THE CROWN: 1154–1177

1. Lyons and Jackson 1982 pp. 42–3; Phillips, J. 2019 pp. 68–9; Barber 2012 pp. 256–7.
2. WT II pp. 397–8.
3. Warren 2000 pp. 509–12.
4. Lloyd 1988 p. 24. For an erudite and very entertaining overview of the complex relationship of Henry II (and other English kings) with the crusading movement, see Edbury 2020.
5. Gatti 2005 pp. 32–5.
6. Lord 2002 pp. 204–8.
7. Inquest pp. 15–16 and 58; Walker 1990 p. 96.
8. The London rents were at the Old Temple; Inquest pp. lv, 10, 80, 138, 142–3 and 174; Walker 1990 pp. 94–6; Nicholson 2009 p. 229; Hurlock 2011 p. 145.
9. Wilson 2010 pp. 20, 23, 35–6 and 41.
10. Walker 1990 pp. 63–4 and 171–9; Inquest pp. xc, 1, 16, 26, 31–2, 35, 53, 63, 79, 128, 166–9, 172–3.
11. Hurlock 2012 pp. 84–5.
12. Hurlock 2012 p. 157.
13. Walker 1990 p. 77.
14. Hurlock 2012 p. 160; Walker 1990 pp. 96, 186–7 and 265; Inquest p. 16.
15. Gatti 2005 pp. 27–38.
16. Inquest pp. 263–4 and 276; Gatti 2005 p. 29.
17. Warren 2000 pp. 82–91; Gatti 2005 pp. 36–8.
18. Inquest pp. 157–8.
19. Warren 2000 pp. 88–90; Gatti 2005 p. 37; Lord 2002 pp. 207–8; Roger of Howden – Chronica I p. 218.
20. Gatti 2005 p. 38.
21. Warren 2000 pp. 447–517.
22. Gatti 2005 p. 39.
23. Geoffrey Fulcher was Preceptor (or Procurator) of the Temple (1164–71) and Commander of the Templar houses in France (1171–9).
24. Gatti 2005 pp. 39–40; *Materials for the History of Thomas Becket* V pp. 220–1.
25. Gatti 2005 p. 41; *Recueil des historiens des Gaules et de la France* 16 pp. 430–2.
26. Gatti 2005 pp. 40–1.
27. Warren 2000 pp. 509–11; Lord 2002 p. 208; Tyerman 1988 pp. 43 and 55.
28. Gatti 2005 pp. 32–5.
29. Warren 2000 pp. 187–206.
30. Tibble 2018 pp. 101–3; Gatti 2005 pp. 33–4.
31. Tibble 2018 pp. 200–4; Barber 2012 p. 198; Riley-Smith 1969.
32. Tibble 2020 pp. 176–220. See the excellent Fulton 2022 pp. 45–141.
33. WT II p. 332; Phillips, J. 1996 p. 154; Fulton 2022 pp. 62–7.
34. Tyerman 1988 p. 36; Phillips, J. 1996 p. 173.
35. Walker 1990 pp. 61–4; WT II p. 306; Barber 2012 p. 240; Nicholson 2009 p. 230.
36. Inquest p. 70; Walker 1990 p. 63.
37. Inquest pp. 49, 128 and 263; Walker 1990 pp. 44–5.
38. WT II p. 319.
39. Phillips, J. 2019 pp. 69–72; Lyons and Jackson 1982 pp. 44–6.

8. HENRY II – THE TEMPLARS IN IRELAND

1. Proceedings II pp. 319–81; Warren 2000 pp. 187–206; Gatti 2005 pp. 43–4; Lord 2002 pp. 178–9; Hosler 2007 pp. 66–76; Nicholson 2016b pp. 1–22.
2. Though note that there is some modern debate about the true extent of Pope Alexander's endorsement. See Duggan 2007.

3. Brown 2016.
4. Nicholson 2003 p. 234.
5. Proceedings II pp. 421–2; Gooder 1995 p. 122.
6. Nicholson 2003 p. 245; Nicholson 2016b p. 13; Barber 2006 pp. 227–8.
7. Warren 2000 pp. 200–6.
8. Lord 2002 pp. 177–85.
9. Lord 2002 p. 183; O'Conor and Naessens 2016 pp. 124–50.
10. Nicholson 2003 p. 234; Nicholson 2009 pp. 222 and 232; Nicholson 2016b pp. 7–9. The Templars' main patron in Ireland was the king. The Hospitallers, on the other hand, received gifts from many different lords. Neither order was given much, if any, property by the native Irish.
11. Nicholson 2003 p. 234 n. 4; O'Conor and Naessens 2016 pp. 124–50; Wightman 1966; Veach 2014.
12. Lord 2002 pp. 178–9 and 183–4; Nicholson 2009 pp. 233–4.
13. Murphy 2016 pp. 167–83.
14. Roger of Wendover II pp. 586–92; Matthew Paris – Chronica III pp. 288–9; Nicholson 2003 p. 236; Gatti 2005 p. 128; Crouch 2014 pp. 393–404.
15. La Torre 2008 pp. 121–7; Nicholson 2003 pp. 244–6; Nicholson 2016b pp. 15–16.
16. Gatti 2005 pp. 107–8; Nicholson 2003 p. 236.
17. Gatti 2005 p. 162; Nicholson 2003 p. 237; Nicholson 2016b pp. 14–15; La Torre 2008 pp. 125–6.
18. Nicholson 2003 p. 237.
19. Nicholson 2003 p. 237.
20. Proceedings II pp. 30 and 95; Barber 2006 pp. 221 and 225; Nicholson 2009 pp. 96, 104, 154, 158 and 177–8.

9. HENRY II – PREPARING FOR WAR: 1177–1189

1. IA II p. 253. See the marvellous Phillips, J. 2019.
2. Nicholson 2016a p. 6.
3. Quoted in Nicholson 2016a p. 6; Ralph of Diceto I pp. 423–4.
4. IA II p. 253.
5. Barber 2012 pp. 270–1; Tibble 2018 pp. 300–13.
6. Barber 2012 pp. 271–3; Tibble 2020 pp. 246–54.
7. Gatti 2005 pp. 27–9 and 32–48.
8. Warren 2000 pp. 122–5; Gatti 2005 pp. 44–5.
9. Roger of Howden – Chronica II pp. 64–5; Gatti 2005 p. 45.
10. Roger of Howden – Gesta I pp. 190–4; Roger of Howden – Chronica II pp. 144–6; Gatti 2005 p. 45.
11. Gatti 2005 pp. 12, 29–30 and 52–3.
12. Gatti 2005 pp. 29 and 46–7.
13. Warren 2000 pp. 615–17.
14. Metcalf 1995.
15. Roger of Howden – Gesta II pp. 30–1 and 47–8; Roger of Howden – Chronica II p. 354; Walter of Coventry I pp. 359–60; Gatti 2005 p. 47.
16. Roger of Howden – Gesta I p. 116; Gervase of Canterbury I pp. 298–300; Walter Map pp. 482–5; Tyerman 1988 pp. 40 and 46; Warren 2000 p. 148.
17. Itinerarium p. 42.
18. Gervase of Canterbury I pp. 198–9; Roger of Howden – Chronica II p. 354; Roger of Howden – Gesta II pp. 30–1 and 47–8; Walter of Coventry I pp. 359–60; Gatti 2005 pp. 33–4. As with so much else, the remit of the Templar bankers with regard to Henry's money is unclear. If it had been sent East to be stockpiled as his war chest for when he eventually went on crusade, then, in allowing King Guy of Jerusalem to use the money to buy troops in 1187, it might be claimed that the Templars were betraying their trust as Henry's bankers.

19. Roger of Howden – Gesta I p. 159; Mayer 1982 pp. 721–39; Phillips, J. 1996 pp. 258–63; Hamilton, B. 2000 pp. 212–14.
20. Tyerman 1988 pp. 45–6. Note that the extension of such taxation to Wales or Ireland was much more limited, as royal administration was lacking in those areas.
21. *Recueil des historiens des Gaules et de la France* 18 pp. 135–6 and 704–5; Tyerman 1988 p. 47.
22. Gatti 2005 p. 48.
23. La Torre 2008 p. 125; Gatti 2005 p. 35.
24. Roger of Howden – Chronica II p. 307; Ralph of Diceto II pp. 27–8; BD pp. 64–5. This reconstruction also relies for context on two other main sources: Bennett, M. 1992 pp. 175–88; Usama pp. 25–6.
25. Roger of Howden – Chronica II p. 307; Ralph of Diceto II pp. 27–8; BD pp. 64–5.
26. For Eraclius's visit, see Hamilton, B. 2000 pp. 212–14; Ralph of Diceto II pp. 32–4; Roger of Howden – Gesta I pp. 328–38; Roger of Howden – Chronica II p. 299–304; William of Newburgh I pp. 244–7; Warren 2000 pp. 221 and 604–7.
27. Wilson 2010 p. 20.
28. Barber 2012 pp. 286–8; Tyerman 1988 p. 52.
29. Tyerman 1988 p. 36.
30. Roger of Howden – Gesta I p. 359 and II p. 22; Inquest pp. 33–5, 78–9, 111, 125, 132, 254–8 and 269–70; Tyerman 1988 p. 52.
31. Roger of Howden – Gesta I p. 359 and II p. 22; Inquest pp. 70, 128 and 131; Walker 1990 pp. 44–5.
32. Tyerman 1988 pp. 36–8.
33. This was a year's income for five knights, so the gift, given to a man who had recently been supporting Henry II's rebellious son, may not have been quite as miserly as *The History of William Marshal* would like to suggest.
34. Asbridge 2015 pp. 160–71 and 373–4.
35. Tibble 2020 pp. 1–7; Barber 2012 p. 297–9; IA II p. 319.
36. WT Cont pp. 160–2.
37. France 2015; Tibble 2018 pp. 321–39; Barber 2012 pp. 302–6.
38. We do not know Gerard's exact remit as Henry's banker in Jerusalem, but he may, of course, have been exceeding his instructions in releasing the money.
39. Letters pp. 78–9.
40. Letters pp. 83–4.
41. Roger of Howden – Chronica III p. 42; Gillingham 1999 pp. 114–16; Gatti 2005 p. 49; Tyerman 1988 p. 61.
42. Tyerman 1988 pp. 75–80; Barber 2012 pp. 339–40.
43. Gatti 2005 pp. 34–5 and 48. There were, of course, regional variations. See, for instance, Edbury 2014.
44. Tyerman 1988 pp. 54–6.
45. Roger of Howden – Gesta II pp. 30 and 47–8; Roger of Howden – Chronica II p. 354; Walter of Coventry I p. 360; Lord 2002 p. 208.
46. Gillingham 1999 pp. 89–100.

10. RICHARD THE LIONHEART – THE VANGUARD OF CHRISTENDOM: 1189–1199

1. Gillingham 1999 p. 89; Edbury 2020 p. 6.
2. Tyerman 1988 p. 83.
3. Roger of Howden – Gesta II pp. 76–7.
4. Richard of Devizes p. 9; Gillingham 1999 pp. 114–6.
5. Roger of Howden – Chronica III pp. 7–8; Tyerman 1988 p. 80; Barber 2012 p. 339.
6. Tyerman 1988 p. 201.

7. Richard of Devizes p. 9.
8. Inquest pp. 169–71; Gatti 2005 pp. 29–30.
9. Roger of Howden – Gesta II pp. 46–7, 110, 115, 119–20, 124 and 134.
10. Gatti 2005 pp. 48–53.
11. Tyerman 1988 p. 60; Gatti 2005 pp. 87–91.
12. Roger of Howden – Gesta II p. 110–11; Richard of Devizes p. 28. For the issue of maritime transportation, particularly with regard to horses; see Pryor 1988 and 2008.
13. Barber 2012 pp. 340–1; Barber 1994 pp. 119 and 122–3.
14. Itinerarium pp. 164–5.
15. Ambroise p. 43 and n. 75. Note that the year of his death is not entirely clear – it is possible that he died on 28 September 1192.
16. Gerald of Wales – Journey pp. 114, 140 and 204; Gerald of Wales – Opera I pp. 73–6; Tyerman 1988 p. 69.
17. Gerald of Wales – Journey p. 114; Barber 2012 p. 339. There was, of course, a hiatus between the preaching in 1188 and Richard's departure in 1190. We can only speculate about how many of the Welsh recruits actually went on crusade. See Edbury 2014.
18. Gerald of Wales – Journey p. 42.
19. Richard of Devizes pp. 15–16 and 28; Roger of Howden – Gesta II pp. 89–90, 112, 115 and 117; Roger of Howden – Chronica III p. 43; Ralph of Diceto II pp. 65–6 and 88; Gillingham 1999 pp. 128–9 and 143–4; Tyerman 1988 pp. 63 and 66.
20. Letters pp. 90–1; Gillingham 1999 pp. 130–54.
21. Ambroise pp. 154–5 n. 584; Boas 2006 p. 8; Gillingham 1999 pp. 196–7; Edbury 2015 pp. 29–52.
22. Hosler 2018.
23. Gillingham 1999 pp. 166–71; Gatti 2005 p. 51.
24. Letters pp. 90–1; Gillingham 1999 pp. 164–6.
25. Gillingham 1999 pp. 172–80.
26. Ambroise p. 115.
27. Letters p. 91; Ambroise p. 115.
28. Gillingham 1999 pp. 175–8.
29. Bennett, S. 2016 pp. 44–53; Tibble 2018 pp. 143–9.
30. BD pp. 175–6.
31. Ambroise p. 125.
32. Ambroise pp. 129–30; Gillingham 1999 p. 186.
33. Gillingham 1999 pp. 190–1; Gatti 2005 pp. 51–2.
34. Ambroise pp. 135–6.
35. Ambroise pp. 135–6.
36. Gillingham 1999 pp. 217–19; Barber 2012 pp. 349–55; Tyerman 1988 pp. 57–8.
37. Inquest pp. 139–44; Walker 1990 pp. 96–7; Lord 2002 p. 208.
38. Gilbert Malet: Inquest pp. cxxxv and 61; Robert III of Stafford: Inquest pp. 28–9, 86 and 92. See also Walker 1990 pp. 47–8 and 89.
39. Inquest pp. 32 and 52. Note that there is a chance the mill had been given to the Templars by his father, who was also named Robert, earl of Leicester; Walker 1990 p. 46.
40. Inquest pp. 80 and 92; Walker 1990 pp. 45–8.
41. Tyerman 1988 pp. 68–9.
42. Roger of Wendover II pp. 123–4.
43. Walker 1990 p. 47.
44. Gillingham 1999 pp. 222–53; Lord 2002 p. 209.
45. Barber 2012 pp. 351–5; Nicholson 1989 pp. 285–8.

11. JOHN – STRANGE TIMES, STRANGE PARTNERS: 1199–1216

1. Webster 2012 pp. 214–15.
2. Nicholson 1998b p. 208; Webster 2012 p. 216.

3. Church 2015; Nicholson 1998b pp. 205–12.
4. Church 2015 pp. 82–3.
5. Webster 2016.
6. Tyerman 1988 p. 96; Roger of Howden – Chronica IV pp. 165–7.
7. Walker 1990 p. 48; Nicholson 2009 pp. 237–8.
8. Lord 2002 pp. 210–12.
9. Church 2015 pp. 71–2.
10. Church 2015 pp. 101–11; Warren 1997 pp. 81–4.
11. Church 2015 pp. 117–27.
12. Gatti 2005 p. 57; Nicholson 1998b pp. 205–7.
13. Gervase of Canterbury II pp. 95–6; Ralph of Coggeshall p. 144; Gatti 2005 pp. 57–8; Church 2015 pp. 111–3; Warren 1997 pp. 93–9.
14. Gatti 2005 pp. 58–60.
15. Church 2015 pp. 198–200; Gatti 2005 p. 62.
16. Warren 1997 pp. 217–23; Church 2015 pp. 205–8; Gatti 2005 pp. 62–4.
17. Church 2015 pp. 208–12; Warren 1997 pp. 223–4; Gatti 2005 pp. 63–4.
18. Gatti 2005 p. 65.
19. *Selected Letters of Pope Innocent III* pp. 207–9, 212–16 and 227; Tyerman 1988 pp. 136–7; Church 2015 pp. 216–20; Ralph of Coggeshall pp. 174–5.
20. Gatti 2005 p. 68.
21. Roger of Wendover II p. 309.
22. Gatti 2005 pp. 68 and 71; Church 2015 pp. 235–6.
23. Gatti 2005 pp. 67–9.
24. Gatti 2005 p. 71; *Rotuli Litterarum* p. 275; Church 2015 pp. 244–5.
25. Gatti 2005 pp. 79–80.
26. Gatti 2005 p. 71.
27. Gatti 2005 pp. 87–8.
28. Roger of Wendover II p. 272; Gatti 2005 p. 62; Church 2015 pp. 198–201.
29. Gatti 2005 p. 90.
30. Gatti 2005 pp. 87–91.
31. Lord 2002 pp. 153–4.
32. Lord 2002 pp. 155–6.
33. Lord 2002 pp. 156–7.
34. Nicholson 1998b pp. 211–12; Gatti 2005 pp. 88–90.
35. Nicholson 1998b pp. 212–15; Gatti 2005 p. 112.
36. Gatti 2005 pp. 112–14; Lord 2002 pp. 156–7.
37. Gatti 2005 pp. 74 and 83–5; La Torre 2008 p. 125.
38. Gatti 2005 pp. 55 and 74.
39. Gatti 2005 p. 48.
40. Gatti 2005 pp. 75, 105 and p. 105 n. 60; Lord 2002 p. 234.
41. Lord 2002 p. 234.
42. Nicholson 2017 pp. 98–9; Gatti 2005 p. 85.
43. Gatti 2005 p. 74.
44. Gatti 2005 p. 75.
45. *Rotuli Litterarum* pp. 54–5; Church 2015 pp. 129–31.
46. Gatti 2005 p. 75.
47. Gatti 2005 p. 78.
48. Gatti 2005 pp. 79–80.
49. Gatti 2005 p. 80.
50. Gatti 2005 pp. 76–7.
51. Nicholson 2017 pp. 99–100.
52. Nicholson 2017 pp. 99–100.

12. HENRY III – REBUILDING BRITAIN: 1216–1269

1. Roger of Wendover II p. 378; Church 2015 p. 246.
2. *The Register of Walter Gray* p. 24; Nicholson 1998b p. 207.
3. Church 2015 pp. 247–52; Carpenter 1996 and 2020.
4. Gatti 2005 p. 101.
5. Gatti 2005 p. 94; Crouch 1990 pp. 117–32; Asbridge 2015 pp. 343–75.
6. Walker 1990 pp. 189–95 and 263; Strickland 2016 p. 308; *The History of William Marshal* pp. 99–104; Barber 2012 p. 286; Crouch 1990 pp. 48–52; Asbridge 2015 pp. 160–71 and 373–4.
7. Park 2010 pp. 79–80; Lankester 2010 pp. 93–134; Griffith-Jones and Park 2010 plates 45 and 57.
8. Walker 1990 p. 85.
9. Nicholson 1998b p. 207; Carpenter 2020 pp. 331–2.
10. Jansen 2010 pp. 45–8.
11. Calendar of the Charter Rolls I 1226–1257 p. 135; Walker 1990 pp. 84–5; Lord 2002 pp. 212–14. Seeking burial in a Templar church was not altogether unusual. Henry III's contemporary and namesake, Henry I of Cyprus (died 1253), was buried in the Temple church in Nicosia.
12. Wild 2010 p. 535.
13. Tyerman 1988 pp. 111–13 and 116–18; Carpenter 2020 pp. 512–67.
14. Lloyd 1988 p. 28; Tyerman 1988 pp. 120 and 123.
15. Lloyd 1988 pp. 239–41; Carpenter 1988 pp. 61–88; Carpenter 1996 pp. 107–36; Carpenter 2020 pp. 547–8, 661–3 and 667–9.
16. Walker 1990 pp. 97–8; Nicholson 2009 p. 238.
17. Tyerman 1988 p. 202.
18. Walker 1990 pp. 49–50; Tyerman 1988 p. 205.
19. Lloyd 1988 p. 161; Nicholson 2009 pp. 239–40; Walker 1990 pp. 50–1.
20. Tyerman 1988 pp. 207–8.
21. Walker 1990 p. 50.
22. Lord 2002 pp. 55–6.
23. Alexander III reigned from 1249 to 1286; Gatti 2005 pp. 169–74 and 184.
24. Gatti 2005 p. 179.
25. Gatti 2005 pp. 98–9; Carpenter 2020 pp. 29–40.
26. Gatti 2005 p. 100.
27. Gatti 2005 p. 93; Lord 2002 pp. 212–14 and 226–8.
28. Hurlock 2012 p. 160.
29. La Torre 2008 pp. 124–5.
30. Lord 2002 p. 213; Gatti 2005 pp. 93 and 95.
31. Gatti 2005 pp. 103–4 and 109.
32. Gatti 2005 p. 94; Lord 2002 pp. 224–5.
33. Calendar of the Liberate Rolls IV pp. 159, 168, 173, 177, 180 and 201; Calendar of the Patent Rolls AD 1247–1258, p. 386; Lord 2002 pp. 232–4.
34. Tyerman 1988 p. 189.
35. Carpenter 1996 pp. 116–17.
36. Carpenter 1988 pp. 61–88; Carpenter 1996 pp. 107–36; Carpenter 2020 pp. 547–8, 661–3 and 667–9.
37. Perry 2013 pp. 131–2; Perry 2015 pp. 630–1.
38. *The 'Barnwell' Chronicle*, quoted in Perry 2015 pp. 634–5.
39. Perry 2015 p. 635.
40. Lord 2002 pp. 229–31.
41. Lord 2002 pp. 231–2.
42. Lord 2002 pp. 234–5.
43. See Nicholson 1992 pp. 68–85 for a witty examination of Matthew's personality.

44. Carpenter 2020 pp. 193 and 332; Lord 2002 pp. 212–19.
45. Nicholson 1992 pp. 68–85; Nicholson 1998b pp. 217–18; Gatti 2005 pp. 164–9; Lord 2002 pp. 212–14.
46. Nicholson 2009 p. 20; Nicholson 2017 p. 46.
47. Nicholson 2017 pp. 101 and 119.
48. Slavin 2013 pp. 36–49; Nicholson 2017 p. 81; Nicholson and Slavin 2017 pp. 237–8.
49. Nicholson and Slavin 2017 pp. 241–2.
50. Nicholson 2009 pp. 231, 242 and 244; Nicholson 2017 p. 82.
51. Nicholson and Slavin 2017 pp. 243–5.
52. Nicholson 2017 p. 86; Slavin 2013.
53. Nicholson 2017 p. 87.
54. Nicholson 2021 pp. 61–2.
55. Nicholson 2017 p. 98.
56. Nicholson 2009 p. 220; Gooder 1995 pp. 5–7. For Balsall as a whole see Eileen Gooder's marvellous monograph: Gooder 1995.
57. Jefferson 2020 p. 7.
58. Gooder 1995 pp. 8–10.
59. Gooder 1995 pp. 10–13.
60. Gooder 1995 pp. 11–12.
61. Jefferson 2020.
62. Jefferson 2020 p. 229.
63. Nicholson and Slavin 2017 p. 247.
64. Nicholson 2017 pp. 48–50.
65. Nicholson 2009 p. 221; Nicholson 2017 pp. 54–8.

13. MELTDOWN ON THE EASTERN FRONT: 1216–1269

1. Gatti 2005 pp. 21–2, 171–4 and 187–90.
2. Nicholson 2011 pp. 89–90; Nicholson 2007b pp. 411–23.
3. Nicholson 2008 pp. 131–54; Forey 2002 pp. 18–37. Interestingly, the arrests and the testimonies at the trial in Cyprus closely parallel what happened in England – lay witnesses who had good cause to dislike the Templars refused to testify to the truth of the charges.
4. Matthew Paris – Chronica III p. 373, IV p. 175 and V pp. 150–4; Tyerman 1988 p. 91.
5. The Templars pp. 104–5; Lloyd 1988 p. 26.
6. Lloyd 1988 pp. 26–7, 29 and 253–5.
7. Riley-Smith 2014 pp. 197–205.
8. Tyerman 1988 pp. 95–8; Carpenter 2020 pp. 20–1 and 23; Oliver of Paderborn p. 103.
9. Ralph of Coggeshall p. 190; Tyerman 1988 p. 98.
10. Hurlock 2012 p. 85.
11. Walter of Coventry II pp. 242–3; Tyerman 1988 p. 98.
12. Matthew Paris – Chronica III pp. 67–8 and 373; Matthew Paris – English History p. 37; Tyerman 1988 pp. 98–9; Riley-Smith 2014 p. 214.
13. Oliver of Paderborn p. 79; Walter of Coventry II p. 246; Walker 1990 pp. 48–50 and 58–9; Tyerman 1988 p. 98.
14. Walker 1990 pp. 48–50.
15. Roger of Wendover II p. 489; Riley-Smith 2014 pp. 205–7.
16. Tyerman 1988 p. 188.
17. Richard of Devizes p. 6; Tyerman 1988 pp. 99–101.
18. Matthew Paris – Chronica III p. 490; Tyerman 1988 pp. 100–1.
19. Matthew Paris – English History pp. 63–4; Matthew Paris – Chronica III p. 406; Nicholson 1992 pp. 68–85.
20. Riley-Smith 2014 p. 216; Tyerman 1988 pp. 101–8; Lloyd 1988 pp. 92–3.
21. Lloyd 1988 pp. 104–5.
22. Letters pp. 136–40.

23. Walker 1990 pp. 50–1.
24. Matthew Paris – English History p. 396.
25. Letters pp. 142–6; Crusader Syria p. 133.
26. Barber 1994 p. 200.
27. Carpenter 2020 pp. 514–18; Matthew Paris – Hist. Ang. III p. 55; Matthew Paris – Chronica V pp. 76–7 and 130–1; Tyerman 1988 pp. 108–10.
28. TTT pp. 36–7; Crusader Syria p. 142; Barber 1994 pp. 158 and 187–8.
29. TTT pp. 35–6.
30. Ibn 'Abd al-Zahir p. 645; TTT p. 59.

14. EDWARD I – LAST THROW OF THE DICE: 1270–1291

1. Barany 2010 p. 21.
2. *The Political Songs of England* p. 128; Tyerman 1988 p. 85; Prestwich 1997.
3. Barber 1994 p. 200.
4. Tyerman 1988 p. 124; Beebe 1971 pp. 48–85; Lloyd 1988 pp. 113–53; Prestwich 1997 pp. 66–85; Riley-Smith 2014 pp. 237–9.
5. *Annales Monastici* IV pp. 217–18; Tyerman 1988 p. 124.
6. Tyerman 1988 p. 127.
7. Prestwich 1997 pp. 71–2; Lloyd 1988 pp. 113–17; Tyerman 1988 pp. 127–8; Ibn 'Abd al-Zahir pp. 753–4.
8. Walker 1990 p. 51.
9. Lloyd 1988 pp. 144–5.
10. Tyerman 1988 p. 129; Gatti 2005 p. 201.
11. La Torre 2008 p. 125.
12. Lloyd 1988 p. 194; Gatti 2005 p. 194.
13. Lloyd 1988 pp. 139–44; Tyerman 1988 p. 125.
14. TTT p. 68; Ibn 'Abd al-Zahir p. 762.
15. TTT p. 68.
16. Tyerman 1988 p. 125.
17. Ibn 'Abd al-Zahir pp. 772–4 and 836–7.
18. TTT pp. 68–9; Ibn 'Abd al-Zahir pp. 776–7; Prestwich 1997 pp. 77–9.
19. TTT pp. 68–9.
20. TTT pp. 68–9; Walter of Guisborough pp. 208–10.
21. TTT pp. 68–9; Ibn 'Abd al-Zahir pp. 776–7.
22. Walter of Guisborough p. 209; Beebe 1971 pp. 82–3; Gatti 2005 p. 194 n. 6.
23. Lloyd 1988 p. 34; Tyerman 1988 p.125; Hurlock 2012 p. 85.
24. Barany 2010 pp. 7–22; Prestwich 1997 pp. 329–33.
25. Gatti 2005 pp. 202–5.
26. Gatti 2005 p. 198; Walker 1990 p. 98.
27. Proceedings II pp. 21, 80–2, 101, 129–30, 164–5, 164 n. 38 and 182–3; Gooder 1995 p. 93; Lord 2002 pp. 82–3.
28. Gooder 1995 pp. 60–1.
29. Gooder 1995 p. 82.
30. Gooder 1995 p. 83.
31. Gooder 1995 p. 84.
32. Gooder 1995 pp. 85–6; Nicholson 2009 p. 239.
33. Nicholson 2009 p. 71.
34. Lord 2002 pp. 172–4; Forey 1987 pp. 56–9. It should be noted, however, that this decline in donations was also experienced by many other religious foundations at this period.
35. Lord 2002 pp. 103–4.
36. Lord 2002 pp. 49–50.
37. Nicholson 2017 p. 21.
38. WT I pp. 526–7.

39. Lord 2002 pp. 76–7.
40. Barber 2006 pp. 21–2. It should be noted that fewer than 100 Templars (knights and sergeants) were rounded up in Cyprus and testified when the order was eventually suppressed. The majority of the brothers at the Nicosia meeting in 1291 were clearly from the order's other provinces.
41. Letters pp. 162–3.
42. Prestwich 1997 pp. 327–9.
43. TTT pp. 98–101; Marshall 1992 pp. 232–4; Nicholson 2016a p. 16.

15. DECLINE: 1291–1307

1. TTT pp. 110–17; Barber 2006 p. 7.
2. Gatti 2005 pp. 197–8, 204–6 and 206 n. 91; Lord 2002 pp. 107–8.
3. Lord 2002 pp. 110–11.
4. Nicholson 2012b p. 110.
5. Nicholson 2012a p. 200; Nicholson 2012b pp. 107 and 118.
6. Barber 2006 pp. 227–8; Lord 2002 p. 148; Nicholson 2012b pp. 107–8.
7. Tyerman 1988 pp. 230–1 and 240.
8. William Rishanger p. 78; *The Political Songs of England* pp. 242–3; Tyerman 1988 p. 233.
9. Luttrell 2010 pp. 21–31; Gatti 2005 pp. 196 and 221.
10. Gatti 2005 pp. 205–9. Edward I may have shown some slight preference for the Hospitallers, but this seems to have been driven by practical matters rather than anything more fundamental. Gatti 2005 pp. 194, 198 and 211.
11. Nicholson 2017 p. 19.
12. Nicholson 2017 pp. 19–20.
13. Nicholson 1989 pp. 288–9.
14. Nicholson 1989 p. 298.
15. Barber 2006 p. 19–23.
16. TTT pp. 157–8 and 161; Barber 2006 pp. 22–3.
17. Barber 2006 pp. 34–5.
18. Barber 2006 pp. 19–23.
19. Tibble 2018 pp. 323–4. All numbers are, of course, estimates.
20. Barber 2006 pp. 35–7.
21. Matthew Paris – Chronica IV p. 291; Tyerman 1988 p. 185.
22. Barber 2006 pp. 19–23.
23. Barber 2006 pp. 36–7.
24. Saul 2011 pp. 203–4; Prestwich 1997 pp. 556–8.

16. FALL: 1307–1312

1. Luttrell 2015 pp. 365–72; Menache 1993 pp. 1–21.
2. Riley-Smith 2014 p. 278.
3. Barber 2006 pp. 59–87.
4. Phillips, Seymour 2010 pp. 125–60; Tyerman 1988 pp. 240–1. For a detailed examination of the British trials see the excellent Nicholson 2009.
5. Barber 2006 pp. 217–29; Nicholson 2008 pp. 131–54; Gatti 2005 pp. 212–13.
6. Hamilton, J. S. 2010 pp. 215–16.
7. Barber 2006 pp. 217–18.
8. Nicholson 2009 p. 45.
9. The Templars had relatively little property in Wales, certainly compared to the Hospitallers. The Hospitallers, who had fewer close links to the English crown, tended to receive more extensive donations, though the Templars had substantial estates just the other side of the border, on the Welsh marches. Nicholson 2012a pp. 189–90 and 207; Barber 2006 p. 219; Hamilton, J. S. 2010 p. 217; Nicholson 2009 pp. 45–6 and 49.

10. Nicholson 2017 pp. 43–4.
11. Barber 2006 pp. 219–20; Hamilton, J. S. 2010 p. 217; Nicholson 2009 pp. 45–9.
12. Barber 2006 pp. 217–29; Lord 2002 pp 250–1.
13. Barber 2006 pp. 217–19.
14. Hamilton, J. S. 2010 pp. 220–1; Lord 2002 pp. 250–1.
15. Barber 2006 p. 220.
16. Nicholson 2009 pp. 31–8.
17. Barber 2006 p. 221.
18. Nicholson 2009 p. 54.
19. Barber 2006 pp. 220–1; Lord 2002 p. 253.
20. Barber 2006 p. 221.
21. Barber 2006 p. 222; Nicholson 2009 p. 99. Their complaints were made on 16 June 1310.
22. Nicholson 2009 pp. 58 and 61.
23. Nicholson 2009 p. 60.
24. Nicholson 2009 pp. 96–7.
25. Nicholson 2009 pp. 106–7.
26. Proceedings II pp. 21–3; Lord 2002 p. 252.
27. Nicholson 2009 pp. 106–7.
28. Nicholson 2009 pp. 107–9; Lord 2002 pp. 254–5.
29. Nicholson 2016b pp. 10–11.
30. Nicholson 2009 pp. 146, 152 and 154.
31. Nicholson 2009 pp. 155–7.
32. Nicholson 2010a pp. 229–30; Nicholson 2007b pp. 411–23; Nicholson 2016b pp. 10–11; Lord 2002 p. 260.
33. Nicholson 2016b pp. 10–11. As far as we know, Templar chaplains were already ordained to the priesthood when they joined the order; recruits were not sent for ordination.
34. Nicholson 2010a pp. 229–30; Nicholson 2007b pp. 411–23.
35. Nicholson 2009 pp. 158–63.
36. Nicholson 2010a pp. 232–4.
37. Proceedings II pp. 30 and 95; Barber 2006 pp. 221 and 225; Nicholson 2009 pp. 96, 104, 154, 158 and 177–8.
38. Lord 2002 p. 181; Gooder 1995 pp. 93–5.
39. Nicholson 2010a pp. 234–5.
40. Nicholson 2009 p. 164; Nicholson 2016b pp. 10–11.
41. Nicholson 2009 pp. 133–42.
42. Nicholson 2009 pp. 170 and 176–7.
43. Nicholson 2009 pp. 177–80 and 182.
44. Nicholson 2009 pp. 197 and 207; Barber 2006 p. 227.
45. Barber 2006 pp. 281–2.
46. Nicholson 2009 p. 199; Nicholson 2008 pp. 131–54; Hill 1987 pp. 123–8; Forey 2002 pp. 18–37.
47. Nicholson 2016b p. 11.
48. Gooder 1995 p. 97.
49. Nicholson 2009 p. 53.
50. Gooder 1995 p. 123; Nicholson 2009 p. 53.

17. MEDIEVAL CONSPIRACIES – GUILTY AS CHARGED?

1. Barber 2006 pp. 203–16.
2. Walter Map pp. 118–20.
3. Barber 2006 pp. 203–16.
4. Nicholson 2009 p. 24.
5. Barber 2006 pp. 146–8.

6. Lord 2002 pp. 255 and 257.
7. Proceedings II pp. 189–90 and 189–90 n. 23.
8. Proceedings II p. 189.
9. Proceedings II pp. 191, 448 and 453; Nicholson 2009 pp. 235.
10. Proceedings II pp. 487–8 and 487 n. 148.
11. Nicholson 2009 p. 37.
12. Tibble 2020 pp. 88–100; Nicholson 2011 pp. 92–4.
13. El-Merheb forthcoming.
14. Nicholson 2016a p. 8. Even the apostate Robert of St Albans is only known through western sources.
15. Nicholson 2017 pp. 105–6.
16. Proceedings II pp. 209 and 209 n. 141. See Nicholson 2011 pp. 94–5 for a discussion of the plot and whether the two high-profile contemporary Carmelites, 'Robert of Maidenesford' and 'Robert of Maydenford' were one and the same person. It seems very likely that they were.
17. Proceedings II pp. 213–14, 218–19 and 219 n. 200; Nicholson 2011 pp. 95–7.
18. Nicholson 2011 pp. 95–7.
19. Nicholson 2017 pp. 105–6.
20. Gilmour-Bryson 2008 pp. 173–4.
21. Nicholson 2017 pp. 105–6.
22. Felix Fabri, writing in 1480–83, quoted in Barber 1994 p. 315.
23. Gilmour-Bryson 2008 pp. 171–2.
24. Nicholson 2008 pp. 131–54.
25. Nicholson 2009 pp. 232–3; Nicholson 2017 p. 62.
26. Nicholson 2017 pp. 67–9.
27. Lord 2002 pp. 84–5 and 167–70.
28. Nicholson 2008 pp. 131–54.
29. Nicholson 2007a pp. 198–9.
30. Nicholson 2009 pp. 81–2.
31. Nicholson 2010b pp. 5–6 and 14–17; Nicholson 2007a pp. 198–9; Nicholson 2007c pp. 225–33; Lewer and Dark 1997; Griffith-Jones and Park 2010.
32. Nicholson 2016c pp. 85–98.
33. Forey 2010 pp. 11–19.
34. Nicholson 2009 pp. 227–8; Nicholson 2016c pp. 85–98.
35. Barber 2006 p. 169.
36. Forey 2010 pp. 11–19; Burgtorf 2010 pp. 105–16.
37. Proceedings II pp. 504, 528, 530 and 558; Nicholson 2017 p. 103. The controversial Gerard of Ridefort was another Templar master who rose rapidly.
38. Nicholson 2017 p. 103.
39. Gilmour-Bryson 1996 p. 165; Gilmour-Bryson 2008 pp. 169–70.
40. Such accusations were also a cheap way of undermining the Templars' idealised gender role and 'masculinity'. See Hodgson et al 2019. For the order's ironic reputation as heterosexual lovers, see Nicholson 1994 pp. 340–5.
41. Nicholson 2017 pp. 57–8.
42. Nicholson 2017 p. 107; Nicholson 2009 p. 196; Forey 2008.
43. Gilmour-Bryson 1996 p. 183.

18. MODERN CONSPIRACIES – DREAMS NEVER END

1. As Umberto Eco wrote in *Foucault's Pendulum* (1990 Picador paperback edition), p. 67: 'The lunatic is all *idée fixe* . . . sooner or later he brings up the Templars.'
2. Shapiro 2010.
3. Barber 2006 pp. 208–15; Wood 2012 pp. 450–1; Barber 1982 pp. 206–25.
4. Barber 1994 pp. 317–18.

5. Barber 1994 pp. 323–31.
6. Barber 1994 p. 320.
7. M. Baigent, R. Leigh and H. Lincoln (2006) *The Holy Blood and the Holy Grail*, London, rev. edn; D. Brown (2003) *The Da Vinci Code*, London; Wood 2012 p. 460; Walker 2012 pp. 439–47.
   Walker 2017 pp. 360–71.
8. Walker 2010 pp. 347–9; Gooder 1995 pp. 84–5; Nicholson 2009 pp. 242–3.
9. Nicholson 2009 p. 50.
10. Nicholson 2009 p. 56.
11. Nicholson 2009 pp. 50–2.
12. Proceedings II pp. 21, 80–1, 101, 129–30, 164–5, 164 n. 38, 182–3, 420 and 420 n. 96; Gooder 1995 pp. 92–3; Nicholson 2009 p. 50.
13. Nicholson 2009 p. 16.
14. Walker 2010 pp. 347–53; Lord 2002 pp. 199–200.
15. Walker 2010 pp. 353–4; Lord 2002 pp. 195–9.
16. Lord 2002 pp. 188–91.
17. Barber 1994 pp. 310–13.

SELECT BIBLIOGRAPHY

PRIMARY SOURCES

Albert of Aachen, *Historia Ierosolimitana*, ed. and tr. S. B. Edgington, Oxford, 2007

Ambroise, *The History of the Holy War*, ed. and tr. M. Ailes and M. Barber, 2 vols, Woodbridge, 2003

The Anglo-Saxon Chronicle, ed. G. Garmonsway, London, 1986

Annales Monastici, ed. H. R. Luard, 5 vols, Rolls Series, London, 1864–9

Baha al-Din Ibn Shaddad, *The Rare and Excellent History of Saladin*, tr. D. S. Richards, Crusade Texts in Translation, 7, Aldershot, 2001

Barber, M., and K. Bate, tr., *The Templars*, Manchester Medieval Sources, Manchester, 2002

——, *Letters from the East: Crusaders, Pilgrims and Settlers in the 12th–13th Centuries*, Crusade Texts in Translation, 18, Farnham, 2010

Bernard of Clairvaux, *Sancti Bernardi Opera*, vol. 8, *Epistolae*, ed. J. Leclercq and H. M. Rochais, Rome, 1977

——, *The Letters of St Bernard of Clairvaux*, tr. B. S. James, intro. B. M. Kienzle, Stroud, 1998

Calendar of the Charter Rolls, vol. I, Henry III AD 1226–1257, London, 1903

Calendar of the Liberate Rolls, vol. IV, 1251–1260, London, 1959

Calendar of the Patent Rolls, Henry III, AD 1247–1258, London, 1908

Cartulaire général de l'Ordre du Temple 1119?–1150: Recueil des chartes et des bulles relatives à l'ordre du Temple, ed. G. d'Albon, Paris, 1913

Chronicle of the Third Crusade: A Translation of the Itinerarium Peregrinorum et Gesta Regis Ricardi, tr. H. Nicholson, Crusade Texts in Translation 3, Aldershot, 1997

The Conquest of the Holy Land by Salah al-Din: A critical edition and translation of the anonymous Libellus de expugnatione Terrae Sanctae per Saladinum, ed. K. Brewer and J. H. Kane, Abingdon, 2019

The Conquest of Jerusalem and the Third Crusade: Sources in Translation, tr. P. W. Edbury, Aldershot, 1996

The Conquest of Lisbon: De Expugnatione Lyxbonensi, ed. C. W. David, New York, 2001

Crusader Syria in the Thirteenth Century: The Rothelin Continuation of the History of William of Tyre with part of the Eracles or Acre text, tr. J. Shirley, Crusade Texts in Translation, 5, Aldershot, 1999

Delaville le Roulx, J., ed., *Documents concernant les Templiers, extraits des archives de Malte*, Paris, 1882

Fulcher of Chartres, *A History of the Expedition to Jerusalem, 1095–1127*, tr. F. Ryan, ed. H. Fink, Knoxville, TN, 1969

Gerald of Wales, *Opera*, ed. J. S. Brewer, 8 vols, RS, London, 1861–91

——, *The Journey through Wales and the Description of Wales*, tr. L. Thorpe, Harmondsworth, 1978

Gervase of Canterbury, *The Gesta Regum with its continuation*, ed. W. Stubbs, 2 vols, London, 1880

Gesta Normannorum Ducum of William of Jumièges, Orderic Vitalis, and Robert of Torigni, ed. and tr. Elizabeth M. C. Van Houts, 2 vols, Oxford, 1992–5

The Great Roll of the Pipe, 1184–8, London, 1913

Guibert de Nogent, *Dei Gesta per Francos et cinq autres texts*, ed. R. B. C. Huygens, Corpus Christianorum, 127A, Turnhout, 1996

The History of William Marshal, tr. N. Bryant, Woodbridge, 2016

Ibn 'Abd al-Zahir, 'A Critical Edition of an Unknown Arabic Source for the Life of al-Malik al-Zahir Baybars [by Ibn 'Abd al-Zahir]', ed. A. A. Khowayter, vol. 2, unpublished PhD thesis, London University, 1960

Ibn al-Athir, *The Chronicle of Ibn al-Athir for the Crusading Period from al-Kamil fi'l Ta'rikh*, parts 1 and 2, tr. D. S. Richards, Crusade Texts in Translation, 13, 15, Aldershot, 2006, 2007

'Imâd ad-Din al-Isfahânî, *Conquête de la Syrie et de Palestine par Saladin*, tr. H. Massé, Paris, 1972

Johannis de Fordun, *Chronica Gentis Scottorum*, ed. and tr. W. F. Skene, Edinburgh, 1872

John of Salisbury, *Historia Pontificalis*, ed. and tr. M. Chibnall, London, 1956

——, *Letters*, ed. W. J. Miller and H. I. Butler, 2 vols, rev. C. N. L. Brooke, vol. II, *The Later Letters, 1163–1180*, Oxford, 1979

John of Worcester, *The Chronicle of John of Worcester, III, The Annals from 1067 to 1140*, ed. P. McGurk, Oxford, 1998

The Knights Hospitallers in England: The 1338 Inquest, Camden Society, vol. 65, Larking, L. B., 1857

Lees, B. A., ed., *Records of the Templars in England in the Twelfth Century: The Inquest of 1185 with Illustrative Charters and Documents*, London, 1935

MacNiocaill, G., 'Documents Relating to the Suppression of the Templars in Ireland', *Analecta Hibernica*, 24, 1967, pp. 183–226

Materials for the History of Thomas Becket, Archbishop of Canterbury, ed. J. C. Robertson, vol. V, London, 1881

Matthew Paris, *Matthew Paris's English History*, vol. 1, tr. J. A. Giles, London, 1852

——, *Historia Anglorum sive historia minor*, ed. F. Madden, 3 vols, London, 1866–9

——, *Chronica Majora*, ed. H. Richards Luard, RS 57, 7 vols, London, 1872–83

Odo of Deuil, *De profectione Ludovici VII in Orientem*, ed. and tr. V. G. Berry, New York, 1948

Oliver of Paderborn, 'Capture of Damietta', tr. in E. Peters, *Christian Society and the Crusades, 1198–1229*, Philadelphia, PA, 1971

Orderic Vitalis, *Ecclesiastical History*, vols II, V, VI, ed. and tr. M. Chibnall, Oxford, 1969–78

The Political Songs of England, from the Reign of John to that of Edward II, ed. T. Wright, London, 1839

The Proceedings Against the Templars in the British Isles, ed. H. Nicholson, 2 vols, Farnham, 2011

Ralph of Coggeshall: *Chronicon Anglicanum*, ed. J. Stevenson, RS, London, 1875

Ralph of Diceto, *The Historical Works of Master Ralph de Diceto*, ed. W. Stubbs, 2 vols, Rolls Series 68, London, 1876

Raymond d'Aguilers, *Historia Francorum Qui Ceperunt Iherusalem*, tr. J. H. and H. H. Hill, Philadelphia, PA, 1968

Recueil des historiens des Gaules et de la France, ed. M. Bouquet et al., 24 vols, Paris, 1738–1876

Regesta Regum Anglo-Normannorum, ed. H. W. C. Davis and others, 4 vols, Oxford, 1913–69

Regesta Regum Scottorum, vol. I, ed. G. W. S. Barrow, Edinburgh, 1960

The Register of Walter Gray, Lord Archbishop of York, ed. James Raine, Surtees Society 56, Durham, 1872

Richard of Devizes, *Chronicle*, ed. J. T. Appleby, London, 1963

Roger of Howden, *Gesta Regis Henrici Secundi*, ed. W. Stubbs, 2 vols, RS 49, London, 1867 (published as Benedict of Peterborough)

SELECT BIBLIOGRAPHY

——, *Chronica*, vols 1–3, ed. W. Stubbs, RS 51, London, 1869

Roger of Wendover, *Roger of Wendover's Flowers of History*, tr. J. A. Giles, 2 vols, London, 1849

Rotuli Litterarum Patentium in Turri Londonensi Asservati, ed. T. Duffus Hardy, vol. I, part 1, Record Commission, London, 1835

The Rule of the Templars: The French Text of the Rule of the Order of the Knights Templar, tr. J. M. Upton-Ward, Woodbridge, 1992

Selected Letters of Pope Innocent III, ed. C. R. Cheney and W. H. Semple, London, 1953

The 'Templar of Tyre': Part III of the 'Deeds of the Cypriots', ed. P. Crawford, Abingdon, 2016

Usama Ibn-Munqidh, *The Book of Contemplation*, tr. P. M. Cobb, London, 2008

Walter of Coventry, *Historical Collections*, ed. W. Stubbs, 2 vols, London, 1872–3

Walter of Guisborough, *The Chronicle of Walter of Guisborough*, ed. H. Rothwell, Camden Society, 3rd Series, lxxxix, 1957

Walter Map, *De Nugis Curialium*, ed. M. R. James, rev. C. N. Brooke and R. A. B. Mynors, Oxford, 1983

William of Newburgh, 'Historia Rerum Anglicarum', in *Chronicles and Memorials of the Reigns of Stephen, Henry II and Richard I*, vol. 1, ed. R. Howlett, RS 82, London, 1884

William Rishanger, *Chronica*, ed. H. T. Riley, London, 1865

William of Tyre, *A History of Deeds done beyond the Sea*, tr. E. A. Babcock and A. C. Krey, 2 vols, Records of Civilization, Sources and Studies 35, New York, 1943

SECONDARY SOURCES

Andrews, D. D., *Cressing Temple: A Templar and Hospitaller Manor in Essex*, Chelmsford, 1993

Asbridge, T., *The Greatest Knight*, London, 2015

Barany, A., 'The Last *Rex Crucesignatus* – Edward I and the Mongol Alliance', *Annual of Medieval Studies at Central European University*, 16, 2010, pp. 1– 22

Barber, M., 'The Templars and the Turin Shroud', *Catholic Historical Review*, 68/2, Apr. 1982, pp. 206–25

——, 'The Social Context of the Templars', *Transactions of the Royal Historical Society*, 1984, vol. 34, 1984, pp. 27–46

——, 'Supplying the Crusader States: The Role of the Templars', in *The Horns of Hattin*, ed. B. Z. Kedar, London, 1992, pp. 314–26

——, *The New Knighthood: A History of the Order of the Temple*, Cambridge, 1994

——, *The Trial of the Templars*, 2nd edn, Cambridge, 2006

——, *The Crusader States*, London, 2012

Barratt, N., 'The English Revenue of Richard', *English Historical Review*, 116, 2001, pp. 636–41

Barrow, G. W. S., *The Anglo-Norman Era in Scottish History*, Oxford, 1980

Beebe, B., 'Edward I and the Crusades', unpublished PhD thesis, University of St Andrews, 1971

Bennett, M., 'La Règle du Temple as a military manual or how to deliver a cavalry charge, appendix', in *The Rule of the Templars: The French Text of the Rule of the Order of the Knights Templar*, tr. J. M. Upton-Ward, Woodbridge, 1992, pp. 175–88

Bennett, S., 'The Battle of Arsuf: A Reappraisal of the Charge of the Hospitallers', in *The Military Orders*, vol. 6 (part 1), ed. J. Schenk and M. Carr, Abingdon, 2016, pp. 44–53

Boas, A. J., *Archaeology of the Military Orders: A Survey of the Urban Centres, Rural Settlement and Castles of the Military Orders in the Latin East (c. 1120–1291)*, London, 2006

Britnell, R., 'The Making of Witham', *History Studies* (1), 1968

——, 'Agriculture in a Region of Ancient Enclosure, 1185–1500', *Nottingham Medieval Studies*, XXVII, 1983, pp. 317–55

Brown, D., *Hugh de Lacy, First Earl of Ulster: Rising and Falling in Angevin Ireland*, Woodbridge, 2016

Brundage, J., 'The Lawyers of the Military Orders', in *The Military Orders*, vol. 1, ed. M. C. Barber, Aldershot, 1994, pp. 346–57

314

Burgtorf, J. 'The Trial Inventories of the Templars' Houses in France: Select Aspects', in *The Debate on the Trial of the Templars (1307–1314)*, ed. J. Burgtorf, P. F. Crawford and H. J. Nicholson, Farnham, 2010, pp. 105–16

Burton, J., 'Knights Templars in Yorkshire in the Twelfth Century: A Reassessment', *Northern History*, 27, 1991, pp. 26–40

Carpenter, D. A., 'The Gold Treasure of Henry III', in *Thirteenth Century England*, ed. P. R. Cross and S. Lloyd, Woodbridge, 1988, pp. 61–88

——, *The Minority of Henry III*, Berkeley, CA, 1990

——, *The Reign of Henry III*, London, 1996

——, *Henry III: The Rise to Power and Personal Rule 1207–1258*, London, 2020

Church, S., *King John: England, Magna Carta and the Making of a Tyrant*, London, 2015

Cobb, P. M., *The Race for Paradise: An Islamic History of the Crusades*, Oxford, 2014

Crouch, D., *William Marshal: Court, Career and Chivalry in the Angevin Empire*, London, 1990

——, *The Reign of King Stephen, 1135–1154*, Harlow, 2000

——, 'Earl Gilbert Marshal and his Mortal Enemies', *Historical Research*, 87/237, August 2014, pp. 393–404

Doherty, J., 'Count Hugh of Troyes and the Prestige of Jerusalem', *History: The Journal of the Historical Association*, 2017, pp. 874–88

Duggan, A. J., 'The Making of a Myth: Gerald Cambrensis, Laudabiliter, and Henry II's Lordship of Ireland', *Studies in Medieval and Renaissance History*, 3/4, 2007, pp. 107–69

Edbury, P. W., 'Preaching the Crusade in Wales', reprinted in his Variorum volume, *Law and History in the Latin East* XXIII, 2014

——, 'Ernoul, Eracles and the Beginnings of Frankish Rule in Cyprus, 1191–1231', in *Medieval Cyprus: A Place of Cultural Encounter*, ed. S. Rogge and M. Grünbart, 2015, pp. 29–52

——, 'The Latin East and the English Crown', *The Henry Loyn Memorial Lecture for 2020*, 2020, published online on academia.edu

Ellenblum, R., *Crusader Castles and Modern Histories*, Cambridge, 2007

El-Merheb, M., *Louis IX and the Transition from Ayyubid to Mamluk Sultanate*, Part I, forthcoming

Forey, A. J., 'Recruitment to the Military Orders (twelfth to mid-fourteenth centuries)', in *Viator*, XVII, University of California, 1986, pp. 139–71

——, 'Women and the Military Orders in the 12th and 13th Centuries', *Studia Monastica*, 29, 1987

——, 'Ex-Templars in England', *Journal of Ecclesiastical History*, 53, 2002, pp. 18–37

——, 'Milites ad terminum in the Military Orders during the Twelfth and Thirteenth Centuries', in *The Military Orders*, vol. 4, ed. J. Upton-Ward, Aldershot, 2008, pp. 5–11

——, 'Could Alleged Templar Malpractices Have Remained Undetected for Decades?', in *The Debate on the Trial of the Templars (1307–1314)*, ed. J. Burgtorf, P. F. Crawford and H. J. Nicholson, Farnham, 2010, pp. 11–19

——, 'Paid Troops in the Service of Military Orders during the Twelfth and Thirteenth Centuries', in *The Crusader World*, ed. A. J. Boas, London, 2016, pp. 84–97

France, J., *Hattin*, Oxford, 2015

Fulton, M. S., *Contest for Egypt: The Collapse of the Fatimid Caliphate, the Ebb of Crusader Influence, and the Rise of Saladin*, Leiden, 2022

Gatti, I., 'The Relationship Between the Knights Templar and the Kings of England: From the Order's Foundation to the Reign of Edward', unpublished PhD thesis, Reading University, 2005

Gervers, M., *The Hospitaller Cartulary in the British Library (Cotton MS Nero E VI): A Study of the Manuscript and its Composition with a critical edition of two fragments of earlier cartularies for Essex*, Toronto, 1981

——, 'Pro defensione Terre Sancte: The Development and Exploitation of the Hospitaller Landed Estate in Essex', in *The Military Orders*, vol. 1, ed. M. C. Barber, Aldershot, 1994, pp. 3–20

——, ed., *The Cartulary of the Knights of St John of Jerusalem in England*, Part 2, *Prima Camera: Essex*, Oxford, 1996

Gillingham, J., 'Roger of Howden on Crusade', in *Richard Coeur de Lion: Kingship, Chivalry and War in the Twelfth Century*, London, 1994, pp. 141–53

——, *Richard I*, London, 1999

Gilmour-Bryson, A., 'Sodomy and the Knights Templar', *Journal of the History of Sexuality*, 7/2, Oct. 1996, pp. 151–83

——, 'Templar Trial Testimony: Voices from 1307 to 1311', in *The Military Orders*, vol. 4, ed. J. Upton-Ward, Aldershot, 2008, pp. 163–74

Gooder, E., *Temple Balsall: The Warwickshire Preceptory of the Templars and their Fate*, Chichester, 1995

Griffith-Jones, R., and D. Park, eds, *The Temple Church in London: History, Architecture, Art*, Woodbridge, 2010

Haag, M., *The Templars : History & Myth*, London, 2008

Hamilton, B., *The Leper King and His Heirs: Baldwin IV and the Crusader Kingdom of Jerusalem*, Cambridge, 2000

Hamilton, J. S., 'King Edward II of England and the Templars', in *The Debate on the Trial of the Templars (1307–1314)*, ed. J. Burgtorf, P. F. Crawford and H. J. Nicholson, Farnham, 2010, pp. 215–24

Hill, R., 'Fourpenny Retirement: The Yorkshire Templars in the Fourteenth Century', in *The Church and Wealth: Papers read at the 1986 Summer Meeting and the 1987 Winter Meeting of the Ecclesiastical History Society*, ed. W. J. Sheils and Diana Wood, Oxford, 1987, pp. 123–8

Hodgson, N. R., K. J. Lewis and M. M. Mesley, eds, *Crusading and Masculinities*, Abingdon, 2019

Hollister, C. W., *Henry I*, London, 2001

Hopkinson, N., *End of Empire: The Loss of Normandy and the End of the Anglo-Norman Realm*, Oxford, forthcoming

Hosler, J. D., *Henry II: A Medieval Soldier at War, 1147–1189*, Leiden, 2007

——, *The Siege of Acre, 1189–1191*, London, 2018

Hunter, J., 'The Historic Landscape of Cressing Temple and its Environs', in *Cressing Temple*, ed. D. Andrews, Chelmsford, 1993, pp. 25–35

Hurlock, K., *Wales and the Crusades*, Cardiff, 2011

——, *Britain, Ireland and the Crusades*, Cardiff, 2012

Jansen, V., 'Light and Pure: The Templars' New Choir', in *The Temple Church in London: History, Architecture, Art*, ed. R. Griffith-Jones and D. Park, Woodbridge, 2010, pp. 45–66

Jefferson, J. M., *The Templar Estates in Lincolnshire 1185–1565: Agriculture and Economy*, Martlesham, 2020

Kennedy, H., *Crusader Castles*, Cambridge, 1994

King, E., ed., *The Anarchy of King Stephen's Reign*, Oxford, 1994

——, *King Stephen*, London, 2012

La Torre, I. de, 'The London and Paris Temples: A Comparative Analysis of their Financial Services for the Kings during the Thirteenth Century', in *The Military Orders*, vol. 4, ed. J. Upton-Ward, Aldershot, 2008, pp. 121–7

Lankester, P. J., 'The Thirteenth-Century Effigies in the Temple Church', in *The Temple Church in London: History, Architecture, Art*, ed. R. Griffith-Jones, and D. Park, Woodbridge, 2010, pp. 93–134

Le Strange, H., *Le Strange Records*, London, 1916

Levett, A., *Studies in Manorial History*, Oxford, 1938

Lewer, D., and R. Dark, *The Temple Church in London*, Whitstable, 1997

Lloyd, S., 'The Lord Edward's Crusade of 1270–2', in *War and Government in the Middle Ages*, ed. J. Gillingham and J. C. Holt, Woodbridge, 1984

——, *English Society and the Crusade, 1216–1307*, Oxford 1988

Lord, E., *The Knights Templar in Britain*, Harlow, 2002 [page references are to the Routledge edition of 2013]

Luttrell, A., 'The Election of the Templar Master Jacques de Molay', in *The Debate on the Trial of the Templars (1307–1314)*, ed. Jochen Burgtorf, Paul F. Crawford and Helen J. Nicholson, Farnham, 2010, pp. 21–31

——, 'Observations on the Fall of the Temple', in *Élites et ordres militaires au Moyen Âge: Rencontre autour d'Alain Demurger,* ed. Philippe Josserand, Luís Filipe Oliveira and Damien Carraz, Madrid, 2015, pp. 365–72

Lyons, M. C., and D. E. P. Jackson, *Saladin: The Politics of the Holy War,* Cambridge, 1982

Macquarrie, A., *Scotland and the Crusades, 1095–1560,* Edinburgh, 1985

Marshall, C., *Warfare in the Latin East, 1192–1291,* Cambridge, 1992

Mayer, H. E., 'Henry II of England and the Holy Land', *English Historical Review,* 97, 1982, pp. 721–39

Menache, S., 'The Templar Order: A Failed Ideal?', *Catholic Historical Review,* 79/1, Jan. 1993, pp. 1–21

Metcalf, D. M., 'The Templars as Bankers and Monetary Transfers Between East and West in the Twelfth Century', in *Coinage in the Latin East,* London, 1995

Murphy, M., 'From Swords to Ploughshares: Evidence for Templar Agriculture in Medieval Ireland,' in *Soldiers of Christ: The Knights Templar and the Knights Hospitaller in Medieval Ireland,* ed. M. Browne and C. O. Clabaigh, Dublin, 2016, pp. 167–83

Murray, A. V., *The Crusader Kingdom of Jerusalem: A Dynastic History 1099–1125,* Oxford, 2000

Nicholson, H., 'Images of the Military Orders 1128–129: Spiritual, Secular, Romantic', PhD thesis, University of Leicester, 1989

——, 'Steamy Syrian Scandals: Matthew Paris on the Templars and Hospitallers', *Medieval History,* 2/2, 1992, pp. 68–85

——, 'Knights and Lovers: The Military Orders in the Romantic Literature of the Thirteenth Century', in *The Military Orders,* vol. 1, ed. M. C. Barber, Aldershot, 1994, pp. 340–5

——, 'Before William of Tyre: European Reports on the Military Order: Deeds in the East, 1150–1185', in *The Military Orders,* vol. 2, ed. H. Nicholson, Aldershot, 1998a, pp. 111–18

——, 'The Military Orders and the Kings of England in the Twelfth and Thirteenth Centuries', in *From Clermont to Jerusalem: The Crusades and Crusader Societies, 1095–1500,* ed. A. V. Murray, Turnhout, 1998b, pp. 203–18

——, 'Serving King and Crusade: The Military Orders in Royal Service in Ireland, 1220–1400', in *The Experience of Crusading, Volume One: Western Approaches,* ed. M. Bull and N. Housley, Cambridge, 2003, pp. 233–52

——, 'Relations between Houses of the Order of the Temple in Britain and their Local Communities, as indicated during the Trial of the Templars, 1307–1312', in *Knighthoods of Christ: Essays on the History of the Crusades and the Knights Templar presented to Malcolm Barber,* ed. N. Housley, Aldershot, 2007a, pp. 195–207

——, 'The Testimony of Brother Henry Danet and the Trial of the Templars in Ireland', in *In Laudem Hierosolymitani: Studies in Crusades and Medieval Culture in Honour of Benjamin Z. Kedar,* ed. I. Shagrir, R. Ellenblum and J. Riley-Smith, Aldershot, 2007b, pp. 401–23

——, 'The Hospitallers and the "Peasants' Revolt" of 1381 Revisited', in *The Military Orders,* vol. 3, ed. Victor Mallia-Milanes, Aldershot, 2007c, pp. 225–33

——, 'The Trial of the Templars in the British Isles', in *Religiones militares: Contributi alla storia degli Ordini religioso-militari nel medioevo,* ed. Anthony Luttrell and Francesco Tommasi, Città di Castello, 2008, pp. 131–54

——, *The Knights Templar on Trial: The Trial of the Knights Templar in the British Isles, 1308–1311,* Stroud, 2009

——, 'The Trial of the Templars in Ireland', in *The Debate on the Trial of the Templars (1307–1314),* ed. J. Burgtorf, P. F. Crawford and H. J. Nicholson, Farnham, 2010a, pp. 225–35

——, 'At the Heart of Medieval London: The New Temple in the Middle Ages', in *The Temple Church in London: History, Architecture, Art,* ed. R. Griffith-Jones and D. Park, Woodbridge, 2010b, pp. 1–18

——, 'Myths and Reality: The Crusades and the Latin East as Presented in the Trial of the Templars in the British Isles, 1308–1311', in *On the Margins of Crusading: The Military Orders, the Papacy and the Christian World,* Farnham, 2011, pp. 89–99

——, 'The Military Orders in Wales and the Welsh March in the Middle Ages', in *The Military Orders*, vol. 5, ed. P. W. Edbury, Farnham, 2012a, pp. 189–207

——, 'The Hospitallers' and Templars' Involvement in Warfare on the Frontiers of the British Isles in the Late Thirteenth and Early Fourteenth Centuries', in *Ordines Militares: Colloquia Torunensia Historica: Yearbook for the Study of the Military Orders*, 17, Torun, 2012b, 105–19

——, 'Knights of Christ: The Templars, Hospitallers and Other Military Orders in the Eyes of Contemporaries, 1128–1291', 2016a, http://the-orb.arlima.net/encyclop/religion/monastic/knights.html

——, 'A Long Way from Jerusalem: The Templars and Hospitallers in Ireland. *c.* 1172–1348', in *Soldiers of Christ: The Knights Templar and the Knights Hospitaller in Medieval Ireland*, ed. M. Browne and C. O. Clabaigh, Dublin, 2016b, pp. 1–22

——, 'How Secret was the Templar Admission Ceremony? Evidence from the Proceedings in the British Isles', in *Commilitones Christi: Miscellanea di studi per il Centro Italiano di Documenttzione sull'Ordine del Tempio, MMXI–MMXVI*, ed. Sergio Sammarco, Rome, 2016c, pp. 85–98

——, *The Everyday Life of the Templars: The Knights Templar at Home*, Stroud, 2017

——, *The Knights Templar*, Leeds, 2021

Nicholson, H., and P. Slavin, ' "The Real Da Vinci Code": The Accounts of Templars' Estates in England and Wales during the Suppression of the Order', in *The Templars and Their Sources*, ed. K. Borchardt, K. Döring, P. Josserand and H. J. Nicholson, 2017, pp. 237–47

O'Conor, K., and P. Naessens, 'Temple House: From Templar Castle to New English Mansion', in *Soldiers of Christ: The Knights Templar and the Knights Hospitaller in Medieval Ireland*, ed. M. Browne and C. O. Clabaigh, Dublin, 2016, pp. 124–50

Park, D., 'Medieval Burials and Monuments', in *The Temple Church in London: History, Architecture, Art*, ed. R. Griffith-Jones and D. Park, Woodbridge, 2010, pp. 67–92

Perry, G., *John of Brienne: King of Jerusalem, Emperor of Constantinople, c. 1175–1237*, Cambridge, 2013

——, 'A King of Jerusalem in England', *History*, 100/5 (343), December 2015, pp. 627–39

Phillips, J., 'Hugh of Payns and the 1129 Damascus Crusade', in *The Military Orders*, vol. 1, ed. M. C. Barber, Aldershot, 1994, pp. 141–62

——, *Defenders of the Holy Land: Relations between the Latin East and the West, 1119–1187*, Oxford, 1996

——, *The Second Crusade: Extending the Frontiers of Christendom*, London, 2007

——, *Holy Warriors: A Modern History of the Crusades*, London, 2009

——, *The Life and Legend of the Sultan Saladin*, London, 2019

Phillips, Seymour, *Edward II*, London, 2010

Phillips, Simon, 'The Hospitallers' Acquisition of the Templar Lands in England', in *The Debate on the Trial of the Templars (1307–1314)*, ed. J. Burgtorf, P. F. Crawford and H. J. Nicholson, Farnham, 2010, pp. 237–46

Prestwich, M., *Edward I*, London, 1997

Pringle, D., 'Templar Castles on the Road to the Jordan', in *The Military Orders*, vol. 1, ed. M. Barber, Aldershot, 1994, pp. 148–66

——, *Secular Buildings in the Crusader Kingdom of Jerusalem: An Archaeological Gazetteer*, Cambridge, 1997

——, 'Templar Castles between Jaffa and Jerusalem', in *The Military Orders*, vol. 2, ed. H. Nicholson, Aldershot, 1998, pp. 89–109

Pryor, J. H., *Geography, Technology and War: Studies in the Maritime History of the Mediterranean, 649–1571*, Cambridge, 1988

——, 'A View from a Masthead: The First Crusade from the Sea', *Crusades*, 7, 2008, pp. 87–151

Riley-Smith. J., 'The Templars and the Castle of Tortosa in Syria: An Unknown Document Concerning the Acquisition of the Fortress, *English Historical Review*, 74, 1969, pp. 278–88

——, *The Feudal Nobility and the Kingdom of Jerusalem 1174–1277*, London, 1973

——, 'Crusading as an Act of Love', *History*, 65/214, 1980, pp. 177–92

——, *The Crusades: A History*, 3rd edn, London, 2014

Ritook, P., 'The Architecture of the Knights Templars in England', in *The Military Orders*, vol. 1, ed. M. C. Barber, Aldershot, 1994, pp. 167–78

Rodwell, W., *The Origins and Early Development of Witham, Essex*, Oxford, 1993

Ryan, P., 'Cressing Temple: Its History from Documents', in *Cressing Temple*, ed. D. Andrews, Chelmsford, 1993, pp. 11–24

Saul, N., *Chivalry in Medieval England*, London, 2011

Schenk, J., 'Forms of Lay Association with the Order of the Temple', *Journal of Medieval History*, 34/1, 2008, pp. 79–103

——, 'Nomadic Violence in the First Latin Kingdom of Jerusalem and the Military Orders', *Reading Medieval Studies*, 36, 2010, pp. 39–55

——, *Templar Families: Landowning Families and the Order of the Temple in France, c. 1120–1307*, Cambridge, 2012

Shapiro, J., *Contested Will: Who Wrote Shakespeare?*, London, 2010

Slavin, P., 'Landed Estates of the Knights Templar in England and Wales and their Management in the Early Fourteenth Century', *Journal of Historical Geography*, 42, 2013, pp. 36–49

Strickland, M., *Henry the Young King, 1155–1183*, London, 2016

Tibble, S., *The Crusader Armies*, London, 2018

——, *The Crusader Strategy*, London, 2020

Tyerman, C. J., *England and the Crusades, 1095–1588*, Chicago, 1988

Upton-Ward, J., 'The Surrender of Gaston and the Rule of the Templars', in *The Military Orders*, vol. 1, ed. M. C. Barber, Aldershot, 1994, pp. 179–88

Veach, C., *Lordship in Four Realms: The Lacy Family, 1166–1241*, Manchester, 2014

Walker, J., 'The Patronage of the Templars and of the Order of St. Lazarus in England in the Twelfth and Thirteenth Centuries', unpublished PhD thesis, University of St Andrews, 1990

——, '"The Templars are Everywhere": An Examination of the Myths Behind Templar Survival after 1307', in *The Debate on the Trial of the Templars (1307–1314)*, ed. J. Burgtorf, P. D. Crawford and H. J. Nicholson, Farnham, 2010, pp. 347–57

——, '"From the Holy Grail and the Ark of the Covenant to Freemasonry and the Priory of Sion": An Introduction to the "After-History" of the Templars', in *The Military Orders*, vol. 5, ed. P. W. Edbury, Farnham, 2012, pp. 439–447

——, 'Sources for the Templar Myth', in *The Templars and their Sources*, ed. K. Borchardt, K. Döring, P. Josserand and H. Nicholson, London, 2017, pp. 360–71

Warren, W. L., *King John*, London, 1997

——, *Henry II*, London, 2000

Webster, P., 'The Military Orders at the Court of King John', in *The Military Orders*, vol. 5, ed. P. W. Edbury, Farnham, 2012, pp. 209–18

——, *King John and Religion*, Woodbridge, 2016

Wightman, W. E., *The Lacy Family in England and Normandy 1066–1194*, Oxford, 1966

Wild, B. J., 'A Gift Inventory from the Reign of Henry III', *English Historical Review*, 125/514, June 2010, pp. 529–69

Wilson, C., 'Gothic Architecture Transplanted: The Nave of the Temple Church in London', in *The Temple Church in London: History, Architecture, Art*, ed. R. Griffith-Jones and D. Park, Woodbridge, 2010, pp. 19–44

Wood, J., 'The Myth of Secret History, or "It's not just the Templars involved in absolutely everything"', in *The Military Orders*, vol. 5, ed. P. W. Edbury, Farnham, 2012, pp. 449–60

INDEX